CONTENTS

Author's Notes	iv
Foreword by the Chief Scout	vi
The Adventures Begin	1
The Auchengillan Chronicles	13
The Glasgow Fair Fortnight Equals Summer Camp	41
Secrets, Smiles and Dramas	89
Never a Dull Moment	111
Competitive Scouting	129
A Place of Our Own	144
Fun and Games in the Hall	158
Spreading our Wings	174
Leaving the Stage	196
Final Thoughts	216

AUTHOR'S NOTE

This memoir has been put together from the scrambled memories of mature Boy Scouts, plus a couple of old log books from past times. Some newspaper cuttings have also been of use. Time has blurred the edges of memory and there are unavoidable gaps in the narrative but, overall, it is a great yarn. Enjoy it as much as we enjoyed our madcap days of long ago when we were Boy Scouts of the 131 of the City of Glasgow.

All profits made from this book will be paid into the Clyde Scouts Outdoor Pursuits Training Fund.

Illustrations are by Rosie Cunningham (www.illustrationetc.co.uk).

The photographs have been provided from the 131 Troop Log Books, the Scout Association and old Scouts.

For Jack Banks, Tommy McWilliams and Jimmy McNeillie

The Troop Song

We are the Boy Scouts of the 131
Of the City of Glasgow
We do a deed a day without accepting pay
As is written in our Law
We are loyal and true to the red, white and blue
And our God, Queen and Country too
So if there's ever a feed you don't really need
Just call on St Robert's Boy Scouts!

(Music – March of the US Marine Corps.
Words – Jimmy McNeillie)

FOREWORD BY THE CHIEF SCOUT

Scouting has been in action for more than 115 years preparing young people with skills for life. This refreshing book tells the heartening story of a group of youngsters and their twenty-seven years of adventure, friendship and hard work in a tough social environment.

Their Scouting achievements were excellent and their journey was hard; filled with challenge, success and disappointment along the way. But the benefits for their later lives from their Scout days was remarkable. Scouting gave them the confidence to recognise their own ability and to make a positive impact on the world.

This really is a true Scouting legend.

Bear Grylls OBE, Chief Scout

THE ADVENTURES BEGIN

The Ambush

Tommy McWilliams was laying a terrazzo floor in the new St Robert's Church in Househillwood when the Parish Priest crept up behind him and asked him to set up a Parish Boy Scout Group. Tommy was trapped. He knew nothing about Scouting but agreed to "have a go."

The 131st Glasgow Boy Scout Group was born and Tommy was its leader for the next 20 years.

The parish priest gave him a sheet of paper from Glasgow Scout Headquarters with an address. Tommy wrote a letter of introduction and racked his brains for ideas to help him in his new, untrained, unpaid role.

The first requirement was for more Leaders. An appeal was made from the pulpit the next Sunday and several ex-military lads contacted Tommy. They were all trained on a local one-day Scoutmaster course for their new roles and the 131 was registered on 2 September 1946. Twenty-seven years of carefree adventure was now under way for local boys.

Tommy was a constant beacon of good behaviour for the lads. His five daughters always assisted at Scout fundraising events and his sixth and final child was a boy who naturally joined the 131. It was a true Scout family.

The Spread of Scouting in Glasgow

The Second World War brought about huge changes in society. The population and the politicians were determined that the tremendous hardships they had endured should lead to a better lifestyle for its citizens – our parents and us, their children.

The Glasgow City housing stock was old and lots of it was decaying. New housing estates were laid out in the final years of the conflict and Pollok, in the deep South West of the city, grew in the years after 1945. Some of this work was done by Prisoners of War who laid out streets and drainage systems in its locality.

Families were moved out of the sub-standard housing into the new schemes. The men were back from war service and ready to build a better standard of living with their families and were keen for a fresh start. The adults who moved to the wide spaces and cleanliness of the Priesthill/Pollok area in the 1950s were resolved to change their lives for the better. And most of them did.

Priesthill and the surrounding parts of Pollok were a bit monotonous, with no town centre or pubs and only a small row of essential shops. This did not inconvenience the newcomers, as they were much stronger than their environment might have suggested. They were resilient and tough.

Glasgow Scouting also joined in this post-war development. Local churches helped to establish new Scout Groups. An agreement was reached with the Catholic Church that Catholic boys should join the nearest Catholic Scout Troop which would be sponsored by the church. The entire community was involved.

This was a radical change as previously only the middle-class areas of the city had Scouts. The first registered Scout Group in the world was the First Glasgow in the West End. This was based on boys from the four main private schools in the city – Glasgow High School, Glasgow Academy, Kelvinside Academy and Hutchesons.

In the early postwar years, society had changed and many working-class boys were now members of the worldwide Scout Movement. Pollok now had five Scout Groups, including the 131 at Househillwood. But regrettably, there was now an imbalance between ambition and reality – namely the lack of finance.

These new Scout Groups met in local church halls or schools. However, over time, many 'poor' Scout Groups achieved superb results with limited resources. The 131 was one of these.

Early Days

Initially, the Troop meetings were held in Tommy's back garden on Peat Road where he would line up the Scouts and give them various tasks to complete. It must have been good fun as the Scout Troop was always full, with about thirty or so boys. They roamed across the woods and lanes of the surrounding areas. Sadly there are no records of their early escapades as notebooks and extensive diaries were not common in Pollok – or any working-class areas at that time.

Chats with old Scouts shed some light on the early-1950s activities. Tony Quinn recalled hikes through Darnley and then on up to the dams. The war-time Army camp was still there and they would sneak in for a look, pretending that they were soldiers. This patch of land was to become a much-travelled path for most Scouts of the 131.

The early Scouts appear to have camped al fresco – there were no official sites in the local area, only farms or spaces at the back of old Army camps. One of the tales I heard as a young Scout involved a camp held beside the Brock Burn where a Patrol would try to climb the big railway bridge. This bridge had stone pillars, with the railway line at the top and sometimes when they were climbing upwards, the train would pass over. This sounded a wee bit scary but I can't remember hearing about any accidents.

Glasgow Scouting was keen to develop more Scout Groups and started to put funds and resources into activities in the Pollok area. By 1951, a new Pollok Scout Association had been formed and was backed by the Tenants' Associations. Other funding had been directed to the building of Scout Halls.

Unfortunately, these commendable efforts bypassed the 131 who were totally reliant on the parish for limited assistance. Regardless, Tommy and his gang plodded on with the Pollok version of *Scouting for Boys*.

This intriguing book was the start point for Scouting and, although Baden-Powell was very England-centric and tended to be a bit priggish and preachy, its fundamentals were sound and related directly to life in Pollok.

By the mid-1950s, Glasgow Corporation started to allow community groups to use school buildings free of charge. Tommy and the Troop took advantage of this. All meetings were then held in the St Bernard's School together with a Cub Pack run by a lady called Pat Haran.

I was one of the keen youngsters who turned up at a Cub meeting in February 1955 with a school friend and began a lifetime in Scouting. I knew absolutely nothing about the Cubs. We played lots of games and practised exciting new activities such as tracking through the long grass. I was hooked.

Fun and Games in the Kelvin Hall

The 131 were in good heart by the time of the Fifty Years of Scouting celebrations in 1957 and took part in the great Jamboree show at the Kelvin Hall.

Scouts from all over the city performed a variety of activities, many of which would be banned nowadays. During this great show, the 131 were getting stuck into quarterstaff fighting – a useful skill in the scheme. Brian Dineley and George Sproule were the Leaders who organised this battle and we mostly battered each other with Scout staves. Bruised knuckles were avoided by the use of boxing gloves, but nobody wore a helmet or body armour. You had to be light on your feet – and prepared for a few sharp blows.

The 131 boxing display was a great crowd-puller. Pollok boys were quite cocky and thumped a few others in the ring. Some of them got a bloody nose, others got black eyes and a few lost teeth as well. No gumshields were available but then again, most of our parents had false teeth anyway.

My own job at this grand Jamboree was to demonstrate the art of bed making. That was one of the Cub tests and I displayed my expertise in full public view.

The show ran for a week. One Troop built an indoor pool and performed canoeing skills, while another climbed up and down the inside of the building. This was all to show that Scouts did exciting things! And the 131 looked at all of these activities. It opened their eyes to a wider world which existed beyond Pollok.

Young lads roamed the Kelvin Hall looking at the various stands, especially the camp sites. These were tantalising for the 131 boys, as our regular camping exploits took place in far simpler surroundings.

Our kit was a collection of dilapidated ex-Army tents and big cooking pots. The 131's most precious possession was an old Army bell tent and this could hold at least 12 Scouts, as Brian McGuire remembered, 'We would usually be camped on a slope and in the morning we would all have rolled round into a heap at the foot of the slope. It was a bit like a dosshouse I suppose.'

Jack Arrives – Badges Appear

By 1957 numbers had grown to about forty Scouts and thirty Cubs. They went off camping most weekends. But none of them had any badges, as Brian McGuire pointed out, 'We had been Scouts for years and camped every weekend, but we didn't have a badge between us.'

Then it all changed. A new Scoutmaster arrived – a big guy from the Gorbals, Jack Banks. It was a pivotal moment. From the outset it was now very clear who was running the show.

A young Jack Banks in 1959 (Photo – Margaret Banks)

Jack had served two years in Malaya during his National Service. He had been a sergeant, quite an achievement for a national serviceman. His military service had a big effect on him. He never forgot the wounded soldiers he had treated in the field hospital. These casualties were flown in by helicopter and his team would rush to the helipad to unload the stretchers. A bit like MASH. Seventy years later he still talked about this seminal time of his life as well as his days with the 131.

Jack stood six feet two inches tall. The average size for a Scotsman at that time was five feet seven inches, so he was a true giant among Glasgow youths. The Troop changed dramatically. Jack's mentoring produced twenty-three Scouts who reached Queen's Scout level, the top of the tree in Scouting. His effect was tremendous and he was Scoutmaster of the 131 for the next eight years.

During his time in charge, the 131 Scouts travelled to summer camps in the Lake District, Guernsey, Torquay and the famous Gilwell Park in Essex. They made these journeys on trains, double decker buses, boats and lorries. All the weekly meetings were still being held in an old school building which was reaching the end of its useful life. This was never hard and Jack looked back fondly on this time, 'We did OK, I think.'

Danny Houston was one of the early 131 Scouts and remembered the change when Jack arrived, 'It was some Troop. We had to pay for our own proficiency badges when we passed them as the Troop did not have any money and we were passing so many badges.'

This rush to qualify for badges often led to comic situations. Two Scouts, who shall remain nameless, set off on their Second Class hike. This was a straightforward activity – hike ten miles and camp overnight. One of the Scouts was new from the Cubs and the other was a grizzled veteran from the old gang. After completing the hike from Dumbarton Rock to Auchengillan, the older Scout decided that they would just take the bus back to Glasgow and return to Pollok and he would be in time to finish his paper round. Sound economics. And in any case, they had already camped at Auchengillan the previous weekend. The younger, keen, new lad, was terrified that they would be seen by 'somebody' and then reported for not having camped overnight. So he crouched down in his seat for the entire bus journey! Both passed the badge.

During this time the first Queen's Scout badges were gained by Brian McGuire, Jimmy McNeillie, Len Ashforth, Robert McGuire, George Lyden, Tommy Maguire and Danny Houston. 'We had so many that we could have got into the Guinness Book of Records,' said Danny.

Jack and Tommy had decided that it would be nice to send these high-achieving Scouts down to the Queen's Scout parade at Windsor Castle to march past the Queen. However, the lads had other ideas as Brian McGuire recalled, 'We weren't interested in going down to London for a parade. Instead we convinced Jack and Tommy that we should spend this money on Scouting things. I bought a camera for use by the Troop and I remember somebody else bought a Primus stove. We were Scouts, not chocolate soldiers.'

Most of the early photos in this book were taken with Brian's camera which he later donated to the Troop.

Bush Hats and Tam o' Shanters

Camping was the 131's Holy Grail. Various camp sites were used. Some of these were local spots where the 131 stuck up a tent and lived rough for the weekend. These were always popular as the boys could hike to the site carrying their tent and cooking pots. It probably took about an hour to get there. Going away to Auchengillan was a real treat.

Summer Camps were held, normally for two weeks in the local Lanarkshire and Renfrewshire countryside. These were attended by a dozen or so Scouts, all dressed in a motley collection of uniforms. Brian McGuire was one of this gang, 'We all got our scout shirts from the Army Surplus stores. They were made from hairy, itchy material. This was so that they would soak up sweat in hot countries. In Scotland they just itched like mad. Some of us would get hold of old Army battledress tunics and the older lads all had kilts.'

A few of the boys wore old-fashioned Scout bush hats with wide brims. Pete McGuire recalled one of his older brothers ironing this hat before church parade, 'It was either Brian or Robert, I can't remember which one it was. The kettle was boiled and then poured into a soup plate then the big hat was sat on top of it. The steam soaked into it and once it was all soaked in he would start to iron it and carefully squeeze the top to make the four dents in it. He would sprinkle some sugar around the brim and then iron this with a wet cloth on top. He claimed that the starch from the sugar made the brim as hard as Oddjob's hat. Thankfully I never had to wear one as the Troop had switched to more sensible hats by the time I was a Scout.'

The reason for this change was simple. The bush hats were too expensive and eventually were only worn by PLs as a badge of office, so Jack decided that Scottish headgear would be worn. These were a mixture of Glengarry and Balmoral hats for the Leaders and Tam o' Shanter hats for the Scouts, 'They were cheap and could be bought at the Army Surplus store,' said Jack. And they were easy to iron.

The big Scout bush hats were a regular source of glee for the 131 at Auchengillan. Noel Carson was one of the gang who would sneak up on a deserted camp site. Some Troops kept their big hats hanging on the outside wall of the tent, so the 131 would run into the camp and smack all the big hats with a wooden mallet. This would flatten them completely. At other times they would grab the hats and fling them away like frisbees.

Many years later, I was telling this daft tale to a friend. He had been a Scout in another Troop in those days and roared with laughter before informing me that he had been smacked on the head with one of these mallets! It had been sore at the time and now, fifty years later, he had caught up with the culprit.

By 1959, the Troop had formed a very solid camping gang – Brian McGuire, Jimmy McNeillie, Len Ashforth, Danny Houston, Frank Rodden, Robert McGuire, George Lyden, Jimmy Carson, Henry Watts and me. Most weekends we would be off to Auchengillan, setting the pattern for later years in the 131.

Lack of cash was always a problem and we were forever finding novel ways to raise funds. One of these had been explained to me by Jimmy McNeillie. In those days, working-class schemes would have lots of people with bikes. These were for getting to work but also for leisure such as cycle rides at the weekends or even cycle racing. There was a local cycle racing club, the Red Hills Racers, and Scouts used to go along to their race days. In fact, some former 131 Scouts were in the team.

THE ADVENTURES BEGIN

Two Scout Troops of the 1950s

A well-equipped Scout Troop

Scouts from Pollok – the 131

The 131 would set up a cooking stall and sell cups of tea and bacon rolls. Tommy was normally with them and gave some of the cash to the cycle club and put the rest into the Troop bank.

The Troop also helped out in an illicit activity at the cycle races. Bookmaking was illegal but it still thrived. Jack's father had been a bookie in the Gorbals, so he had a chat with the bookmaker at the races who would engage a couple of big Scouts as his 'runners.' They would take the bet money from the punter to the bookmaker and then return with the winnings. It was good, sneaky, exciting work and the lads enjoyed it, keeping watch for any approaching police patrols. And of course, the bookie made a donation to the Troop funds!

The Journey to becoming a Queen's Scout – The Early Steps

The Queen's Scout Badge

Each 131 Scout wanted to become a Queen's Scout (now known as King's Scouts). There was a clear pathway leading from two years as a Cub followed by six Years as a Scout to reach this target. Many got there in the end and are as proud of their achievement in their seventies as they were as eighteen-years old lads. They all set out on this journey in great anticipation.

Moving up to the Scouts from the Cubs was a big step as most of the Troop were at a different school. For Jimmy Carson, Henry Watts and me, it was memorable. There was another Cub who came up with us but he did not return the next week. He probably thought it was too rough for him. We were introduced to Bulldog, the Troop's welcome ceremony for new members. This was basically a mad charge from one end of the Hall to the other with some Scouts in the middle trying to catch other Scouts. Eventually it was most of the Troop in the middle with a few survivors trying to break through. A rough beginning which normally chased away a few new recruits but many others thought this was great fun and stayed on.

Once in the Troop, the Tenderfoot badge, involving First Aid and knotting, was the first goal and we all passed this within a few weeks.

Scout Parties – the Half Pound Night

Troop meetings were great fun – and hard work! Once during each school term we had a Half Pound Night. Each boy (because there were only boys in those days) would bring half a pound of something to the meeting. The Leaders would collect all the offerings and serve up a great feast.

It was still a Scout meeting, with games which had edible prizes instead of points. The half-pound offerings were varied – and interesting. There were biscuits (loose, not pre-packed as now), sometimes a cake (a rarity in those days), tea (yes, even wee jokers drank tea as there was nothing else), rhubarb, apples and nuts. And on one occasion, Henry Watts recalled someone bringing potatoes, 'These wee parties were great fun. Parties were few and far between in those days and normally only at birthdays and Xmas.'

Having a drink of Ribena or American Cream Soda was a luxury for most of the boys. Some Scout would bring a jar of Bovril and this would be dished out to the gang. This was unknown to most of us. But some had already tasted it on Saturday mornings at the Fifty Pitches when they went there to play football for the school team. Tasting different foods was exciting – apart from cooked tripe which was produced one Half Pound Night!

There were plenty of rough games as well. This was party time at the hard edge – thumps and bumps with something nice to eat. Sheer delight!

One of the games which was reserved for Half Pound Nights was two-handed quarterstaff – whacking one another with Scout staves. But there were rules to limit the damage as Robert McGuire explained to me, 'You had to use both hands on the staff and flail away at the other guy.' We thought we were knights of old, though, and most of the boys did not flinch although there were some sore knuckles at times. All good, clean fun.

Jack Banks laughed at this memory, 'People nowadays must think we were mad but that was life back then. Very little extra money so biscuits, probably digestives, would be two per boy per week at home and chocolate biscuits were a real treat. The boys really loved these nights, especially those who came from the poorest families. You have to remember that some families had seven or eight kids with only the father working. Life was tough and we could bring a wee bit of stardust into it by these Half-Pound nights.'

THE AUCHENGILLAN CHRONICLES

The Field of Our Youth

One of the highlights for any 131 Scout was to go to Auchengillan, the Glasgow Scout camp site. Although, this was only fifteen miles north of the city, for boys from Pollok, it was a trip to the mighty Highlands. They could almost hear the roar of the clansmen, particularly the mighty Rob Roy McGregor who had inhabited those parts in days gone by. (On investigation, he appears to have been a bit of a gangster. But the 131 Scouts were happy with the legend.)

Over the years, Auchengillan has brought the great outdoors to hundreds of thousands of the city's youngsters. The land had been gifted in the early days of Scouting and many international Scout events have been held there. In the 1950s and 1960s it was glamorous – and primitive. Auchengillan was the weekend home to hundreds of Glasgow Scouts, with at least at least thirty Troops regularly camping there. It was a popular, cheap holiday. The bus fare and the camp fees were affordable for young guys. We used our pocket money to fund our Scout camps and it also encouraged many of us to get part-time jobs to help with the cost.

The camping kit was kept at Tommy's house. Tents, poles, pegs, cooking pots, big ex-Army dixies, axes and saws – all lived beneath Tommy's kitchen floor.

The overall journey would take more than two hours and involved travelling on two different buses as well as staggering up through Glasgow city centre with camping kit and rucksacks. The heavy tent would be carried by the PL who would be a young working man with a full-time job.

Our regular and unchanging menu was easily split up between the boys – Co-op pie, tin of Irish stew, tin of Ambrosia creamed rice. Slices of bacon were provided by lads like Eddie Mallan and George Coll who had a Saturday morning job in the local butchers.

They would cut the bacon to the thinnest number to enable everyone to have two slices – in reality it was like tissue paper and would shrivel up when cooked.

Some parts of the journey were memorable, like the drive through Bearsden where we could see the smart houses with a wee burn running through their back gardens. A different world from the scheme! When the bus crested summits on its way to Carbeth we would be thrown from our seats in glee. And there was always music for the journey, mainly Patsy Cline songs from the older lads. The Kingfisher Patrol song *Honky Tonk Angels* was belted out on every journey.

Then we would come through Carbeth, with its amazing collection of huts. These were weekend pieds a terre for legions of Glaswegians. Pete McGuire loved them, 'For us, having a hut at Carbeth would have been like winning the lottery. Loads of working-class guys and gals would head to Carbeth at the weekend carrying guitars, banjos, accordions, harmonicas and fiddles. The place was a great big party then.'

Jim Donnelly was laughing as he recounted one trip, 'I remember four of us left on a Friday night to head to Auchengillan by bus. We got on the wrong bus and ended up in Blanefield. We had a big tent with us and were struggling. Our only option was to carry it up a country road in the dark. This was a very steep road. We knew if we got to the top of the road and turned right we'd eventually get to the camp. We did not know that four wee boys would take all night lugging the gear. Fortunately, a local resident saw us pass his house and took pity on us. He appeared with his car and gave us a lift.'

At the more conventional journey's end, more than 60 Scouts would spill out of the bus, grab their kit and trudge the final 200 yards up to Auchengillan. The serious business was about to begin.

Next stage was to book in at the Providore. This was an amazing L-shaped building. It had two halls – one on either side of the camp office – and the central link had a big diorama of the hills opposite. It was a wonderland for us. We learned all the names of these hills and all of the others which lay in front of us all the way past Loch Lomond to the far north.

The Providore at Auchengillan (Photo – David Scott)

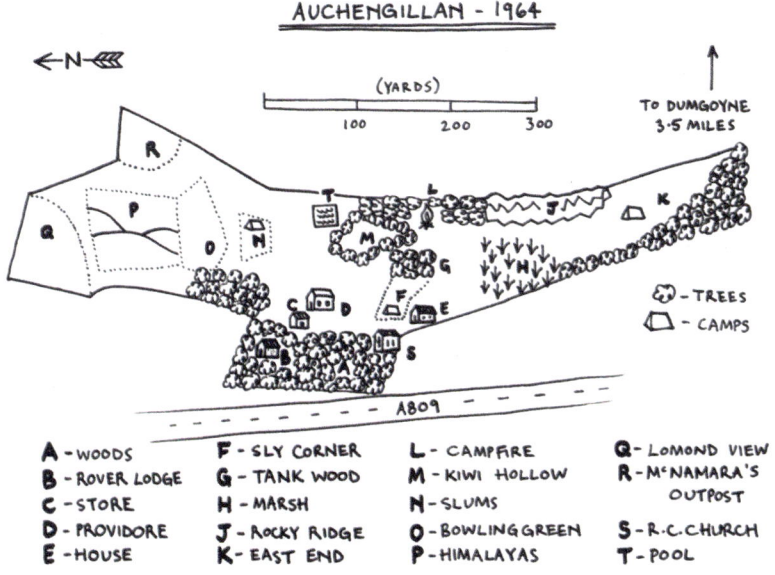

Auchengillan map 1964 (Rosie Cunningham)

Having booked in, we would then move along to our allotted camp site. We would often ask for the one at Rocky Ridge. We don't know why this particular spot was given this name, because all of Auchengillan was a huge rocky ridge with only a shallow covering of earth. Many tent pegs were ruined every weekend. Anyway, we would tramp along to this spot and set up camp. From there, it was about two hundred yards to the nearest water point and even further to the latrines.

There was a routine to every camp. First of all, some Scouts – normally the smallest – would be sent for wood and water. The water trip needed two boys to carry the huge, ex-Army dixie and most of it would be spilled on the way back. The wood party had much more fun and an older Scout would take this group to the wood store.

This was crammed with offcuts from a nearby wood mill. Jim Donnelly was well acquainted with this, 'To one side of the Providore block was a massive log pile of firewood. We used to go there every day to chop some wood for our camp site. These bits were very handy as one side was tree bark and the other was smooth. They were great for building camp gadgets.'

The next task was to cut this wood into sensible lengths – about six feet – and take them back to camp. This was done by using camp saws or hand axes, skills which we had already learned. Occasionally, the big Scout would use the felling axe. Over time, we all learned to use all of these tools. I can only recall one Scout hitting their own hand with the butt end of the hand axe when he was using it to hammer in a tent peg. He had to wear one of his spare socks to protect it for the rest of the weekend.

On his first camping trip, the young Scout would enter this enchanted world. It was a huge experience for an eleven-years old boy from the far south side of Glasgow. There were great views of mountains and rivers. But there wasn't any time to stand around and admire the view – the midges were everywhere. We would scratch our legs until they were bleeding and then pull up our white kilt socks to cover our knees. The blood just seeped through the socks. A bit gruesome for modern tastes, I suppose, but imprinted on the memory of many old 131 Scouts.

At night, the young campers would stare in amazement at the stars. Auchengillan was far away from the street light glow of Glasgow. We learned constellations and even took measurements on the ground of star movements. Nothing scientific, though this was exciting none the less – and was one of the regular educational moments at camp.

All the camp staff, apart from the full-time Warden, were weekend volunteers. Auchengillan was run by Scouts for Scouts. This crew manned a small hut which served as the shop in those days and the 131 were regular clients. This hut was actually a sweetie shop and only opened for one hour each day. There would be a long queue of youngsters eager to spend their pocket money there. The choice was simple – either a Mars Bar or a bottle of Coca Cola or a bag of crisps. Us 131 lads could only afford one – for the whole weekend. The Coca Cola bottle would be opened by the buckle on the Scout belt. As our PL told us, the belt buckle had been designed to do just that. Brilliant!

September weekend at Auchengillan 1961; including Jimmy Carson, David Mackay, Eddie Mallan, Len Ashforth and others unidentified (Photo – Brian McGuire)

The 131 boys were wildly keen to attend camps. The living was rough, cooking your own food was challenging but the freedom was complete. A Scout had to be tough minded and adaptable to get on at camp and there were many benefits. We learned how to play cards for wee stones but never for money as nobody had any. Sometimes it was for sweeties. Then there were the sweary words. We certainly never heard these words at home. It could be described as an al fresco learning experience. A lot of the boys started to smoke there as well. Just being at camp and away from home was a great event. Going for wood and water took up most of our time as we were young boys and we could not carry very much. Cooking on wood fires, and eating, took up the rest of the day.

The 131 were nosey and adventurous. We were also good at protecting ourselves against other Scout Troops, all of whom were regarded as potential enemies. As a result we became boys of the Wild West. Like all young lads, we would form ourselves into a tight team, our own Pollok posse. Us against them. We would disguise ourselves by pulling our neckies across our faces and ambush the water carriers from other Troops, tip over their water and run away. When we got back to our camp site, we would find their Scoutmaster waiting for us. Of course, they knew who we were. Our neckie colour, maroon – with the Papal Keys badge, was noted and the mystery was quickly solved. The punishment was always to replace the water.

Our camp site was like home to us. It was really great when we were able to sleep in our new tent, which was amazing for a Troop like the 131. We had no money, no Scout Hall and our parents all worked in lowly-paid jobs. But we had saved up money from jumble sales and dances and bought a new tent. This was a Nijer from Blacks of Greenock.

The Nijer was superb and could hold eight boys without any problem. They would sleep in blankets in the early days – on the ground. Only a couple of the older lads would have sleeping bags. My PL had what he called a bivvy bag. This was actually a canvas tent bag. It had rope laced through eyeholes to pull it tight for some warmth. And another of the PLs (Brian McGuire) had a wartime flying suit which he wore like padded pyjamas. It had loads of insulation and was very warm. He would lend it out to other Scouts when he was not at camp.

All 131 camp sites were expected to be smart. We would line off our site with sisal (hairy string). The fire would also be lined off, as well as the wood chopping area. These would have to be at least ten yards away from the rest of the site. Everything had to be kept tidy and we even picked up the wood chips. Cooking pots and personal plates were scoured with mud and rinsed clean – B-P had told us that one and it worked.

Hugh Mullaney, Len McKinnon and Michael O'Neill, Auchengillan 1963
– watching out for Pop Whitelaw

Auchengillan was haunted by a ghost…

On the first night in camp the tent would be dark and quiet while the PL narrated the grisly tale of Pop Whitelaw. Jim Mackay was one of those who heard this story, 'It was probably at my first camp. Our PL (Len Ashforth) was sitting on the groundsheet and we were gathered around him listening to the tale. We did not know it was a ghost story. We thought it was just some old fairy tale about Auchengillan. He told us about the various places we had visited that day and wove them all into the story. We were listening intently. Nobody moved and nobody spoke. We were just beginning to get scared when he finished the story by switching on his torch which he held under his chin. We all screamed and jumped up in terror. I don't think any of us could sleep that night. For years afterwards I would always think about Pop Whitelaw when I passed these places at 'Gillan, especially in the dark.

Jim was not the only 131 Scout who was terrified by stories about Pop Whitelaw. Graeme O'Neill was another, 'What a scare I had when I was told the tale about Pop Whitelaw. Mine was when we had an indoor weekend at 'Gillan during the winter. We listened to the tale during campfire and then went straight to bed having been warned by the Leaders that Pop Whitelaw was always on the prowl looking for victims and could come into the dormitory and snatch away his prey. I couldn't sleep at all that night or the next one as there were lots of ghostly sounds outside the building. Low moans, wild cackles and horrible rasping sounds. I was really terrified. The Leaders really did a good job on us and we all kept quiet. We were even too scared to get up and go to the toilet!'

Ian McKelvie recalled his introduction to the Ghost of 'Gillan, 'I had just turned ten years old the first time I went to Auchengillan. Because we were Cubs we were not allowed to sleep in the 131 tents so we used a big shed and we all crawled into it for our sleep. Akela told us the tale and he was pretty convincing because I was absolutely terrified and could not sleep. In the morning I told my brother Eric who was one of the Scouts. He burst out laughing and told me it was Pop Whitelaw and I had to be careful around the site because he might capture me!'

So, who was Pop Whitelaw? 'Well,' remembered Graeme. 'He was a hermit who lived in a remote cottage on the Stockiemuir road and lured travellers into his home to murder them. All very believable for young boys. And we would spend the next few years at Auchengillan looking for blood stains on any piles of stones as evidence of his old hut.'

Danny Houston summed up the allure of Auchengillan, 'We felt really special as we left the scheme at the weekend and went camping to the Highlands. Everybody else just stayed at home and played in the streets. They had a drab existence but our weekends had these great splashes of vivid colour.'

Jim Donnelly went to Auchengillan many times during his seven years in the 131, 'The first time I was there was as a Cub, staying in the Cub Lodge. It was a new build at that time, at the bottom end of the camp. The dormitory had a two-tier bunk system made of pine. Each level held loads of kids. We all screamed and cheered when we were in the bunks and then we fell asleep absolutely knackered.'

This Cub building was the Frank McAleer Chalet and the 131 had been involved in its construction. We had done manual tasks like lifting beams and laying kerb stones.

Part of most camp programmes involved a wide game in the evening – an excuse for letting the lads run around the camp site in the dark. In reality a wide game was a chance for the Leaders to relax while the Scouts dashed madly across fields and woods trying to murder one another. There were obviously rules, but these were normally pretty useless. It was marauding gangs against each other.

Jim Donnelly remembered, 'The night hunts! I think they were called wide games – it was really a carry-on in the dark for us. The whole camp (about thirty lads) were split into two teams. Each team member had a match. The Hunters had to locate each member of the other team and seize the matches. It was rough, but a good laugh.'

The mention of wide games caused Graeme O'Neill to chuckle. 'Good grief! I loved wide games. They were great. We would sneak about all over the camp site and jump on anybody we thought was one of the enemy. I remember once at Auchengillan that we pounced on a Leader from another Troop. He told us to let him go as he was not in the game but we ignored him. We tied him to a tree and tied a neckie round his mouth to keep him quiet. Then we shot off into the night never to be caught.'

The Auchengillan pool regularly hosted Scouting activities as recalled by Jim Donnelly, 'Competing in the pool in a raft building competition was something else we did. The instructions were simple. Build the raft – use staves and anything buoyant then get on board and paddle it to the other end. We managed this but we were up to our waists in water by the time we got to the deep end. And we quite often camped on a hill just up from the pool in a bunch of pine trees quite near to the pool. I think it was called Tank Wood or something similar.'

Jim provided further memories, 'As Catholics, we had to go to Mass on Sundays. At camp, this was not like going to Mass in St Robert's church in Househillwood. We even had a Catholic Chapel at Auchengillan and this was quite near the Providore, in the woods. The Chapel was big enough for the priest and the altar but everyone else was out in the open air. I later found out that the Chapel had been built by the 131.'

Further along the Drymen road from Auchengillan was the Queen's View, a point from which Queen Victoria is said to have viewed Loch Lomond. This explanation was never accepted by guys like Eddie Mallan as it was not much of a view. To get the best view you have to climb the Whangie hill which is just beside it. The 131 did this umpteen times, as Jim Donnelly explained.

'The Whangie was a big rock which had been split in two by the Devil's tail when he was jumping across from Dumbarton Rock to Dumgoyne – so said my PL and of course we all believed him. So another of my memories is when the older Scouts would do a hike to the Whangie hill. They would not let us trail along. I later discovered they made a stop at the pub!' It would not be misleading to state that most of the 131 lads learned to drink alcohol as part of their Scouting education – at the Carbeth Inn. Definitely a transferrable skill.

The Brotherhood of the Muddy Splash

Every 131 Scout who was bold enough to go to Auchengillan had to be initiated on their first visit, as described by Roberto McLellan, 'There was a concrete swimming pool in the middle of the site. This was filled by a couple of burns and the water was brown and muddy. There was no way of telling how deep it was by looking at it. In fact, it was probably only about three feet deep at most, but this was quite deep – probably chest high for a wee guy.'

Once Roberto had walked to the edge of the pond, the ceremony began, 'The big Scouts grabbed handfuls of mud and rubbed it all over my body, including into my mouth. My hair was given the full treatment as well. Then, when I was completely covered with mud, they grabbed me and swung me out in time, releasing me on the count of three. I seemed to fly through the air and splashed into the water on my back. I sank to the bottom and then started flapping my arms wildly to save myself from drowning. One of the big guys reached down and pulled me to the side. I was able to put my legs on the bottom of the pool. Safe at last!'

It was the same for every Scout and I can still vividly recall my own initiation, sixty-five years later. We all had to be initiated. That was how it operated. I'd say it was harmless fun, but for the victim, it was a wee bit scary.

This picture shows an epic 131 moment – an initiation ceremony beside the pool at Auchengillan. Eddie Mallan, Brian McIntyre, Pete McGuire, Roberto McLellan and the victim Michael O'Neill are all in there somewhere (Photo – Jim Mackay)

Once initiated, life had changed for the young Scout, 'I was a keen member of initiation gangs from then on,' Roberto recalled. 'I always got stuck into them after that. After all, it was just a shallow pool, although there were rocks and bits of wood and even old dixies, lying along the bottom. We would build rafts and wobble about on them in the pool. Other Scouts would build bridges. I don't remember it being used for swimming at any time. In winter it would be frozen over. Frozen solid sometimes. And always muddy.'

More laughter came from Graeme O'Neill when he recalled his swimming pool antics, 'When you jumped into the pool it was pot luck. You couldn't see anything because of the muddy water and there would be lots of debris lying on the bottom. It was a bit of a lucky dip I suppose.'

It was a good test. If a Scout couldn't handle being thrown into the pond, he was not tough enough to be a Scout in the 131 or any other Troop.

Our Home from Home

Every 131 Scout camped at Auchengillan several times each year and some of them went there nearly every weekend. There was great glee when a storage locker became available. Jack was delighted, 'We now had enough in our funds to pay for the rental and the kit was moved out there smartly. It was a big change when we finally got a locker. Until then we had to take our tents and dixies home every weekend and then carry them back the following weekend.'

The lockers at Auchengillan were a treasure trove. Each was about twice the size of a phone box. It was a great idea and loudly appreciated by one of the parents who had been a pre-war Scout in the Gorbals and would recount the tales of loading camping gear on to a trek cart and pushing this all the way to Auchengillan for a camp (well, there was a wee bit of a train ride as well, but it was still a long journey).

The lockers block produced some comical activity. As most other Troops did not camp every weekend, this meant that we could sneak some kit out of their lockers and use it ourselves. We would always return it fully cleaned before we went back home. We could even access their food supplies, such as tea and sugar, as well as stuff like tent pegs and sisal. We would use it, replace it and drop it back into the other Troop's locker. Len Ashforth mentioned at the time that he learned to pick the padlocks. And others, like Noel Carson, learned how to use a wire coat hanger as a hook. We had seen this trick on films and so we just copied it in the lockers. A very handy tool it was.

Camping made us very confident. We could camp anywhere in any weather. A five-minute chat on Troop night was all that was needed. The senior Scout, usually a PL, would pass the word. We would decide what bits of the menu each one of us would bring and then we would meet at the bus stop on Saturday.

The camping season opened at Easter and ran until the September Weekend. We would go out every week and spend two nights under canvas, with the exception of the Glasgow Fair fortnight – when we would be away at another camp site for 13 nights summer camp. There were also winter weekends. Being outdoors in bad weather never bothered us. So, as Scouts we would camp probably for about 30 nights every year with the really keen ones hitting 50 or 60 nights away.

Jack Banks summarised it, 'Camping wasn't difficult. It wasn't hard. It wasn't dangerous. Mothers didn't weep as their son went off to camp. That was life in those days. They were just doing good sensible activities. And learning how to face the world on its terms. Going camping was about learning to stand on their own two feet away from their parents and the boys learned to look after themselves, enjoy it and become self-reliant.'

The 131 were such regular campers at Auchengillan that eventually we were able to leave our tent standing when we left for home on a Sunday afternoon. Pete McGuire remembered this. 'Our tent was a huge ex-Army tent, about 15 feet long and the same across. It was made of very heavy bulletproof brown canvas and was murder to carry and it was very dark inside. But we were so good at camping that one of us big guys could carry the tent and erect it on our own, although somebody else had to carry the poles and pegs. But we could leave it standing on our favourite site at Tank Wood. We would move it around the site to make sure we did not kill off the grass underneath.'

Moving tents was recalled by Roberto McLellan, 'Getting the tents from the bus stop was something which the 131 rapidly mastered. I can still remember carrying the big tents up from the bus stop at Auchengillan. We must have easily carried them for more than half a mile, normally two big Scouts were needed to carry each tent.'

'I loved going there. It was our home for many weekends. No adults were involved in organising the camps. This was all done by the boys. On certain weekends a Leader would come out, but this was normally only for a day as most of them were married and would want to spend their weekends at home. In those days, they still worked on Saturday morning anyway.'

Pete had managed to save up his money from navvying during the college holidays and bought a wee Mini. None of us really knew anything about car engines but we would all try to assist with the vehicle. It could fit four Leaders and all their kit into it but it was really tight. Also it could hardly get above thirty miles an hour and that was only downhill.

Every time we got to the first hill outside Milngavie on our way to Auchengillan, the passengers would have to get out and walk behind as it struggled to get up the hill. There were lots of occasions when we would have to push it to the top. But it was a car and Pete was the only guy we knew who had one. The roof rack was crammed with our rucksacks and sometimes we had to push against the Mini to stop it from rolling backwards down the hill or we would empty the kit and carry the rucksacks ourselves up the hill.

Len McKinnon's uncle was a motor mechanic and he got hold of a wee van for him. We all worked on it and he was able to use it when he turned seventeen and got his provisional licence. We could squeeze five or six Scouts inside. Needless to say, though, none of us had a full driving licence and Len used to live in fear of being stopped by the cops and losing his licence.

Scouting for us was a great adventure to be enjoyed at all times and in all weather conditions. Auchengillan was the 'Happy Land' as far as Graeme O'Neill was concerned. 'It was such a good place and I loved going there. We cooked our own food and it seemed to taste much better there. At times we would climb trees and fix up swings and have a great time. Probably a wee bit hair-raising for some people!'

The Kings of Camping

Our camping skills were under scrutiny every weekend as part of the Sassenach Trophy competition. This prize was awarded to the Troop which had gained the highest number of First Class camp awards during the camping season. For us, this was really the Champions' League of camping.

The Sassenach Trophy

Lots of other Troops camped regularly and all strove to be awarded a First Class camp site. For the weekend camp Leader, whether he was a PL or ASM, failure to get this rating was unthinkable. One PL came home with a Second Class grade, so had to go out the following weekend and sort it out – and achieved a First Class camp mark.

The camp site gradings were marked up on a blackboard on the side of the sweetie shop at Auchengillan. Our PL would wait with Scouts from other Troops beside the hut for the Camp Skipper to chalk up the results. This was probably our first experience of stress at an early age. Once our score had been posted – First Class of course – we would race away jumping up and down in delight. That's how much it meant to us.

The First Class rating was so important that the PL had to phone Jack at home on the Sunday after the result was published. Jack would also want to know the ratings for various other Troops as well, our main rivals for the trophy.

We had finished second in the Sassenach Trophy in 1961 (having won it the previous year), so our victory in 1962 was celebrated enthusiastically. By the middle weekend in September we knew that we were the winners, as we had been awarded 12 First Class camps by then and nobody else could catch us over the remaining two weekends. But we were not allowed to take the trophy home with us, so Jack had to go out to 'Gillan and bring it up to show the Troop the following week. A great memory for all of us.

Another win for Jack Banks, the Alex Ferguson of Glasgow Scouting.

Danny Houston was one of these champion campers, 'We did win the best camping Troop at Auchengillan for five or six years in a row.'

In fact, the 131 were so successful that we were asked to allow somebody else to win it. Jack reluctantly agreed to this request. There were plenty of mutterings about a stitch-up and poor losers, but he knew it was part of the bigger picture. Our Troop camp sites were still inspected on the Sunday morning and the result notified to the PL, but it was not logged in the competition scorecard.

Camping enabled the boys from the scheme to get away and be confident, competent youngsters ruling their own domain.

This enthusiasm for camping continued throughout our history. Joe McEwan remembered it well, 'All I had to do was to pass the word to Skipper and he would tell the Troop that I was taking a camp at the weekend. After that it was easy.' This point was emphasised by Alan McCombes, 'I remember the mad camps at Auchengillan. There was always something daft going on there and we loved it. Away with our pals and having great fun.'

Eddie Mallan was one of our gang of veteran campers who roamed around the site in T-shirts, khaki shorts rolled up and boots with two pairs of socks. They were always interested when they saw other Troops with different tents and gadgets. The 131 would meander all over 'Gillan to check on the opposition and learn from them if they could. If some Troop had something interesting they would ask how to make it, etc. They were nosey and would copy these ideas for themselves.

An early camp at Auchengillan – note the headwear!

Training PLs

The Easter Camp was one of the building blocks of the 131 programme. To ensure there were enough Leaders, Jack would organise a joint camp with another Troop. This was a special training weekend and only PLs and Seconds would attend.

Advanced training would be tackled and standards were high. It was probably a bit like the pre-season sessions for football and rugby teams. All the PLs were expected to turn up and work hard. New skills were learned and everything was practised rigorously. Pete McGuire remembers it well, 'We got stuck in right away as soon as we reached 'Gillan. All our kit in the lockers would be sorted out and repaired. Axes and saws were sharpened and cooking dixies were thoroughly cleaned. We were getting ready for the new season. There was no time for faffing about. It was hard work but good training for us. We felt we were special guys.'

Serious pioneering projects were also practised, such as the Troop favourite, the aerial runway. Experience was used and knowledge was gained. 'These training camps were a great boon to us,' remembered Jim Mackay. 'We came home tired and happy as we had done lots of serious Scout work and learned a lot as well.'

Jack explained his thinking behind these training weekends, 'I felt it was important that the older boys, the PLs, could get away from looking after their own Patrols at camp and get some good, hard training which was suitable for their age. You have to remember that these young guys were 15, 16, 17 and most of them had started out in the adult workplace as well. They were not kids but young adults.'

'We would always do a long session on the aerial runways as this was a big part of our regular Troop night and camp activities. It was a challenge for them as they needed to really have the knowledge and guts to build it, and to climb up high trees. Not everybody could do that easily but they all did their bit. I made them check out their work before anybody else could use the runway. There was never any problem as they had the skills and the toughness for it.'

The Court of Honour (COH) was also held at this camp. This was the management meeting of the PLs and Seconds, along with the Leaders. All upcoming matters were discussed and arrangements were made. The 131 worked well because all the senior Scouts were involved in the management and planning of activities. Jack or Jimmy McNeillie would suggest some activities and we would have a look at them, agree the dates and decide who was responsible.

In reality, this was simple forward planning. It always produced a lot of discussion, and we came away from the COH feeling very important. We had been given tasks to organise for the whole Troop. This was serious responsibility for us at that age. Once more, B-P's guidance was being put into practical use – Make the boys themselves manage the affairs… let them make their mistakes and learn sense and responsibility.

Other matters were decided at the COH, such as which Scouts were now eligible for promotion to Second or PL. Little did the keen PLs realise that Jack and Jimmy had already made these decisions. 'But we knew that if the PLs discussed it and came to the same decision we had strengthened the system,' chuckled Jack. 'So we would always slant the decision to get the desired result.'

In the 1990s, the Scout training system included attendance at PL training camps as a required skill. The 131 had led the way years earlier.

Climb Every Mountain

A regular outing at Auchengillan was an expedition to the top of the great hill of Dumgoyne (1,400 feet). We would climb over the camp site drystone wall and walk down into the Blane valley. The river Ettrick was the next obstacle, but there was a well-used path which crossed it at a low point. Boots were tied round necks to do this bit. Then we had to avoid being seen by the ghillie at Edmonstone Castle – or so we imagined as nobody can ever recall being chased by him – or ever seeing him!

The next stage of the journey was to cross the quiet A81 road – nowadays full of traffic – and to get up the hill beside Glengoyne Distillery. I can still remember there was an AA Box on this stretch of the road and we would wave to the motorcycle AA man. He would salute back. We used to think that it was the same man every time and we called him 'Andy the AA Man.' This was a glamorous job as far as the 131 were concerned – all we had experienced were a couple of mopeds.

The 131 climbers were just wee lads, although the PL would be sixteen or seventeen. They had no formal training in hillwalking or mountaineering. And they did not bother with a map as the route was obvious – down the hill, across the river and then cross the road and go up the big hill. Turn around at the top and return to the camp site. A round trip of about 8 miles.

Dumgoyne is actually a very steep hill. There is an easy route which follows the ridge line and curves gently upwards. But this took too long for impatient Pollok Diehards. Instead, we went straight up the front of the hill like Sherpas.

The route was hard on the way up and a wee bit dangerous coming back. Stumbles and slides were often part of the trip. But all the 131 lads ever collected were grazed knees and sore hands. They were full of energy, as well as very watery Coca Cola.

Quite often there would be a couple of Scout groups on Dumgoyne, all striving to be the first to the top or first to the bottom.

We loved it. We felt like we were real mountaineers. Mount Everest had only been climbed a few years earlier. We never worried about falling down or getting injured. It was just another Auchengillan experience.

The other regular rock-climbing activity was the shorter trip to the Whangie. This rock face could be reached by climbing the wall at McNamara's Outpost and walking half a mile along the Stockiemuir road. This treat was always reserved for the older Scouts as they were less likely to freeze once on the rock face. Most of them, like Eddie Mallan and Brian McIntyre, learned to climb here.

It was always great fun on the Whangie as we could normally see for about thirty miles in any direction. This also meant that it was a wee bit windy and cold so we didn't stay too long on the top and would hike back through Auchineden farm and then back up the farm road to 'Gillan. The Whangie helped to toughen up wavering Scouts through a basic process of rock climbing on a 30-foot rock face.

The hillwalking breakthrough came after 1966. The 131 got access to climbing kit when three of the Rover Scouts became PE students and were able to bring formal knowledge into the 131. The older lads loved this and became a reasonable group of hillwalkers, albeit normally wearing an exotic selection of outdoor clothing.

Building Projects

Service For Auchengillan was carried out most weekends. This could involve digging ditches, litter cleaning, tidying out the murky pond and even cutting the grass. The latrine blocks also benefitted from our robust assistance.

Having older Scouts who were apprentices meant that some serious work could be tackled too. A lot of these work-centred weekends were done during the winter months. The lads would be accommodated in the Providore building or they would camp.

One of the early projects we helped with was the building of a Rover Lodge in the woods. Glasgow Scouting had no separate Rover centre at Auchengillan. So, in the early 1960s they decided to build their own hut at Auchengillan. It started off as a small hut like those down at Carbeth but within a few years it needed to be upgraded (in fact, it had actually sunk into the boggy ground). The Glasgow Rover Scouts got hold of a much bigger wooden building and had it delivered to Auchengillan.

Although it was of prefabricated construction, it still had to be assembled. But before that could be done, it needed proper foundations to avoid the fate of its predecessor and most weekends would see various tradesmen and helpers, all Scouts, working on the site. The 131, of course, joined in on this project.

One of these working weekends was in January 1965. We were inside the building, sorting out the floorboards and painting the walls, while listening to the radio commentary of the Scotland versus England rugby international at Twickenham. Scotland were winning with only one minute to go and were pummelling England's line when Hancock, one of the England players, got hold of the ball and raced the full length of the pitch. We were screaming for somebody to tackle him but he evaded all attempts and scored.

Despite the collapse of productivity caused by this disappointment, the new Rover Lodge was fully erected on the site and used on several occasions by the 131's Rover Crew. But we would always hear the ghostly squawks of the radio commentator and see the phantom English player run away and dash our hopes.

St Kentigern of Auchengillan

The Glasgow Catholic Scout Leaders decided that they wanted to have a specific Catholic Church at Auchengillan. A site was selected in the woods, close to the track which led up from the main road. After an initial visit by a senior priest to bless the site, the hard work began on St Kentigern's.

The 131 were among the main movers. With an overdose of enthusiasm, about six or seven of us would turn up and start work on the boggy ground, pulling up bushes and digging ditches. The students amongst us did this sort of work during the college holidays. Michael O'Neill was a regular member of this team, 'We would dig away for about two or three hours every weekend. It was our Service for Auchengillan and we enjoyed it, apart from the midges!'

Scouts of any religion could take part and many did. Both these buildings served their purpose and were regularly frequented by the 131, although both have now disappeared. In the late 1960s, the Rover Lodge was replaced by the huge Allander Chalet and St Kentigern sadly sank into the bog.

Highland Games and the Cunning Relay Race

By the end of the 1966 camping season, the 131 had won the Sassenach Trophy yet again. As ever, they were miles ahead of the second place Troop and a bunch of the lads went out for the final weekend to collect the trophy and the very tasty Scout Shop voucher for the winners. The £5 prize, worth almost £120 in today's money, was a well-earned reward for our regular appearances on the site that year.

'Gillan was mobbed with many other Troops. Some of these had brought along their whole Troop, as there was also a centralised programme for the weekend – the Auchengillan Highland Games. This was a great attraction for the Pollok boys.

Tossing the caber was one of the events and we were good enough to take first and second. Although our shot-putters (small rocks) were equally vigorous, their accuracy was dismal and too many shots went sideways instead of forward. We were not so good at the high jump, tug-o-war or the discus (throwing a cooking pot lid) but came back strongly in the long jump.

By the end of Sunday morning, we were just leading the competition with only the relay race to be completed. There was no racing track, only the rocky fields of Auchengillan, so it involved running around the camp site with a team of four runners. The Troop which won the overall competition would get another Scout Shop voucher for £5.

Tactics now came into play. A good plan was needed as some of the other Troops had six or eight older Scouts whereas we only had three. This meant they would probably beat us in the relay. The Pollok lads wanted to win to achieve some fund-raising without any parental assistance. So we came up with a cunning plan which needed a lot of hard work to succeed.

We explained to the camp staff that we only had three runners available as the younger Scouts had to leave early. The race was a simple cross-country run with four legs of about 500 yards each.

I ran the first leg from the Providore to the East End. Pete ran to the Campfire Circle and handed over to Roberto. He then ran the longest leg to McNamara's Outpost and back to the Himalayas where Pete was now waiting, having run across from Campfire Circle. Pete was too fast on the final leg and we won the competition and a Scout Shop voucher for £5 as well. A most profitable weekend.

'Gillan, 1965

Spectacular Stunts

For the 131, there was never a dull camp. We would cook mainly on wood fires and sometimes used the few Primus (paraffin) stoves we owned. Their use was limited to experienced campers as paraffin stoves could be dangerous. I still remember my personal introduction to this scenario when I ran a Troop camp at Auchengillan in May 1968.

About Thirty Scouts were camping that weekend. Cubs and parents arrived by bus on the Sunday. The wee jokers were led away to various distant points to keep them out of mischief and the parents, were given cups of tea, sandwiches and biscuits. The Leaders were inside a large tent counting the camp money and heating an urn on a Primus stove. Suddenly spurts of flame started shooting from the stove.

It was obvious that something was wrong, so Len McKinnon and Michael O'Neill, lifted the urn and started to walk away with it. A good safety measure. Besides, the water had boiled and would now be used to make tea for the parents. Then there was a huge jet of flame, about three feet high, from the stove. Lenny and Michael fell over, spilling hot water on the floor of the tent, and the other Leaders raced out of the inferno.

But there were still two Leaders inside the tent. I was one and Michael McGee was the other. He was counting the camp money. The burning stove had blocked our escape route and the rear tent door was firmly laced up, so I grabbed him and jumped down towards the bottom wall of the tent. I tore away at the pegs to create an opening and we finally crawled out into the daylight, while he was still cramming the camp cash into his anorak pocket.

We looked around at the bewildered crowd of parents. There were no injuries, apart from my singed eyebrows and beard. The parents gave us a round of applause as they thought this was a fire rescue stunt we had prepared for their entertainment. So, rather than spoil the narrative, we all lined up and bowed to the cheering audience.

Stove dramas were few and far between for the 131 and wood fires seldom caused accidents, despite their constant smoke and sparks. The pine wood which had been harvested from the postwar Forestry Commission forests near Auchengillan had an added delight. Fiery sparks of sap would fly regularly from the burning wood and damage anything near to the fire. 'It was madness when we put on this wood,' remembered Eddie Mallan. 'Big sparks would spurt off from it and we would have to jump away to avoid being burned. When it was dark we could see this technicolour display from all the other fires at 'Gillan as well.'

The 131 Scouts were quite able to perform impromptu camp stunts and Gerard Doherty was the star of one of these, 'I went to Auchengillan camp quite a few times, occasionally ending in me being injured. I once chased George Coll, who was annoying me, around the water tower at Tank Wood. I misjudged the height of an iron strut which George ran under. I ran into it and was knocked out. When I came to I couldn't see anything but heard an adult voice saying – 'It's only a scratch.' Meanwhile behind me younger voices, probably from the 131, were saying – 'Look at aw that blood, he's probably deid.' I was taken to hospital (Killearn?) where I had stiches on the bridge of my nose and eyelid. Naturally I returned to camp as quickly as possible and finished off the weekend. My Mum almost fainted when I came up the stairs with bandages round my head and looking like the Invisible Man. Another 131 camp with another great story to tell. I bear the scars to this day. Quite proudly. I have retold this story many times over the years.'

Blades of Steel

Scout knives have always been a sharp topic. Strapping a knife to a Scout belt was a rite of passage – it meant that the Scout had been trained in its use. It was a formal test and most Scouts thought that it was the authority for them to carry a knife. Obviously something had been lost in translation as it only meant that the Scout was trained in its use for camping requirements such as cutting sisal and rope and perhaps whittling some sticks for use as pegs or such likes. Nevertheless, it was worn proudly as a badge of attainment.

The 131 boys naturally graduated to the next level of knifemanship – taking part in knife competitions. This was a simple activity, known as knifey. A couple of Scouts would get together and throw a knife into the ground. As near to their feet as possible. The winner had to throw his knife very close to his own foot. Of course, this could go wrong.

At various times boots were hit but there is no memory of anybody receiving a foot wound.

There was of course another version of knifey and this used a nearby tree as the target. I remember one session in particular. My PL, Robert McGuire, had gifted me a knife as I did not have one. This was a Swedish hunting knife with a long bone handle. It was most impressive and claimed to be perfect for throwing at deer when hunting them. Of course we believed this story, although there were no deer to test this claim.

My first throw was perfect and the knife stuck in the tree. My second, however, went a wee bit off target, bounced off the tree and landed in my arm. Blood galore and off we went to the camp medical room where I was bandaged up. No more knifey at that camp.

Hand axes were most useful items and were used to chop wood and occasionally hammer in tent pegs. Various Scouts such as Jimmy Carson, Bobby Moore and yours truly managed to miss the tent peg and hammer our hands instead. Regardless of this diversion, hand axes were also worn on Scout belts and wrapped in a leather holster. Many bystanders gaped at this display of Scouting expertise when we made our way down the street.

However, we would not carry our knives or axes into church and would hand them over at the front door.

Battling Through The Gorbals

As Catholics we were supposed to go to Mass, but this was often impossible at camp. I can remember that some weekends at 'Gillan we would go down to Blanefield for Mass. This trip took almost two hours in total. On return to the camp, we would still be running around full of energy as usual, showing no ill effects of our long trudge up the steep hill back.

And going to Mass was important, as it was part of the Scout Promise –

On my honour I promise that I will do my best to do duty to God and the Queen…

Therefore, there was no dodging this requirement, as Jack Banks explained, 'As Scoutmaster I was always very strict about getting them to Mass. The parents had entrusted them to our care and fully expected that this would be done even though they didn't have a clue how hard it was most of the time. I think we were very good on this point. Many of these weekends, when at distant camp sites, there would have to be a Scouts Own service in the field, where a few prayers were said and then everybody got back to camping.'

At other times, the boys would go to evening Mass once they got back into Glasgow. Sometimes this would be at the Catholic cathedral beside the river, but most often it would be at St Francis Church in the Gorbals. When we went there for Mass, we would walk about two miles down the road to the church after getting off the bus at Buchanan Street.

This was not a problem for fit lads. However, we often carried tents and other equipment with us, as well as our rucksacks. We would be wearing kilts and would attract yells of abuse from local youths and often a fusillade of stones – 'Kiltie, kiltie cauld bum' being a regular chant. Suitably needled, we would dump the kit and race after these pests, often catching the slower ones and give them a few smacks. Another tribal warfare situation.

Sometimes we would go to this Church along with Scouts from the local Troop, the 182nd Glasgow. This was Jack's old Troop and he had great affection for it, 'Without the Scouts, I would just have become another wild guy from the Gorbals.'

Occasionally, on the way to Mass, the 131 could store their kit in the 182 Scout Hall. It was an amazing Scout headquarters, covering two floors of a tenement building next to the river. A few walls had been removed to make room for lots of Scouts. To the 131 lads it was sensational. We were mesmerised by it. Imagine having such an interesting place for your Scout Hall. They also had a pipe band, which practised there as well. This band would always be at the head of the big parade which the 131 also attended every year at Bishopbriggs.

For Brendan McLeod and others, attending evening Mass was a waste of time after being at camp. Once we were seated on the pews, we would all fall asleep and miss all the words of wisdom. But we could faithfully report to our parents that we had attended Mass. But the lads were never spoken to by any priests or members of the congregation for falling asleep. Everyone who witnessed it seemed to realise that they were decent lads doing the right thing – apart from the wild snoring coming from the sleeping 131 faithful.

THE GLASGOW FAIR FORTNIGHT EQUALS SUMMER CAMP

The Big Build-Up

Baden-Powell described Summer Camp as the Scoutmaster's great opportunity to train the Troop. It meant two weeks away from home at an unknown destination. The whole year built up to this great expedition. Camp money had been taken to Troop meetings and marked up in the individual Scout's bank book. In the early 60s, the cost for the whole camp was about £15 for each Scout – more than half of their Dad's weekly wage.

The boys funded their Summer Camp payments by unusual methods as Jim Mackay explained, 'We lived next to the countryside and there were plenty of cows so there were plenty of cow pats. This was the era when most families had a small allotment – or a plot as we called them in Glasgow. Manure was very good for the plot and for some reason it was used on vegetables and roses. So we would head off to the nearest fields with a wheelbarrow and a small coal shovel and shovel the cow pats aboard. Normally we would have made an arrangement with a local guy who wanted some manure for his plot and we would deliver it. The cash would go into the camp bank on Troop nights.'

Robert Allan and Brian Carson, found other ways to earn funds. It was still the days of coal fires and they would collect wood to sell on as firewood. One of the fathers would also bring home various lengths of wood and they would chop them into bundles, tie them up and go around the closes looking for customers.

Paper rounds were another source of income for camp funds. Eddie Mallan protected his earnings by hiding it in a sock, ready to thump any Pollok hoodlum who might try to 'jump' him.

Another fund raising initiative took place on a Friday night when various Scouts would rescue drunk men who had fallen flat on their faces and would return them to their embarrassed families. A few pennies would be donated to Scouts for their help.

Funding a Summer Camp was not easy, especially if there were a couple of Scouts from the same family and only one wage going into the home, as Jack pointed out, 'The 131 were all from poor families. Their parents did not have any savings. Every penny was precious. They were all just normal families in the scheme. When a Scout activity came along that was too expensive for two brothers to attend, neither attended. No moans. No feelings of injustice. As the 131 raised more funds we were able to assist these lads. We felt good about that.'

The Summer Camps always coincided with the Glasgow Fair holiday, when the city closed down and hundreds of thousands of its inhabitants headed for the holiday spots such as Rothesay, Dunoon, Ayr, Girvan and Blackpool.

Stand-Offs, Scuffles and Rain

Just getting out of Pollok was always an adventure and I remember my first Summer Camp in the Lake District in 1959.

There would always be somebody's father or uncle who drove a lorry and this would be parked outside Tommy's house, so we packed it with our kit and rucksacks. Some of the older Scouts climbed aboard and sat on top of this huge bundle, while the wee jokers like me got on the Corporation bus. We were first into Central Station.

On the teeming platforms, people carried suitcases and shopping bags full of holiday clothing, as well as other bags with sandwiches to eat on the rail journey. No prisoners were taken, as every little group fought for its place on the overcrowded trains. For the 131 lads, this was an experience which would be repeated many times over.

We had a well-practised method of coping with this chaos. Our equipment was stored in the baggage van and then we boarded the train. Seats had been booked, but other passengers worked on a first-come first-served basis and would not move from our reserved places. Luckily, we had four or five big Scouts, aged eighteen or over. Various scuffles later and we managed to cram into one side of our booked compartment. Eight smaller Scouts were fitted into this, with a few more sitting on the floor and some others standing in the corridor. We were on our way.

Unknown places flashed by as we peeped out of the windows and cheered at all the unfamiliar names. And then we arrived at Oxenholme station and got ready to board another train.

We younger boys threw our bags out on to the platform and jumped down beside them. The bigger lads had to run to the baggage van to unload the kit and get hold of a station trolley. Our task was to scoot down, go through the underpass and get on to the next train. We did this in quick time and climbed aboard.

But the PLs could not make it and were still coming up from the underpass when our train puffed out of the station. They had fallen victim to the railway's version of customer service – trains first, passengers second. Although we had explained the situation to the guard, he ignored us. Panic had set in, but at least we knew where to get off next – at Ambleside. When we got there we lifted our packs on to our backs and off we staggered. We had asked where the Scout Camp was located but most people did not know, as they were tourists, like us. Eventually we were pointed along the correct road.

It was a moment of discovery for those of us who believed the old fairy tale that it only rained heavily in Scotland. We trudged along and the mileposts were carefully checked. At the five-mile point, a small lorry passed us heading in the direction of the camp site. It was loaded with the PLs and our tents. They waved at us, stopped to take our rucksacks and moved on as there were too many of us to pick up.

Then at last the eight wee guys reached the camp. It had been a seven miles trek from Ambleside and there was a long muddy walk along a rough track before we got to the camp site. Jimmy Carson and I were tired, but the PLs had put up the tents and we tumbled into them with our bags. It had been more than twelve hours since we left Pollok.

Some of the 1959 Windermere Summer Camp Scouts –
Danny Houston, Robert McGuire, Len Ashforth,
George Lyden and David Mackay
(Photo – Danny Houston)

Upsetting the Local Wildlife

Within three days of our arrival, the first major drama of the camp occurred. The weather was warm, but the ground was boggy and uncomfortable. At least, there were no midges, so Henry Watts, Jimmy Carson and I set out across the site to chop some wood from live trees for making camp gadgets. These were rough inventions which looked like a table, bench seats, crockery racks and shelves for food storage. Nothing sensational, but they were very practical and filled us with pride.

As we trudged across the field, the older Scouts were about fifty yards ahead of us. They were standing beside a tree, pointing up at its branches. One of them hit the tree with a large stick. Suddenly they scattered in panic. They were racing in all directions, leaping over drainage ditches and waving their hands wildly. They had disturbed a hornet's nest and the hornets were now on a seek and destroy mission.

We fell down laughing. We were far enough away from the mayhem to be safe and decided to run away, back down the track. When things had calmed down, we surveyed the damage. George Lyden and Len Ashforth, had been stung on the arms and legs and we were able to treat them at the camp first aid centre. But Big Danny was different. He had been wearing a bush hat and had taken it off to swipe at the hornets before jamming it back on his head. He had provided an everlasting memory as he sprinted across the field and threw himself into the stream to escape. But he had trapped quite few hornets underneath his hat and his head had been stung many times. They had also gone under his shirt and attacked his upper body. Off to the small local hospital he went on the local bus. Danny returned hours later, his body covered in cream and half of his hair cut off. What a crazy day.

By the middle of the second week, Danny had made good progress and his odd haircut was the only clue to his previous antics. During this time, we had visited Lake Windermere and travelled up and down it on a wooden boat. Even the sun had come out to greet us most days. Then the weather changed again. Heavy rain. Very heavy rain.

This was the start of another mad escapade. We woke up inside our tent and knew something was wrong. Our PL, Robert McGuire, was shouting at us. From the waist down I was soaking wet and so were the others. We checked the inside of the tent, but it was dry. So, where had the water come from? Easy answer. It had flooded up from the ground as it made its way down hill. We were all soaking. The other two tents were in better nick, but there was still a lot of water inside them. We spent the next two nights in the camp hut further up the hill as our bedding could not dry due to the nonstop rain.

Our journey back to Glasgow lacked the drama of the outward trip. The change of trains at Oxenholme was easy this time round as there was a two hours' gap between them. The train back to Glasgow was not crowded, so the PLs decided to entertain the rest of us. In those days, some train coaches had separate compartments which could only be reached from the station platform. Once the train was in motion these were sealed spaces. However, they could actually be reached by climbing along the outside of the coach and opening the door from outside.

A nimble lad with strong arms could reach across and grab hold of the door to the next compartment. He could now swing across and balance on the outside step, open the door and climb inside. It was all safely done by each of the older Scouts while we watched in amazement. Any accident could have been fatal as, of course, the train was moving when these tricks were performed. But not even Big Danny managed to fall off. They were even singing Scout songs during the performance.

And they all came home safely to Pollok.

Tommy's Bad Break

Tommy's wife, Irene, was from Guernsey. She had been evacuated to Scotland at the start of the war before the Germans invaded the island. In 1962, Irene's brothers had arranged for Guernsey Scouts to provide tents and camping equipment for the 131's Channel Islands Summer Camp. Part of the camp was to be a holiday for Tommy's family to go to Guernsey to meet Irene's family for the first time – accompanied by 30 Scouts!

Tommy rode to work each day on a moped. It was economical on fuel but could not go very fast and was just a bit heavier than a large bicycle.

But it was no match for a Glasgow Corporation Albion double-decker bus as Tommy found out when returning home the night before camp. The result was a completely wrecked moped, a broken leg for Tommy, plus two days in the Southern General Hospital.

But Tommy's house did not have a phone and Jack lived many miles away. So, with the assistance of the City of Glasgow Police Force, messages were flashed across the city. The outcome was that there was no holiday in the Channel Islands for Tommy and his eldest daughter who would now have to stay at home to nurse him. And also no Tommy to guide the 131 through London to the Guernsey ferry. The excited campers were oblivious to any of these changes.

Everybody met outside Tommy's house. The PLs loaded all the rucksacks aboard the baggage lorry. Now all the Troop had to do was to travel to Guernsey. A journey of about one thousand miles over two days. Glasgow, as ever on Fair Friday, was mobbed. The 131 were once again back into the Big Fight for seats on the train.

The older Scouts had a list of the booked compartments and made their way aboard the London train. In keeping with local tradition and good manners, the labels had been torn from the windows and determined strangers sat in our pre-booked seats. A short discussion followed and the invaders were chased out. The boys squeezed into the compartments for the twelve-hours journey – the train was certainly not the Flying Scotsman!

The Forgotten Cub and the Sandwiches

Tony McGuire takes up the story of his first Summer Camp, 'I was only 8 years old and I was a Cub at the time. My three brothers were in the Scouts and were going to the camp in Guernsey, as well as my Dad who was a former Scout. Off we went to the Central Station on a Corporation bus. I was gripped tightly as we fought through the mob and finally arrived on our platform for the London train.'

'When the Troop was gathered at Central Station, ready for the long journey south, my brother Robert and George Lyden, as PLs, were in charge of the provisions for the trip, namely a huge wicker basket full of sandwiches and flasks. While helping to organize getting the other Scouts on the train, the pair seemed to have forgotten that they had left me sitting on (guarding, they told me) the hamper. Then, as the train pulled out of the station, Robert and George suddenly remembered the food, not me, and jumped off the moving train.'

'So here were two and a half people with enough food to feed an army, watching the tail end of our train disappear round the gentle curve and across the bridge over the river. I do remember the "two" of the "two and a half", blaming the "half" for some reason as if I had deliberately sat there on the hamper in an effort to get Robert and George into trouble with Jack Banks (The Boss).'

'Every cloud, of course, has a silver lining. A guard had been watching what had been happening and told us not to panic. An express train for London a couple of hours later would get us to Euston right behind the rest of the troop. So here we were on a train with our own compartment and an endless supply of grub. A bit like First Class, really. The fun lasted until we caught up with the rest of the group. My brother Robert got pelters from my parents, who had visions of me being mugged for the hamper.'

The main party had nothing to eat during the journey. No personal bags of sweeties or sandwiches from station stalls. It was a hungry trip and at 6 a.m. the following day, a bleary-eyed group climbed down from the train in London Euston.

Stuck in the Tube

Phase One had been completed. Now for Phase Two – in a totally unfamiliar environment.

Jimmy Carson and Henry Watts were two of the Scouts on this trip. Along with the others, they formed up and set off to the nearest tube station, a big step up from the Glasgow Subway. They were all carrying rucksacks, wearing kilts and generally cheery. Day Two of Summer Camp and they had not even left mainland UK.

We all climbed down many steps to reach the platform. The train pulled in. We rushed aboard and all squeezed in. The train doors started to close and the train moved off. Thankfully it was a long platform, as the next howler was about to unfold.

Robert McGuire had a problem. He had shepherded his Patrol in front of him and squeezed into the coach as it began to move off. Alas, his rucksack jammed in the doors as they closed. He was still strapped into it and could not release himself. Two older Scouts, big lads about 18-years old, jumped to his rescue inside the train. They grabbed at the doors and managed to prise them apart. Robert and his rucksack fell back on to the platform and the train rushed into the tunnel. A big cheer from the chorus of 131 Scouts. Another problem had been overcome. Robert caught the next train. This time he was carrying his rucksack in front of him. Phase Two was now concluded.

We then piled aboard another train at Waterloo. We hurtled through the Surrey countryside on our way to Weymouth, counting up the badges we could claim for the places we had visited or even just passed through on the train. Weymouth station was on the pier and it was easy for us to march straight on to the boat to Guernsey. Lots of the lads were experienced sailors after boarding ferries for their holidays *Doon The Watter* to Rothesay and Dunoon.

The cruise to St Peter's Port was gentle and incident free. Nobody was seasick and the older lads mounted guard to prevent any keen

Scouts from plunging into the Channel. It was rather enjoyable and the boys were able to chat to other passengers who, for a change, did not want to steal their seats. And to add to the enjoyment, Guernsey was bathed in sunshine as the 131 came ashore twenty-four hours after leaving Pollok.

Jack was there to meet us as he and his family had flown over from Glasgow the previous day. He had also brought a local lorry which would carry our kit. The rest of us formed up and marched three miles to the camp site. Along the way we sang all the Scout songs we could remember. The 131 Scouts were abroad and what a carry-on we were having.

Tomatoes and Hangovers

Guernsey is famous for tomatoes and Tommy's relatives turned up at camp next day with a trailer full. How much in weight, nobody had a clue. The 131 lads had only ever tasted tomatoes occasionally, unlike nowadays where globalisation brings them to our local supermarket every day. Nevertheless, we nibbled on them all day long and ate them at every meal.

Guernsey had more surprises in store for us and one of these was a really exciting attraction for many of the boys. The Nazi wartime bunkers were still intact. Glasgow had been bombed during the war – for many months in fact. So, we were all familiar with bomb sites throughout the city. But this was the first time we had actually seen real Nazi handiwork. The locals told us about the war years and the rough treatment they had received. This was only seventeen years after the Germans had been thrown out at the end of the war and memories were still fresh – and raw.

The camp site was not exclusive to Scouts. It was surrounded on two sides by large sheds which were full of even more tomatoes being packed for shipment off the island.

Another youth group arrived the day after us. They left a permanent impression on Michael O'Neill, 'This was a BB group and they were totally different from us. First of all, they wore suits and those odd-looking pill box hats – a bit like the telegram boys who used to cycle around with important messages for people. But the BB were also totally different campers. 'Their big marquee tents had floors!' remembered Tony McGuire. 'I can still see George Lyden and Danny Houston rolling around with laughter when they looked inside the marquee. A wee bit different from us.'

Summer Camp was always a time where young guys flapped their wings and attempted bold things, as they were away from their parents. Bold things such as getting drunk. The boys from Pollok were the same as all the young lads of their age group back home in Glasgow. Drinking alcohol was a dominant part of the culture.

So, it was no surprise that the older Scouts, a group aged from fifteen to eighteen years old, copied their cultural behaviour. Nobody knew them in Guernsey and it was very easy to buy intoxicating liquor, as the locals had the French attitude towards alcohol – mature and sophisticated.

Because some of these Pollok Scouts were small, they had to send another, tall Scout into the off licence to buy the bevvy. Then they all then went down to the wartime bunkers to drink the stuff and had a great time shouting insults to the Nazis. Jack had been expecting this episode, 'It was the same at every Summer Camp I had been to. Basically the PLs get drunk and so I had prepared a big empty tent for them when they came back. For the next two days they were on jankers and had to live there until they had fully recovered. I would do things like telling them I wanted to brush my teeth and they would have to go to the furthest water tap with a big pot and then bring it back to me.' Jack's method definitely cured the hangovers.

Football Glory and Fond Farewells

Guernsey was not the only foreign land conquered by the 131 during this camp. More of continental Europe was visited – and another badge earned. The small island of Herm was invaded for a day's outing. The whole Troop formed up and marched down to St Peter Port to board the small ferry to the island. Sandwiches were taken – mostly filled with tomatoes – along with a football as they were to play a game against the islanders. It was a nice day out, but there was one casualty – Jack.

As a very big guy, Jack would only play in goal as he had received a bad knee injury during his Army parachuting training. He filled the goals – or rather the space between the two jackets – very well. The local football pitch was very like Auchengillan, hilly and bumpy, so the lads were fully at home on its uneven surface. Quite a few of our lads were good players and the locals had no answer to our trcikery, despite all being adults. Alas, during one of Herm's few attacks on the 131 goal, Jack fell over and had to be carried from the pitch by a gang of giggling Scouts – in proper First Aid fashion of course.

To cries of delight, the Troop received a cup from the local Squire. It was rather small and easily fitted into a sporran. Needless to say the victors celebrated with orange juice – and a cup of tea for Jack – but no sympathy. He hobbled around for the remainder of the camp.

The mighty football champions after beating Herm

Many badges were gained at Guernsey and Jim Mackay was one of the Scouts who completed his Backwoodsman Badge, 'Michael O'Neill and I built our Backwoodsman shelter in the field next to the camp. Spent all day putting it together, gathering wood, branches, leaves, etc. We were pretty pleased with it. However we woke up in the middle of the night terrified as the shelter was swaying side to side with a horrible grinding noise. We were too scared to look outside in the pitch black. Eventually it stopped and we plucked up the courage to look out. We were pleased to see a large cow wandering away. It had been scratching itself on our shelter. We were hugely relieved but couldn't sleep a wink after that.'

There was a poignant moment at the end of the camp, fondly recalled by Jim, 'When leaving Guernsey, as we boarded the ship the local choir (from the church maybe) showed up to sing us off on a safe journey. After they sang a couple of songs/hymns, we decided to sing back. So, it became for us anyway "We can sing better and louder than you." We all gathered on deck and went through the full campfire playlist alternating with the choir's contribution. We sang *I Belong to Glasgow, We're no awa tae bide awa* and all the rest. One of the boys was a great singer and he sang a solo *Song of the Clyde*. He sang the verse while we hummed along and joined in the chorus. It finished off with the choir and Scouts singing together a stirring rendering of *Auld Lang Syne* as our ship sailed away. It was a beautiful moment.'

Culture was definitely breaking in to the scheme.

The Lake District Re-Visited

Jimmy McNeillie led the Troop to Great Tower in the Lake District again in 1963. Jack's wife was pregnant, so he remained behind in Glasgow.

Central Station was tackled and Roberto McLellan remembered it well, 'In 1963 our Summer Camp was at Great Tower in the Lake District. Some of the 131 had been there before but for me it was the first time. We travelled by train and had to fight our way through Central Station on Fair Friday. This was normal procedure for Summer Camp. It was like a madhouse with hundreds of people battling through the crowd to get to their train.'

As usual, tents and camping kit went into the luggage van. But this time there was a helpful difference as Roberto explained,

'There were about twenty of us and some of us were allowed to travel in the luggage van. It was exciting as we could see out of a wee window. When we got to the changeover station we jumped down with our rucksacks, grabbed a trolley and loaded the tents on to it. A couple of the big Scouts ran ahead to warn the other train.'

'There was a tunnel we had to get through with the trolley before we got to the next train. It was a bit of a rush but we got there in time and everyone got aboard. I was really excited. All the other Scouts were cheering away and we had a good singsong before the train got to Windermere where we got off. The previous time the 131 had been there, they had to hike to the camp. But this time, there was a lorry for us and our kit, so we climbed aboard and had a peaceful journey to the camp site.'

One of the older Scouts, George Lyden, had been there in 1959 and he was worried that it would rain like the last time. But Roberto was able to report a happier story about the weather this time round, 'The camp was great fun. Of course, it rained, but not too heavily and we were able to stay in our tents. The best bit of the camp was when we were able to chop down some trees, like real lumberjacks, and used the wood to make a wee bridge. I wonder if it's still standing now?'

Needless to say, there was the inevitable accident to a 131 Scout and Roberto was there when it happened, 'Easily the biggest memory I have of that camp was when Eddie Mallan fell and broke his arm. We were just running across a field when he slipped and fell down. When he got up he was yelling and holding his arm. Len McKinnon and I were First Aid trained and had a look at it. We figured that it was broken in two separate places and we bandaged it up with the proper sling and went along to the Camp Warden for assistance. Eddie was doing a wee bit of wailing by this time.'

'The Warden was friendly but a wee bit adventurous. The three of us climbed into the back of the Land Rover and off we went to the nearest hospital. The Land Rover must have been wartime because it was bare inside. And it was also very muddy as it probably hadn't been washed out for weeks – it was manky in fact.'

The hair-raising journey has never been forgotten. Roberto and Len crouched in the back and held on as the warden drove frenetically all the way to the hospital. It swayed around and seemed to hit every bump on the way. Once they got there, Eddie was treated and a big plaster cast was put on his arm. So, for the rest of camp he tried to avoid wet places. All the 131 lads signed the plaster remembered Roberto, 'It was like a trophy for us.'

The rest of the camp passed peacefully. Cooking, pioneering and map-reading were the main activities. There was also another boat trip across Lake Windermere. 'This was a real treat for us and I can't remember any nonsense or daring escapades during it,' recalled Roberto. 'And most evenings, there was a campfire with lots of other Scouts who were camping there. We loved doing our Scottish songs in front of them.'

Then it was back to Glasgow at the end of the two weeks. But this time there was no acrobatic swinging from the carriage doors. The lads were too busy eating Kendal Mint Cake this time.

Great Tower Camp Site, Windermere – the Big Barn used by the 131 in 1959 and 1963

Summer Camp Heats Up

The 131 always aimed for exciting Summer Camp locations and 1964 was no exception. The hardy travellers headed for Watcombe Scout Camp near Torquay, along with other Troops from Penilee and Milton.

Some food had been purchased in advance and this had been brought along in various bags and cardboard boxes. It was loaded on to the bus and guarded by the Penilee Leaders and Pete McGuire was sitting with one of them, 'We, the 131, did not know what was in the big heavy cardboard boxes. Frozen chickens was the answer. Six frozen chickens from the meat market at a cheap price.

Sounded good. Joe Farrell, one of the Penilee Leaders, told me that he believed they would not thaw out before we had reached Torquay the following morning. Fair enough.' But these were the days before cool bags and cool boxes, and the blankets wrapped round the boxes for insulation were not up to the task.

Pete continued the gruesome tale, 'True to form, the chickens began to defrost during the journey and leaked a red-coloured liquid beneath them on to the floor of the bus. We tried to dry this up but it continued.' The rest of the passengers had not noticed this at that point. They soon did.

'Somewhere in the middle of England, the bus suddenly braked. Everybody grabbed on to something to steady themselves but the chicken boxes slipped out from under the seat and slid down the bus. The other Scouts all cheered as this gooey mess swirled along the floor. We mopped up the mess and kept the boxes jammed tight for the rest of the journey. Despite this wee bit of nonsense, we cleaned the chickens up at camp and cooked them that night. They were very tasty as far as I can remember.'

Everybody was relieved to arrive at the camp site after the long journey. The coach was able to drive up the narrow lane to the gate of the campsite, on the cliffs above the Channel. It took about thirty minutes to unload the bus and all the kit, then another thirty minutes for the coach to reverse down the narrow lane back to the main road. The normal camp fun and games were now under way for the next two weeks.

There were plenty of vivid memories for Roberto McLellan, 'Watcombe Camp near Torquay was a great Summer Camp. I can remember the bus journey from Glasgow. It seemed like it would never end but we eventually got there safe and sound. The camp site was in a big field which sloped down to the cliffs beside the sea. It was very hot indeed, a bit like Italy. But we were Scouts and knew how to avoid sunburn. Only one or two Scouts were roasted by the sun and they were not from the 131.'

Every day, two leaders and two older Scouts would walk down to the local village to buy food. This would be carried in rucksacks, with some cardboard boxes being brought back at times. Pete McGuire was doing one of these shopping expeditions when he was caught short. He headed into the nearest public toilet to find out that he did not have a penny for entrance. So he used his initiative. As a future PE teacher, he easily scaled the toilet door, only to find that there were spikes on the top!

These were no obstacle to him and he clambered over. But his watch strap caught in one and his arm was badly gashed. Even worse, his watch had now fallen down outside the cubicle. Tying a handkerchief round his cut arm, Pete opened the door stepped out and retrieved his watch. The door clanged shut behind him and he had to repeat his acrobatics.

To reach the main town, Torquay, we had to walk two miles and then catch a bus. Trips were made there several times during the camp, and the rest of the time was spent doing projects and getting a suntan. Yes, our peely-wally Glasgow bodies were exposed to the burning sun. The Scout rules of health were rigorously followed and everyone gradually tanned up. That was apart from Gilly, one of the young leaders from the Milton Troop. He was red-haired and remained pale, sometimes breaking out in a red puffy rash if he felt brave enough to expose his muscles to the sun. Torquay was definitely the hottest Summer Camp with the nearby Channel acting as a big magnifying glass to increase the heat.

High jinks at Torquay 1964 – Roberto McLellan and Michael O'Neill on top with Brian McIntyre, Pete McGuire, Brendan McLeod and Len McKinnon dangling down

There was the usual full programme of Scout work and plenty of badges were gained, including the Backwoodsman Badge. This involved identifying edible plants and mushrooms – nobody was poisoned. As Roberto recalled, fungi handling was strictly controlled, 'Only a PL was able to let anyone taste the fungi as they had all been well trained to identify the stuff. This was another cool skill for us and made us even more proud of being a member of our special 131 gang.'

This badge also had a section where an overnight shelter had to be constructed and used. So, for Graeme O'Neill, this was a great achievement, 'I can still remember it vividly. We had to spend two days in a forest and build a shelter to sleep in. I think we called it a bivvy. It was made from a small groundsheet and we covered it with branches and ferns to hide it. I think mine looked good. We had to catch fish from the burn that ran down the hill. This was quite easy as we had done some fishing before in the 131 Fishing Club. We cooked the fish and ate it. But we had some normal food as well like digestive biscuits and a bar of chocolate. We also had to find our way out of the forest and back to camp. But the best bit was getting the badge.'

There was plenty more fun and games at the Torquay camp, especially with one daily ritual which had to be completed correctly. This was the thunderbox patrol. Roberto laughed at this performance, 'We had a field latrine with a plumbed in running water supply – and two thunderboxes. These had to be emptied daily and would be carted off to the septic tank which was a wartime brick construction at the top of the field. The thunderbox patrol, for obvious reasons, had to be properly supervised.'

One morning, the Leaders were sitting around drinking tea and talking about the day's programme when suddenly a shout came out from further up the hill. Some Scouts started running towards the Leaders and others ran up the hill, making a lot of noise. Something had happened. The Leaders jumped to their feet and ran up the hill, anticipating the worst.

The mystery was quickly revealed. There had been an incident at the septic tank.

Eddie Mallan had witnessed the epic event and told me the tale at the time. Gilly had been supervising the emptying of the thunderbox contents. To do this, he had to lift open the lid to the septic tank and tip the thunderbox contents into it. This was a straightforward task. But, as he was closing the tank, his arm bashed against the metal rim of the lid. His watch strap was made of fleximetal. It snapped and the watch fell off his wrist. He tried to grab it, but it fell into the sludge below. It didn't sink down, but remained on the surface, almost winking back up at him.

Gilly, determined to retrieve his watch, decided to lean in and try to grab it, but he couldn't reach it. However, Scout Leaders are guys with plenty of bright ideas and Gilly had one. He told the bigger Scouts to hold on to his legs and lower him until he could grasp the watch.

Down he went, head first, legs gripped tightly by the lads. To reach the watch, he had to wriggle a bit and grabbed it successfully. But the boys could not hold him and he plunged from their grasp, head first into the thunderbox pit. He was able to stand up in the mess as it only came up to his waist. Not a pretty sight!

The other Scouts could not help him as they were roaring with laughter. When the Leaders arrived, they set about organising his rescue. They grabbed hold of a couple of ropes and tied a bowline knot in each. With the leaders now holding tight, these were thrown to him in the cesspool. He fitted them around his waist and held on as they pulled away to lift him from his boggy location. He managed to grasp the top edges of the tank and slowly climbed out, covered from top to toe in the pit's residue.

The Leaders pulled the two ropes tight. This kept Gilly about ten yards away from them as he was marched down the hill to the nearest latrine. Once there, he was washed thoroughly with a hose. Only when he appeared to be fully clean, were the ropes were slackened and he was thrown a bar of soap.

The unfortunate youth was then sent into town, to go to the swimming pool which had hot showers. But it was not the end of the story. Gilly returned from town and asked where his clothing was. He had spotted a dry-cleaning shop and wanted to take his shirt and shorts to be properly cleaned. I pointed to the camp fire where they had gone up in flames as soon as he had left the site a few hours earlier.

Gilly had managed to save his watch but it needed serious cleaning at the watchmaker's shop in Torquay. Even sixty years later, any mention of this incident produces great guffaws from those who were there. They also remember the usefulness of the bowline knot.

Eddie Mallan and Michael O'Neill, Torquay 1964

Wild Swimming

The camp site was beside the sea and the 131 had the use of a rowing boat every day. The little cove was nice and peaceful and the boys would normally splash around for a few hours. However, one day the programme changed – dramatically.

Four of the older Scouts were jumping from the boat into deeper water and swimming around. Two of them would jump in and the other two would row the boat and pick them up. Simple and enjoyable. Then it happened. The rest of us were on shore when we heard the yell, *Shark! Shark!* A bit of clowning about by the swimmers we thought. But no, it was real.

Two of the lads had swum about fifty yards from the boat. One of the rowing pair had then spotted something in the water between the boat and the swimmers. He looked again and grabbed the other oarsman. It was a shark! Definitely. A large fin was clearly visible. It must be a shark – not that anybody from Pollok had ever seen one. A warning was shouted to the two swimmers and the boat rapidly made its way towards them.

It reached the swimmers but did not wait for them to climb aboard. The oarsmen thought this would have been too dangerous, in case the boat tipped over. The swimmers had to hold on to the sides of the boat while the oarsmen rowed wildly for the shore. The rest of the Scouts on the beach had run to the water's edge. They were all cheering away. Everybody could still see the shark's fin which was circling some distance behind the swimmers and for them it was terrifying at the time.

One of the panicking swimmers was Eddie Mallan who recalled that he never really saw the shark. He was too scared to look around and just kept thinking that it would bite Noel first. That was his insurance policy and he made sure he was in front of him all the way to the beach.

The crowd on the beach could only hear the faint yells and the shark's fin could only be seen by the taller lads. 'From where I was standing,' recalled Jim Mackay with a smile on his face, 'it certainly looked like a shark. But we had never seen a shark, in fact we had never seen a salmon or even a large trout, so this was real mass entertainment 131-style. It was a great laugh and nobody ever believed that the swimmers would be eaten up by this monster from the deep – apart from them!'

He was correct. All four staggered ashore to loud applause and the shark vanished. Was it really a proper shark with huge teeth? Or was it maybe only a basking shark or even a porpoise? Who knows, but the 131 did not go into the water again for the next few days. Pollok boys are not daft.

But they did explore the local nightlife…

'One night, the older Scouts went to a local hotel which had a band playing,' recalled Roberto McLellan. 'We did not know who the band were until we were inside the hotel. It was the Eric Delaney Band. We were astonished. He was probably the most famous drummer in Britain at the time and we had even seen him on TV as well. His session was fabulous and he played solo on various drums for about twenty minutes. An unexpected touch of culture.' Some of the other lads were introduced to 'scrumpy' cider that night and lived to tell the tale.

There were daft memories for Michael O'Neill as well, 'I remember there was a BB camp on the same site but their version of a camp was wildly different from ours. They had marquees, camp beds, benches, tables and cooks. We were just Scouts and we tried to be friends with them, even helping them to put up their tents, huge marquees, not Nijers like ours. But they were not friendly. In fact, they annoyed us so much that we got up in the middle of their first night on the site and pulled their tent pegs out. Their tents collapsed and we ran away.' Of course, the 131 came back to assist the stricken BB campers half an hour later. A subtle point had been made and the BB welcomed the lads into their company for the rest of the time there.

Good Deeds at Gilwell

In 1965, Jack decided to take the Troop to Gilwell Park in Essex for Summer Camp. For the 131, this was sensational. Gilwell was the most famous camp site in the world of Scouting. It was the principal Leader Training centre for the movement and Scouters from all over the world came to attend its courses. Jack had been one of them.

The 131 hired a double-decker red bus for the journey and the tents and camping kit were loaded into the bottom deck. Most of the Scouts travelled upstairs, sleeping on the long seats or on the metal floor. Some of the older lads stayed downstairs to keep a safety watch and make sure that nobody toppled from the open back of the vehicle. A stove was set up beneath the stairs and an urn boiled away to make soup – the ghastly dried stuff – as well as cups of tea and cocoa.

THE GLASGOW FAIR FORTNIGHT EQUALS SUMMER CAMP

The Mackays going to Gilwell, 1965

For the first three days at Gilwell, the weather was good. Then it rained. It was like a biblical deluge. Most of the camp sites were washed away and about two hundred campers took refuge in the big barn. Jim Mackay always remembered the 131's response to the downpour, 'Everybody else scurried off to the big barn for shelter. Except us. We were top campers. We showed them how to cope with the rain. Stripped to the waist – to keep our shirts dry – and digging trenches all around our camp site, we diverted the water away from our tents. We built a series of duckboards and were able to walk across our very wet site. Our wood fire blazed away for three days. We were quite chuffed with our handiwork. True Scouts. We were complimented by the Camp Skipper, then the Camp Chief who was a famous guy called John Thurman. Jack was pleased, we had shown everybody how good we were at camping.'

In face of this stubborn Pollok resistance, the rain eventually admitted defeat and went away.

The heavy rain had also delayed a long-planned good deed. My cousin Margaret was a nun and she ran a home for abandoned kids quite close to Gilwell. So we had decided to give them a treat and raised some money to buy them sweets and Coca Cola. None of our lads had ever seen so many sweets and we stored them in the Senior Scouts tent.

The plan was derailed by the deluge and over the next few days, the sweets were devoured by hungry Scouts. Another collection was made and a group of about ten Scouts, all in kilts, made the delayed trip to the orphanage. We had so much fun that most of us stayed overnight, organising Scout games like British Bulldog, Port & Starboard, incident trails and a wide game. In the morning we were surrounded by curious faces when we were shaving.

Forty years later, at Margaret's funeral, one of the orphanage boys approached me to thank us for that long ago visit. He was so emotional speaking about it. The kids had been looking forward to meeting these boys from Scotland and our visit had been a great highlight of their young lives. We were a sort of hero gang in their eyes but we didn't have a clue about how important this visit was to them. As far as we were concerned we were just doing a good deed and visiting a group of youngsters who were a lot less fortunate than we were. And we thought that we had come from a tough background!

The Fab Four

During the second week, the older Scouts went into London for a day visit. We needed to pick a meeting point that evening and decided that we could all get to the Eros statue at Piccadilly Circus.

At the agreed time, a couple of Scouts stepped out of the Tube station opposite the statue. 'We were not alone,' said Jim Mackay. 'In fact, we were surrounded by half a million people. The Beatles had just made a film and its premiere was being held in a nearby cinema. We actually heard the Fab Four arriving. An incredible screaming noise arose. Very exciting, but a big problem for us – how could we meet up with the others? We decided to squeeze through the crowd to the nearest Wimpy Bar. The rest of the gang were sitting there and we managed to exit the scene and make our way to the station. The Beatles didn't know that they almost met the 131 that night and they have been regretting it ever since.'

Getting ready to meet the Beatles – Tommy supervises

Queue-Jumping Tourists

Parliament meets the 131

A visit to Parliament provided another vivid memory for Jim Mackay, 'We went to London for another visit and decided to visit the Houses of Parliament. We didn't make an appointment. This would have been impossible as phones were very rare and all contacts in those days were made by letter. We were in a very long queue, with about 100 people ahead of us. One of us kept wandering down to the front to see what was happening. Of course we were in Scout uniform and wearing kilts. One of the stewards asked who we were and how many of us (about 6 or 8, I think). A few minutes later he came along the line to our group and led us to the front and into the building where we were met by Leslie Spriggs MP, chairman of the Commons Scout Association (or something like that) who gave us the grand tour, something which the regular punters didn't get. It was brilliant.'

This parliamentary treat did not inspire any political careers, although a few 131 boys became notable revolutionaries in later years.

Westminster Abbey was also occupied by the kilted 131 Scouts that same day. We all wanted to see the Stone of Scone which had been stolen from Scotland. We finally got alongside and surrounded it, much to the horror of the warden guy who was positioned there. He thought we had come to take it back again.

A Big Red Bus

Needless to record, there were more shenanigans at Gilwell and Jim Mackay was a wee bit hesitant about some of them, 'We went down on a big red double decker bus to Gilwell. Not sure if we had another Troop with us. The bus parked up in one of the camp fields. However, when groups of Scouts headed into town of an evening we developed a habit of collecting street signs on the way back to camp. We planked them under the big red bus. At the end of the camp when we packed up, we drove out of the field exposing our cache of seven or eight street sign trophies – oops!'

Another of these desperadoes was Roberto McLellan, 'Oh yes. Chingford was where the local gnomes disappeared from surrounding gardens and were found on the top deck of our bus just before we were leaving.' It's hard to forget giant gnomes as Michael

O'Neill confirmed, 'I certainly remember lifting a road sign planted in the grass on our way back from the pub and planking it at camp along with a few gnomes at the Gilwell jamboree. I do remember that it was large and took three of us to pull it out then carry it back to the bus.'

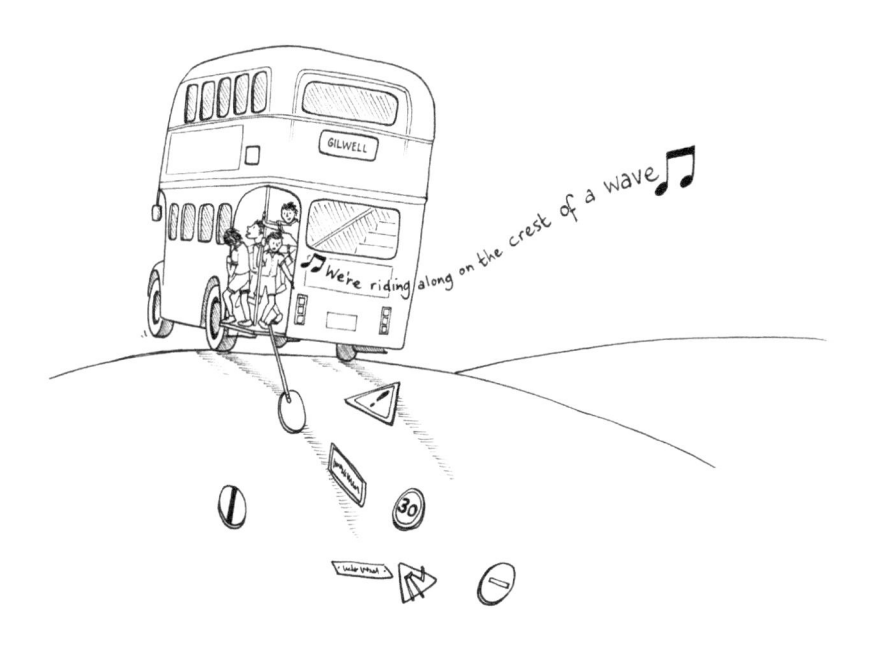

The big red bus featured on another even more adventurous event which Jim recalled, 'We had access to the bus for storage of equipment and the likes, as the driver had gone back to Glasgow. Which meant we also had access to the driver's cab! One afternoon with time on our hands a group of us were hanging about the field with the bus. We entered the bus and took shots each at sitting in the driver's seat pretending to drive it. Then one of our number who had his driving licence and had driven a van previously said he thought he could drive the bus.' The driver's name was confirmed by Roberto, 'LMcK driving a bus. YES.'

'He discovered the starter button and after several attempts the old bus engine spluttered and burst into life. There was no stopping us now, we had to take a spin around the field. We also hadn't appreciated how steep the field was as we trundled at an alarmingly increasing speed. Our driver then realised he had to make a fairly tight turn at the bottom to get us back up the hill. For a few moments we were terrified the bus might topple during the tight turn as we all held on for dear life.'

'However, we made the turn successfully and rumbled back up and across the field to where we started. Or nearly. Our driver missed the spot by several bus widths so we jumped gingerly out of the bus, ran to where it had been previously, dragged the 'borrowed' signs over to the new parking place and hurriedly hid them under the bus again. That done we raced out of the field as fast as we could, looking over our shoulder hoping no-one had seen a thing!'

This madcap episode was confirmed by Michael O'Neill, 'That was absolute madness! I remember the bus going round the field like something from Top Gear!' Needless to say, all of these antics were unknown to Jack and the other Leaders – at least until almost sixty years later.

Beware the Guinness Factory

Going to Dublin for Summer Camp in 1967 was a bold move. We were going to a foreign country and would renew our acquaintance with a ferry journey. It was also the first to set out from the new Hall. The baggage party went ahead on the Dublin boat two days earlier than the rest of the Troop. They were met at Dublin Docks by our Glasgow neighbours, the 30th from Cardonald, who were camping there and helped them to move the kit to Larch Hill Camp, Rathfarnham, on the outskirts of the city. The camp site was prepared in advance for the Troop who would arrive later.

The remaining 131 boys formed up at the Scout Hall, loaded a big van with rucksacks and moved off to the Broomielaw. There were no fighting throngs there, ripping labels from reserved seats and hurling threats. All that had to do be done was to carry personal rucksacks and some sandwiches up the gangplank and find space aboard the ferry to Dublin.

But this was not the usual ferry which sailed a couple of times each week. This was the cheaper boat – a returning cattle boat. Herds of cows had been brought from Dublin and offloaded in Glasgow. This left lots of room for passengers on the return voyage. Graeme O'Neill still has a long-lasting memory of this trip, 'The smell in the hold was awful and that was where we put our rucksacks. I suppose most of the cow pats had been washed out before we got aboard but the smell stayed behind and it was rancid.'

Three young Leaders stayed in the hold to keep watch. Big Frank Steele the camp treasurer sat on top of the bundle of rucksacks, with the camp funds in his anorak pocket.

The other Leaders patrolled the boat, looking for naughty Scouts. It was a busy and popular sailing. Half the population of Glasgow could claim Irish connections and these holiday trips were like a mini carnival. Guitar-playing folk singers, accordion players, fiddle players and a piper were all aboard and were all playing away. There was a general singsong aboard the vessel. The bar stayed open until late. A floating ceilidh, no less.

Several of the younger rascals managed to get in tow with some of the partying passengers. The Leaders captured four of them, all of them aged fourteen, who were drinking bottles of beer. This was confiscated and the ship's purser agreed to stop serving youngsters. After that, the Leaders rounded up all the boys and guarded them in a central point. Even visits to the toilet were escorted.

It was an early morning arrival in Dublin and the baggage party was there waiting for the Troop. The lorry was loaded up with the rucksacks and set off to the campsite. The Troop (thirty-six in total) had to catch the local bus. But the first bus was not for another two hours. Patiently the lads waited at the bus stop, a gang of Scottish Scouts in kilts in early morning Dublin. Another foreign country, even though they spoke English. Another badge for the camp blanket.

Before long, tired wee Scouts sank to the pavement and fell asleep. Then the bus arrived. The Troop climbed aboard and Frank paid the fares. Scottish banknotes were accepted without question. No devaluation was attempted as had been common in past years when at camp in England. The city had started its daily business and the bus chugged through the old parts and out into the far suburbs. Then came the normal fiasco. The camp site was two miles from the bus stop. Lots of wee legs had to trudge up the hill. Surprisingly, all made it safely without any dramatic escapades. The tents had been set up and we settled down to camp routine.

A few days later we made our first cultural trip – a visit the Guinness Brewery. A pilgrimage for the Leaders who were all fond of the dark liquid. The visit was interesting and the wee Scouts found plenty to keep themselves amused as they wandered round the building. The best bit was at the end when the Troop was ushered into a large room and everyone given a half pint of Guinness. For the leaders, this was superb. Drinking Guinness in the Guinness Brewery! However, unknown to them, some of the wee jokers had helped themselves to the glasses of Guinness as well – and then went up to the counter for a refill before being spotted and safely disarmed. Noticeably, three of them were a wee bit merry for the rest of that day's activities.

Graeme O'Neill was one of the lads at the brewery, 'I can still remember the strong smell of the hops they used to make the beer. It had a special tang to it. I'd never smelled hops before.' Most of the boys were infected by the Guinness bug for the rest of their lives.

For the O'Neill brothers, the Dublin camp also brought a chance to meet an elderly aunt whom they had never seen before. 'I think she was some sort of great aunt,' said Michael. 'We knew nothing about her so we had agreed to meet her in the city.' Off went the brothers to see her for the first time. The meeting place was the Gresham Hotel, a famous watering-hole for the well-off.

This visit is still clear in Graeme's memory, 'We walked down the lane from our camp site and caught the bus to Dublin city centre. Then we asked for directions to the Gresham. It was easy to find as it was on O'Connell Street, the main street and was enormous! You couldn't miss it. We approached it nervously and looked out for this aunt we had never seen before. She was tiny and was wearing clothes which she must have borrowed from Queen Victoria.' Michael chuckled as he recalled their encounter, 'She was very polite and asked us lots of interesting questions.' But Graeme's vivid memory is of their meal with her, 'We had afternoon tea with lots of wee cakes and sausage rolls. But the best part was that we ate cucumber sandwiches! We had never eaten these before – spam or corned beef was our normal – but we tore in to everything on offer. A great visit.'

While they were at Summer Camp, the 131 would learn to cook different dishes, mainly because of culinary specialities of the locality. In Dublin there were plenty of potato dishes – boiled, mashed, roasted, fritters and even chips – tricky to do in a big ex-Army dixie. However, another dish which was mastered was bread and butter pudding – with custard, of course. This proved popular and was on the menu many times during the camp.

One of bread and butter pudding's biggest fans was Tony McGuire, 'I really pigged into it when it was on the menu. I would eat loads of it and was always looking for more.' Alas, this craving led to an inevitable outcome. 'We had it for lunch and there was still some left at dinner so I had more. I felt really full and started to feel a wee bit unwell. But it was bed time and we all climbed into the tent and went to sleep.'

'My PL, Graeme O'Neill, was sleeping next to the door and I crawled on top of him trying to unlace the tent flap. He woke up grumpy and told me to stop being stupid and get back to sleep. I tried to tell him that I was feeling sick but I was afraid to open my mouth so I made some hand gestures in the dark. Of course he did not understand what I was trying to tell him and told me to stop pestering him. Needless to say, the inevitable occurred. I was sick all over him.'

Pandemonium! 'Graeme jumped up, unlaced the tent flap and raced across the camp site to the burn and jumped in it to get clean. I staggered after him and we both splashed water all over ourselves. The Leaders thought we were under attack from Martians and soon most of the Troop were awake by this time – and laughing their heads off.'

As for Graeme, his memories of the incident are still pungent, more than fifty years later, 'The worst thing was that the smell would not go away from our tent. We opened both ends and brailed up the sides and washed the groundsheet, as well as sending my sleeping bag and clothes to a laundrette. But the smell just hung around. It was cold and smelly in the tent for the rest of the camp.'

The moral of this story is obvious – don't be greedy with bread and butter pudding or it will fight back!'

One night, the older Scouts paid a visit to a Dublin club. A first for most of them and Jim Mackay was one of the gang,

'Can't remember much but Slattery's Lounge was a hoot. A group of us had headed into Dublin for the night and came across the lounge/club. We queued round the side of the building and climbed a staircase to get in. We paid the guy on the door and swore we were all old enough to get in.' Michael O'Neill picked up the story, 'It was a small dark room with booths around the sides and a small stage in the centre. The guy on the door turned out to be the raffle ticket seller, MC and main act.'

The entertainment on offer was mediocre, to be polite. The acts were dreadful. There was a magician, a singer and a comedian. Jim Mackay still remembers the scene, 'We were helpless with laughter watching them and trying not to bring too much attention to ourselves. The performers gathered next to us and they all bad-mouthed Slattery's and the MC, while congratulating each other on how well each had performed. We were struggling to hold our composure until the killer line came. One of them declared "that's the last time I perform here, not even if he pays £5." That put us on the floor. We were in tears. It was a bit of a *Father Ted* moment, only it was thirty years too early.'

The Gaelic Football Match

As the Troop was in Ireland, it was decided to go to see a Gaelic football match. Some of the Leaders had an idea what it was but none of them had ever seen a game and it didn't feature on TV in Scotland. The 131 turned up at the famous Croke Park to watch an All-Ireland match, joining the thousands of spectators. The stadium was huge – and ancient – it had earth terraces and rusty metal crush barriers. We settled down to watch proceedings.

It proved to be interesting and hilarious, as Jim Mackay recollected, 'Can't remember the teams but it was a big game, big crowd. Must have been a semi-final. When the teams ran out there was the loudest roar I had ever heard! It was amazing. There appeared to be about fifty guys in a team, plus First Aid guys with stretchers and priests who seemed to be the managers. Completely bonkers. The crowd loved it.'

Michael O'Neill was fascinated by the First Aid men, 'I think they were called the St Patrick's First Aid Brigade. They would just run on to the pitch when someone was injured. The game did not stop and kept going on around them. Sometimes they would load the casualty on to a stretcher and trot off with the teams racing by them. Total mayhem!' And we were mesmerized by the physicality of the game. These guys were battering into one another all afternoon. We hadn't a clue about the score but one set of supporters were singing at the end.

Viewing the game was often a problem as the crowd would regularly sway forwards and backwards. But the big difference for the 131 boys was that the playing pitch was enclosed. This safety measure had not yet been introduced into Scottish football grounds. But, here in Dublin at Croke Park, the crowd of 45,000 was kept on the terracing by a metal fence. It was just like one of those big wire mesh fences that surrounded some fields and pig compounds. But it certainly worked.

However, the priests racing on to the pitch was the big memory. They would race around at one end of the pitch and often ran on to it waving their arms and yelling abuse at the referee. We were doubled up at the spectacle as we couldn't imagine our priests at St Robert's behaving like this. It was hilarious.

For the record Meath defeated Mayo and went on to win the final in September 1967. The 131, on the other hand, did not make a return trip for this game. Once was enough for us.

The Hellfire Club
– The Midnight Terror Walk

Tony McGuire was just twelve years old when he, and the rest of the Troop, went into Dublin to see *The Fighting Prince of Donegal* film at one of the city centre cinemas. When the film ended, Tony went to the toilet and when he came back outside the cinema, everyone had already headed back to the campsite.

Tony knew nothing about the city or the bus services. None of the PLs present had remembered to count the Scouts in to the cinema and count them out again. 'I was alone in the city, with no idea how to get back to the campsite. I stopped a bus and asked the conductor for directions, but he told me there were no more buses going in that direction until morning. I was so young the conductor must have felt sorry for me, because he told the driver to take me as close as he could to the campsite and then give me directions before they headed back to the depot.'

'He dropped me off at the end of a mile-long narrow road (Mutton Lane), which was bounded by a high wall on one side and trees and bushes on the other. I had the daunting prospect of walking alone in the almost total darkness of the countryside back to the place where we had set up camp. To make things worse, we had been told a creepy story about a nearby derelict structure on top of a hill known as the Hellfire Club, a notorious 18th-century club for high society where members engaged in debauchery, including animal sacrifices and devil worship, pacts with the devil and supernatural beings. And I was sure it was visible from the lane I was now expected to walk along at around midnight. Even now, I would be afraid to walk alone in such conditions.'

'The bus conductor had told me to take the right-hand branch of the road after about a mile, and that would be the entrance to the camp. As I started off, I was running, but the echo of my footsteps bouncing off the wall gave me the impression I was being followed, so I slowed down, constantly looking behind me. I remember there was a crescent moon which made things even more creepy, but at least it gave me a little light to see something in front of me.'

'After some time, the road widened, and I could see two ghostly figures standing off to my right, and they seemed to be moving slightly. I asked them if they knew the way to the campsite, but they didn't answer. I mustered up the courage to approach them, putting my twelve-year-old life at their mercy. It turned out they were only the white gate posts of the entrance to the campsite glowing in the partial moonlight.'

'By this time, I was in such a state of panic that I just ran in total darkness through the woods, which I knew lay between me and where the troop had set up the tents. I was scratched on the face and legs from the branches of the trees, but I didn't care, all I wanted was to get back to my friends.'

'When I did reach the tents, I was screaming in panic at the top of my voice, trying to untie the fastening of the tent flap before the 'bogeyman' got me. Everybody else seemed quite relaxed about the fact that they had left me behind, and I am probably the only one who recalls it, but it did leave an indelible impression on me for the rest of my life.'

Initially nobody had even noticed that Tony had not returned to camp, not even his big brother who was one of the Leaders. Cocoa was dished out and all the weary lads climbed into their sleeping bags for a good night's sleep. Then the Leaders had started to look for him. They searched the woods and the stream and were sure that he was just playing some daft trick before bed time. They were confident that he would eventually come back into camp.

Yes, he did, but from the opposite direction as he ran up the hill in a wild panic. But all ended well, apart from the bollocking delivered to the PLs for their slackness. And Tony added his own input when this had been done.

'I even thought I should have earned a badge for that ordeal.' Perhaps the Ghost Storyteller would have been suitable if it had existed back then.

Snowdonia Gets the Treatment

Beddgelert, North Wales, was the location for Summer Camp 1968. It was situated in the Snowdon National Forest Park and was surrounded by lots of hills and woods. On Fair Friday, the Troop loaded up on to a coach and set off for Wales. There were about twenty-five Scouts at this camp.

The parents committee had worked hard to raise funds for the purchase of another Nijer tent. The 131 camp would have a smarter look instead of its normal Army surplus appearance. Some of our fund-raising activities of those days are laughable nowadays. Most families would have the *Daily Record* and an evening newspaper; some of these were delivered by Scouts who had a paper round. In fact, we always encouraged Scout parents to use Scout paper boys– a clever bit of niche marketing. But not only did the Scouts deliver the newspapers, but they also collected them.

On designated Troop nights and Cub nights, the boys would bring in bundles of newspapers, then once a month these would be taken to a big shed near Scotland Street School and exchanged for cash.

'Ah yes,' said Pete. 'We would also send out Patrols one night a month to collect old newspapers from the local houses. These were stored in a side room at the bottom of the Hall. The money made from these activities was for the Troop's benefit, so we had to do the leg work as well.' A side issue to the storage of so much paper was the added attraction for the local *ratus ratus*. We would have to shine torches and make a lot of noise to chase out the rats who had made cosy wee nests amongst the old newspapers.

Silver paper was also collected. This was the stuff which lined cigarette packets and various other things. Nobody in my family smoked, but lots of other parents did. When we had collected enough of it, we would exchange this for cash too. These small contributions mounted up and helped to pay for some camping items.

For the North Wales camp, nearly all the Leaders were available and our old coach chugged along in the dark, arriving on the camp site early Saturday morning. Tents were erected and the adventure got under way.

There were a few memorable episodes at Beddgelert. The first of these was when we ventured forth to conquer Snowdon. Correct preparations were carried out to tackle this big hill. The lads were introduced to mountain ropework and were trained in abseiling techniques as several of the Leaders were already competent at this activity. In reality, there would never have been any need to abseil on the mountain but it was definitely good fun learning it. Particularly for Bobby Moore.

He was about twelve at the time and this was his first Summer Camp. Bobby was absolutely terrified and would hardly budge from the safe rock even though he was securely belayed and could not fall far. The Leader, who shall remain nameless, was losing patience with him. Everybody else had managed to abseil that day except for Bobby. The Leader was determined not to fail and eventually managed to convince Bobby to get into the proper abseiling position facing the rock face.

THE GLASGOW FAIR FORTNIGHT EQUALS SUMMER CAMP

But that was as far as Scout Moore got. He froze again. The Leader implored him to lean away from the rock. *No way*, Bobby thought, gripping the rope in both hands. So the Leader resorted to basic principles and stamped on his fingers. Bobby immediately let go then and swayed outwards before realising that he could now abseil down the rock face. It was only about ten feet and he did so easily. His fingers were sore after that but he had passed the test and this was ticked off on his record card. I think we would call it off-the-wall teaching nowadays. But it worked and Bobby was never scared of abseiling ever again – although he always tried to avoid it.

The early stage of the Snowdon climb was easy, with several stops for drinks and navigation checks. Each PL had to take a shot at navigating the route, with a Leader supervising him. It was straightforward. No problems had arisen and all the Scouts were enjoying our day on the hill. Then we hit the steep part. Snowdon was a big mountain. In Scotland it would be classed as a Munro and the route up was hard. This slowed us down for a while, but we were able to sit down on some rocks for a snack break.

There was a huge roar – and two RAF fast-jets zoomed overhead. The lads could actually see the faces of the pilot and navigator. They all waved to the crew and cheered lustily. Huge excitement all round. A bit like a *Maverick* film nowadays, but no sign of Tom Cruise, though.

Upwards we continued, in good conditions, and suddenly, amazingly, we could see there was a café at the top of the mountain! We made our way to the café and after the mandatory posing at the summit, the next sensation was revealed. A train was chugging up the mountain! Once we had recovered from the surprise, everybody climbed aboard and we took the easy route down. Another mountain had been conquered. Another badge had been gained – and there were also mountain railway badges available.

Scouting activities were run every day and many badges were awarded. The Pioneer badge was the most popular as we were able to use lots of the cut timber which was around the site and build a smart bridge over the river.

The camp site was surrounded by woods and hills and was therefore ideal ground for wide games. On one of these,

Tony McGuire paired up with Charlie Stelmaszuc. The wide game was incorporated into the Backwoodsman Badge and had an overnight camp. 'We had a wee two-man tent and a petrol stove,' said Tony. 'So we hid ourselves away and settled down for the night. Charlie started to light the stove and heat up a dixie of water for tea. I told him to move it out of the tent and he lifted the water, which was boiling by this time, and then tripped over a tent peg.'

Matters rapidly became worse, 'We were both covered in scalding water. It was all over my foot but Charlie had spilled it over his arm. He raced out of the tent waving his arm like a windmill to try to cool it down while I wrapped my sock around my foot. As this was a wide game we were carefully hidden in the middle of a wood. Nobody knew where we were. Despite our wounds, we managed to sleep until morning.'

By this time, however, the situation had only deteriorated, 'My foot had a red mark where the water had landed but I could still walk OK. But Charlie's arm had swollen up. It looked like he was wearing one of those fat-suits. And it was very sore. I told him not to burst the blister – we were First Aid trained, but only at the basic level. Help was needed so we packed the tent and I carried it while we limped down the hill.'

Eventually they met a local farmer. But he was of little use, 'He did not want to become involved so he just pointed us towards the main camp site which was about a mile away. Off we went, me like Hopalong Cassidy and Charlie wailing and trying to cool his arm by removing his shirt. The Leaders saw us and took us to our First Aid tent for treatment. Luckily they were fully trained and no further damage was done to either of us.'

Tony and Charlie were then very careful at later wide games and managed to survive them unscathed. Oh yes, most importantly, they both passed the Backwoodsman Badge.

After climbing Snowdon and surviving wide games, a few days later, the 131 set out on their biggest challenge of the camp – pony-trekking, a new activity. First time for most of us, Leaders and Scouts. We were given small ponies and we rampaged across fields and through woods for a couple of hours, cheering and pretending that we were the Lone Ranger or the US Cavalry. A couple of wee Scouts were tipped off, but there were no injuries. Or so we believed.

Leaders posing in Wales, 1968 – Mullaney, O'Neill, McKinnon, Mallan, McLellan and Carson

The moment of truth was revealed the following morning to Hugh Mullaney, the Duty Scouter. When he woke up, he knew something was wrong. He couldn't move. Every time he tried to get up the pain from his ribs was too much. It was the same story for the other Leaders. But the Scouts didn't have any problems. They were all up and running around the camp site. Eventually one of the Leaders was able to supervise them for the rest of the day. We had discovered inter-costal muscles. It took us two days to recover.

Like the rest of the Scouts, Brian Carson could not understand why the Leaders were so sore after the pony-trekking. He had never been on a horse before and didn't think any of the other lads had either. He had just had an interesting time, especially when the instructor told us to trot the ponies. This inevitably turned into the

Charge of the Pollok Brigade and ended with the ponies jumping across a small ditch at the bottom of the field. One or two of our bold horsemen parted company with their steeds at that point. Oh, and by the way, no helmets. A different era.

Pony-trekking did not feature on any other programmes after that episode.

The Cornish Pasty Camp

Summer Camp in 1969 was held in Cornwall. This was probably the furthest away point from Glasgow the 131 could find on the UK mainland and the unknown location raised an obvious question. Was there a pre-visit to check out the locality? No. We just wrote to the local District Commissioner and he provided the details.

I had lived there when I was a wee baby and had then been there on holiday a few years earlier. Therefore, of course, I was an expert about Cornwall. It was a joint camp, this time with the 209th Troop from Milton and 36th Troop from Barmulloch.

Mr McGuire (father of four 131 Scouts) had stepped in as two of the regular Leaders, Pete McGuire and Bill Toal, were unable to come to Cornwall. Economic necessity – they were students and were able to get jobs at a Butlin's camp in Somerset for six weeks. This was a chance to make some much-needed money and they stood down for the camp. 'Our time at Butlin's was also educational,' said Pete. 'We learned how to crack eggs using one hand. A useful skill for later Troop camps where we would gleefully take an egg in each hand and crack them cleanly into the frying pan.'

The epic coach journey seemed to go on for ever before we even got into England, never mind Cornwall. There were plenty of moans and groans from the Troop as we rumbled through the night but everybody was wide awake and buzzing when we finally got there. The bus company was Southern Coaches from Barrhead and I think we were the first long distance trip they had ever done. We could have flown to New York and back in less time. The coach stayed with us for the two weeks, hiring itself out for local trips and the drivers slept inside.

After setting up the tents in the dark, the Troop explored the local area the following day. It was typical Cornwall, bumpy ground, windy roads and cows in every field. The older Scouts decided to join the local 'country club' which had a swimming pool – despite the camp site being beside the beach. The Troop Log Book for 19th July 1969 recorded an interesting occurrence:

> *The older boys took out temporary membership of the local social club, but the locals weren't very sociable, owing to the fact that the boys were from that miniature Chicago named Glasgow. (Probably due to the fact that they were also carrying on in their usual 'Bundy Ya Bass' manner.)*

> *This wee problem was smoothed over by Mr McGuire visiting the club and chatting to the manager, while the wayward Scouts were interviewed by Skipper. Community relations remained a sore point and the older lads were regularly pursued when they went out to the local village, Portscatho. One night, one of the Leaders raced into camp after having had to, regrettably, smack several local louts on his journey home. Shades of Pollok no less.*

> *The next day was Sunday, and despite the usual spate of dirty knees and squinty kilts, we rolled into St Mawes for mass to find out there was none! However, the local priest said a special one for us and then came back to camp with us later. Dinner and campfire followed and, a weary bunch climbed into their beds. The Leaders were still planning the next day's Scout work a few hours later as Neil Armstrong (a former Scout) stepped on to the moon. No TV for us we were in bed sleeping – or being pests.*

The camp programme was varied and designed to give the boys as much Scouting experience as possible, while also providing lots of exercise. The Log Book for 28th July described this:

> *At 11 am we commenced Scout works covering Athletics and the Camper Badge.*

> *When the Scout work was done at 12.30 the lads were given free time up to 2 pm when we had lunch. 'During the queue-up for lunch, we had a series of 3 consecutive fights. Burton v Hutchison, McKelvie v McGuire and Coll v Neilson. The winner in each case being Skipper.'*

THE GLASGOW FAIR FORTNIGHT EQUALS SUMMER CAMP

A camp golf course was set up and consequently we had to look out for flying saucers (frisbees) during the rest of the evening. Campfire was held from 10 pm to 11pm after which the Advance Standard lads went on their hike, returning at 3 am on 30th July.

A day later, when the Troop got back to the site following a coach trip to St Mawes, there was a large marquee at the top of the hill. A church group had arrived for their annual camp. The boys went across and helped them to settle in, doing various chores for these non-campers who were a wee bit bewildered by their all-action neighbours who also appeared to speak a foreign language.

They operated slightly differently from the Pollok boys and brought camp beds, tables, chairs, cutlery, crockery – and a small organ. This was too much temptation for Scout Johnstone, our musical genius. Within a few minutes the campsite was being bombarded with various tunes, including *The Sash* – much to the delight of the nice Anglican folk. Skipper legged it across to try and restrain him but the boy wonder was soon rattling off some hymns. Their organist was very impressed.

By this time, the 131 had fixed on to Cornish pasties as an excellent dinner dish. The local ones were as large as rugby balls, as one of the Leaders claimed. But they were all eaten. Graeme O'Neill was one of the happy eaters, 'It was strange and interesting to eat different food from our normal mince and tatties. The pasties were exotic for us, honestly. They had some spicy stuff and we loved them.'

However, for some of the PLs, the task of cooking a meal for thirty hungry bodies was often a challenge. The Log Book noted:

Porridge, as made by PL Burton, turned out like 'dishwater knocked stupid.' But not a drop was wasted. He was much better at cooking braised liver.

Every day there would be a 'jankers squad.' These were the Scouts, mainly PLs, who had been performing for the crowd and neglecting their duties. This group would carry out tasks such as cleaning the latrines.

Most nights, the tired campers slept soundly, except for some who would talk, laugh and shout well into the night. These were identified by the Duty Scouter and joined the jankers squad the following day.

The local District Commissioner came to visit the camp on 22nd July and this was noted in the Log Book. This was an important matter as the local DC was required to complete a form regarding the standard of camping of the Troop. It was a sort of quality control assessment and this form would find its way back to Glasgow and our own DC. The camp site had to be spotless.

> *About 6 pm the local District Commissioner, Mr Sharp, accompanied by his ADC Mr Hedley and their wives, paid the camp a visit. They were quite a pleasant bunch and they were suitably entertained by Skipper and Mr McGuire.*

Of course, Mr Sharp gave the 131 a First Class rating, both for the tidiness of the camp and for the programme. No other outcome could have been contemplated and the boys had worked well that day to achieve the necessary standard. The planned camp programme continued despite rain, sun and darkness.

And, of course, there was the traditional encounter with a wasp's nest when one of the Leaders was stung when a group of the boys headed for the beach. Vinegar solved this problem:

> *After lunch the lads went down to the beach for a swim but couldn't find the beach! One of the Leaders found a wasps' nest and was well and truly stung! Somewhere in the surrounding woodlands the lads were trying to find their loyal Leader.*

But this was not the biggest drama of the day. That occurred when Mr McGuire was serving soup:

> *We all gathered for dinner at 6.30 and Mr McGuire added a bit of spice to things when his hat fell off his head right into the soup pot! Roars of laughter!*

Rain and Tasty Potatoes

Cornwall was very warm. But rain eventually arrived on 25th July as noted in the Troop Log:

> *The rain started about 3 am and the general activities of the boys and Scouters were confined to within the tents (cards, dominoes, reading books and telling daft stories). Much of this rainy day in Cornwall was spent in slackening guy ropes, securing tent pegs and removing articles from the tent walls.*

There was a Troop games box which held all of these timewasting activities. We would use it at most camps and one of our favourite games was the chess set. Yes, the boys from the scheme played chess.

Several of the older Scouts had been members, indeed founding members of their school chess club. Len McKinnon was one of them and once they had been shown how to play chess, they were hooked. There were about twenty lads in the club and at least six of them were Scouts. They played in competitions against other schools. Another chess fiend was Jim Mackay, 'It was serious for us. We were fifth and sixth year pupils and had to balance our interesting chess matches against adventurous Scout activities. I remember one time when four of us took part in a big match against some chess grand master. It was a great experience and he would just walk round each of the fifty boards and make a move. We all lost, of course, and then made our way up to a Troop meeting later.

But, even for such champion campers, the downpour that day was too much:

> *All four Patrol tents were out of commission. Bus driver Joe got a shock when he returned from the club to find his bus packed with the whole Troop sleeping snugly.*

Mr McGuire was in charge of the cooking tent where he dealt with the Duty Patrol each day and chased them around on their cooking tasks. His most notable contribution was recalled by his son Tony, 'My Dad was at the Cornwall Summer Camp. He had a great story about putting Fairy Liquid in the potatoes instead of salt.

He only noticed when the bubbles overflowed. He quickly emptied the huge ex-army pot and changed the water a few times then added the salt. If you knew, you could still taste the soap but nobody complained.' Another example of the 131's creative approach to camp cooking.

Missing Funds and Folklore

There is a popular misconception that Scouting is full of angelic weans. In reality, Scouting is full of local weans who are full of energy and mischief. The adults tend to be former Scouts. But occasionally a rogue gets into the scene. This was certainly the case when the 131 set out on Summer Camp 1970 to North Wales. It was a joint camp with our regular partners from Penilee, so the camp funds were held in their account.

The 131 Troop was lined up on the pavement outside the Hall when the coach carrying the Penilee Scouts drew up. Their Leader had gone to the bank that afternoon to withdraw the camp funds. But his treasurer had got there first and disappeared off to Blackpool with all the cash. There were no camp funds.

Frank Steele, our 131 treasurer, took charge. First of all, he handed over the personal spending cash he had collected from the boys that evening. This would be used as a cash float until the mess had been sorted out. A few phone calls were made and the true brotherhood of Scouting came into action. Glasgow Scout headquarters made up the missing money. The camp was now fully funded.

Suitably reinvigorated, the Troop made its return to the pleasant mountain scenery at Beddgelert. Frank Roselli still has vivid memories of his first Summer Camp, 'I remember the trip to Wales on the bus down to Snowdonia. It was pretty exciting for a bunch of city kids.'

'The campground was fabulous and the lads headed into the woods and carried down a half dozen good sized tree trunks. We lashed them together and made a gateway for the camp. There was a stream that ran past the camp. I followed it one day and found a really deep pool. The water was crystal clear and I could see huge trout swimming in the pool. I wished I had a fishing rod that day.'

It was also Joe McEwan's first visit there and he recalled it clearly many years later, 'Beddgelert was a small, but historic village. I remember reading at school, about the legendary tale of the local knight who returned from the Holy Wars and mistakenly thought that his dog had killed his baby son. So he killed the dog and then found out the truth that it had been protecting the baby. He was distraught and buried the dog under the weeping willow tree (I think?) and marked the spot with a gravestone which was still there in 1970. It felt really cool to actually be right at the grave site and sense its history. Even though it may only have been folklore.'

'My second memory was definitely of something more in line with the 1970s. Near to our campsite there were a group of young foreign campers from Sweden, who caught our attention. Why? Because they were teenaged, blonde and FEMALE! But the best was yet to come.'

'They appeared on the grass outside their camp site sunbathing, wearing very skimpy swimwear. But the body covering did not extend to the top half of their bodies. They were so open and friendly and the fact that they were topless in a camp full of frisky young boys didn't seem to bother them at all. Needless to say, our lads took a detour past the girls every day after that.'

Frank Roselli also appreciated such unusual camp attractions, 'There were a load of school kids camped next to us from Corby. I met a young lady about my age, and we kept in touch by letter for a couple of years. Don't remember her name now.'

One activity which was a great success for the Troop was the trip to the top of Snowdon on the mountain railway. Pete McGuire had remembered the fun when the 131 had come down the mountain by this means in 1967 and decided this was the most sensible way to get up the hill as it took the weather out of the equation. There were a few decent hillwalkers but the remainder were youngsters: so the train trip would give them something to talk about when they got back to Pollok.

The mountain railway was a memorable trip for the boys – in more ways than one. It was not a real train with coaches but instead there was a long coach which held about fifty people and this was pushed along by a small engine. However, some of the more agile Scouts managed to clamber to the rear of the carriage and were astonished to find that the engine was not attached to the carriage. Every time the carriage hit a bump it would swing away from the engine. Once this was known, all the boys squeezed up to have a look.

One day the older Scouts decided to have a day out in Caernarfon. Joe McEwan provided the story, 'A group of us set off to hike the 13 miles to Caernarfon Castle, the site of Prince Charles' Investiture. Needless to say, the Welsh weather was not cooperating that day, and it rained heavily after we set out. So a unanimous decision was made to try to hitch a ride, even although there were 3 or 4 of us in the group. But we were unable to get any of the local Welsh drivers to take a chance on a group of cheeky young Scottish Boy Scouts in kilts. So we had to walk the whole way there.'

'After finding a local bakery to fuel our tired and hungry bodies, we decided to bolster our cultural knowledge. We visited the grandiose and historical Castle. After exploring the castle's many attractions, we decided to head for the highest vantage point which overlooked the main street and afforded a great view of the city.'

'When we got to the parapet, it was decided, for some probably mischievous, reason, that as we had some fresh eggs left in the food rucksack, we should use them for a dare. There was a fairy tale going round in those days that you could drop eggs on to the ground from any height and as long as they landed properly, they would not break. So, 6 eggs were promptly launched from the tower of the castle onto the street below. We had such a laugh watching the eggs splatter all over the cobblestones. Upon reflection, it was probably not the safest thing to do with the eggs. But we did try to avoid launching whilst tourists were in the firing line. At the end of the day we got away with it and had plenty to talk about on our return hike to the camp site.'

This cultural diversion in Caernarfon was also recalled by Frank Roselli, 'I clearly remember a trip into Caernarfon, and the castle. It was quite spectacular as some celebration was going on and the banners and flags were out.'

The camp finished and it was a quiet coach trip back to the Scout Hall. As they stepped from the bus outside the Hall on their return to Glasgow, none of the group could have imagined that this had been the last time the 131 would return to their Scout Hall after Summer Camp.

SECRETS, SMILES AND DRAMAS

Our Secret Den at the Hurlet

The Hurlet sits on the very edge of Pollok. It had been a tiny mining hamlet and there were still heaps of slate waste around the area. Over time, the hamlet had disappeared and the only old building left was Jean Gebbie's pub about half a mile from the woods. There were no houses for at least a mile in every direction.

There was great excitement at the Troop meeting of 13th May 1963 when Jack announced the news:

We have now acquired a site up at the Hurlet for outdoor Scouting. Farmer Stewart's permission granted.

The woods were remote; they had belonged to Miss Cranston of the Tea Rooms fame and were part of the Househill estate. Michael O'Neill was one of the gang who laughed at this connection, 'It was true. Us 131 guys were camping next to the ruins of a Charles Rennie McIntosh masterpiece. Culture, art, music, they were all closed books to the working class back then. We hadn't even been to the Tea Rooms either as our parents thought they would be too expensive for people like us.'

We would go up there a couple of nights each week during the summer break and also at Easter. Each of the Patrols had its own site in the woods and we would all keep quiet if the signal was given by the look-out that strangers were in the vicinity. This meant nobody could see us or even hear us. We also camped there overnight and could move around the woods easily but other people were frightened to enter in the dark. There was also an old tramp who lived at the top of the woods and we would talk to him.

Regardless of our excitement and pride in having such a great camp site, some of the boys were a wee bit frightened in the woods. Hawkhead Mental Hospital was quite close and we could often see people wandering around wearing big white gowns. We worried that they would climb over the wall and get up to the Hurlet and grab us. What nonsense but we were just daft lads.

Our Hurlet site became a miniature Auchengillan. There was a stand pipe in a field to fill the water trough for the cows. We helped ourselves to the water with the farmer's blessing, as long as we tidied up any mess. Nitshill was the nearest place to buy food and the Patrols would walk down there.

One night, the local police spotted smoke rising from the woods and came in to investigate, remembered Jack, 'They thought it was some troublemakers trying to burn down the woods. They were surprised to find about twenty lads from the 131 camping there so they joined us for an hour or so as both of them had been Scouts. Then it became part of the regular patrol route for the local cops.'

The Hurlet was excellent for us. Many young lads were first introduced to camping in the shade of its trees. Patrols would hold meetings there instead of in someone's house. It was our territory.

Cooking took on another life at the Hurlet. The apprentice chefs, all aged fifteen or so, were able to show the rest of the lads how to prepare easy dishes. But Roberto was adamant about being the instructor for cooking spaghetti Bolognese, 'I am an Italian Scot and I knew how to cook this dish, so the chef guys listened to me. I remember one night when each Patrol had to cook spag bol and it was a riot once they realised that it was really just mince and pasta. But cooking the pasta was not easy to learn as too much water would boil over and put out the wood fire. They all managed to get it right in the end but it was quite dark by then.'

The path into the woods was not obvious and the lads even hid Jack's and Tommy's scooters when they were there. Entry was restricted to the 131 and their pals. The Hurlet was our hidey hole and we would not tell anybody else about it.

There would always be a sentry posted at each end of the woods. 'You had to give the password,' remembered Tony McGuire. 'But you had to ask for it to start with. Bonkers but we were only excited wee guys pretending to be secret agents and the like.'

Roll Up, Roll Up!

One of many memorable Troop trips for the 131 was a visit to the carnival and circus at the Kelvin Hall in the West End of Glasgow. Money was tight and there was seldom any spare cash for such a rare treat.

But one of the parents had pals in the local police and the whole Troop of about thirty guys turned up at the venue's back door and spoke to the cop there. We were waved forward and got inside, right behind the Circus Orchestra. We clambered across the seats while the band was setting up.

A couple of the boys thought that they would try the drums and grabbed a few drumsticks. The band leader threw a complete wobbler and chased us all out. Then we got into the carnival and walked around just looking at the rides as we didn't have any money.

We stopped at the Wall of Death. None of the other visitors would attempt this as they were too scared, so we spoke to the operator and offered to go on it for free to encourage more customers. For the next twenty minutes we whirled around inside the contraption, stuck to the sides by the gravity pull. Quite a few of us were wearing our kilts as we were all in Scout uniform. This added to the mad sight. Nobody else came forward, but we had a great time.

As the evening progressed, a couple of us were walking towards the circus entrance when we saw an elephant! A mighty cheer rose up from the other Scouts and we crowded towards it. The following day we were proudly showing off our souvenirs of elephant manure to admiring schoolmates.

The final escapade was inside the circus tent, where we cheered loudly when the horses came on, followed by the performing seals. But the loudest catcalls were reserved for the lion tamer. Some of the lads jumped out of their seats at this performance. This bloke was strolling around a cage full of lions and they all had big teeth. When he stuck his head inside the lion's mouth the crowd fell silent except for the 131 smart alecks – *come oan the lion, bite his heid aff – huv a good look at the tonsils mister – gie his teeth a good clean*. But there was a real sigh of relief when the act was completed without any more drama – or input from us.

Most of these angelic Scouts were at the Kelvin Hall circus!
(Photo –Jimmy McNeillie)

Bagpipes, Parades and Politics

The 131 Scouts regularly took part in another great spectacle, but this time on their home ground, on church parade Sunday.

Surprisingly, for a housing scheme Group, we had a pipe band. This consisted of a couple of former Scouts from the early days. These guys had done their National Service and probably played in another pipe band but wore 131 neckies over their battledress jackets as the Group marched down Peat Road. One of the Leaders would be ahead of us and another would hang off the back to flag down any vehicles. Sometimes we would be following a bus or one would be only ten yards behind us.

Roberto McLellan was one of these marching Scouts, 'Everyone on the pavements would wave to us and cheer the tunes. For wee guys like me it was really exciting and we would swagger away to the music. Jack or one of the Leaders would try to give us some Army drill before we set off, just to keep us from looking like a rabble. Great days. We were so chuffed that we had a pipe band, just like the posh Scout Troops.' He continued, 'It used to feel great marching down Peat Road behind our own pipe band. There were about sixty Scouts and Cubs, three pipers and a drummer!'

The 131 also marched along behind the Union Flag, the Scout Flag and the Papal Keys, which had all been Jack's first purchase after he had formed the parents' committee, 'In the Army soldiers are very proud to march behind their regimental colours and it builds great team spirit. That's why I thought it was important to get our own set.'

This display of religious allegiance raised a laugh from Michael O'Neill and others, 'It was like having a target on our back, we were just Scouts, we never regarded ourselves as Catholic Scouts, only Scouts.' Brian McGuire was another, 'It was easy to see that we were Catholics. Remember, this was Glasgow in the 1950s. No chance to keep our heads down and just get on with being Scouts.'

Tommy and Jack decided that the Flags needed to be blessed. The ceremony was organised for a Thursday evening Mass – the same night as the regular Scout meeting in St Bernard's school. The Group turned out and paraded outside the church; the parents were already inside and the Glasgow Scout Chaplain, Brother Ronan, was to say the Mass.

But there was an unpleasant incident involving the Union Flag. It has remained in Jim Mackay's memory for more than sixty years, 'I remember the night the Troop flags were to be blessed in St Robert's Church and the parish priest wouldn't allow the Union Flag into the church. What a load of nonsense.'

Still laughing, Jim continued with the story, 'The Colour Party formed up, flags aloft and marched towards the church door. The Irish parish priest stepped forward and held up his hand, a bit like Charlton Heston in the *Ten Commandments* film. His voice boomed out – That flag will not enter this church! He was, of course, pointing to the Union Flag. Tommy, quietly spoken as always, replied – Well, in that case, the Scouts will not enter the Church. We will ask Brother Ronan to come up to the school and bless the flags there.'

The flag entered the church, all three were blessed and the boys marched behind them that night for the first time.

The following year produced a re-run of this nonsense. A new church was being opened by the Archbishop of Glasgow. A large crowd attended, including the Scouts. The boys were lining the route from the Presbytery – a magnificent building which was easily the biggest house on the scheme – to the church doors. The flags were being flown.

It was a happy night for the parish, at least, until one of the priests in the long procession made an insulting remark about the Union Flag and the Scout who was carrying it. There was a commotion but Tommy managed to calm matters down. The procession continued; however the damage had been done. Several Scout parents were incensed and had to be restrained.

The Archbishop was not amused when Tommy and Jack turned up at his palatial offices in Park Circus the following day. Some unknown priest then apologised for the incident. What a palaver about the national flag of Great Britain.

This was sad as the parents were all church-going Catholics who fully supported the parish in all its activities. Jack and Tommy put Scouting first. The 131 was not prepared to be bossed about by priests. Eventually, the young Leaders who had come through this uneasy period decided that Scout activities should be held instead of Church parades.

But the constant turmoil with the parish did not go unnoticed by the boys. Ken McCombes still remembers the antagonism shown towards the Scouts by one of the priests, 'He had another agenda and we were convenient targets for his opinions. It was not nice at all and we were relieved once the Troop decided to stop attending church parades.'

Gradually, the interaction with the parish became more relaxed. The Troop would regularly get a visit from the Scout Chaplain to have a cup of tea and a blether with some of the boys. No friction. No sermons.

This was observed by Alan McCombes, 'There were a couple of guys in the Troop who weren't at Bellarmine School and weren't even Catholics. We just looked at them as Scouts the same as the rest of us. I guess it was a sort of ecumenical moment and we just got on with it.'

Overall, the chaplains became helpful to us. Father Joe Devine had been a Scout himself. He liked testing the Scouts for a specific badge on religious knowledge. Many years later, he became the Bishop of Motherwell and one of the Leaders attended his inauguration. He gave the Leader a Scout salute and a Scout handshake, while still wearing his huge bishop's hat. Father Jim Jamieson, a quiet and amusing young priest, who went off to become a teacher at the Scots College in Rome. The final Chaplain was Father George Bradburn, another ex-Scout. He was very tall and made a decent centre-half for the 131 Rovers football team. He picked up a few yellow cards there – for over-vigorous tackling.

Two members of the colour party in 1959, George Lyden and Robert McGuire

The Pioneering Spirit

Scouting opened a door to an exciting world for the boys. We were introduced to five special activities – Pioneering, Camping, Cooking, Hiking and First Aid. Only Scouting could provide these opportunities in the early 1960s.

Pioneering was a team effort where Scouts tied knots, used poles and built some amazing and practical structures.

Our most popular pioneering project was the construction of the aerial runway – or zip slide as it's now known. This always involved a tall, sturdy tree. Auchengillan had a small clump of suitable trees at Tank Wood. The older lads were regularly in the midst of this. They would climb up the tree and fix the main rope to it. This would be anchored on the ground about 50 yards away. A pulley was threaded along this line and a double-loop rope seat was also fitted. Safety lines were attached. We knew how to build it correctly and did so, always checking each other's work as we went along. Nothing was left to chance.

Testing the aerial runway was important. The line would sag once it was carrying weight and the passenger would often hit the ground. The testing process would result in the line being tightened up to a safer level. Pete McGuire noted, 'The test had to be done by a human being – a live Scout, a sort of test pilot no less. I did this a few times, but our usual tester was Henry. He had red hair and wore specs. A mad keen Scout, along with his brother John, he was at every camp. A few years older than me, he later became a ship's engineer on the oil tankers.'

So, Henry would climb up the tree, wiggle himself into the rope seat and whiz down the rope slide. The technical team would watch carefully, yell encouragement and pull on the brake ropes. More often than not, the line would sag and Henry's backside would caress the ground before he could prepare himself for a crash landing, 'Well,' he said,' somebody had to do it and I always liked doing it.' Michael O'Neill chuckled at the memory, 'Henry's valuable expertise was treasured by the rest of us. He took the bumps and bruises and we did not. Health and safety in glorious action.'

In later years, the Scout Association decided that aerial runways were too dangerous. Nowadays it is seldom done and adults need to attend a two-day course to learn all the skills involved. Aerial runway veterans Pete and Michael scoffed at this, 'What a shame. We were able to do this activity with the skills we had learned and practiced on a weekly basis. Young lads aged sixteen to nineteen.'

Pioneering skills were also useful on our camp site. We would always want to have a proper entrance and this had to look smart. For this we would use logs, at least ten feet long. Sometimes we would have to make do with a wigwam-like shape, but other times we managed to get hold of longer logs and make a square gate, with a platform at the top: this provided rigidity to the structure. We worked safely and it was simple to do.

We would construct a rugby goalpost and this would be raised, dug in at the bottom and secured by guy ropes. The second goalpost then followed; it was identical to the first, then shorter logs would be lashed across both, creating the gateway support platform. Jimmy McNeillie often supervised these projects. Occasionally the gateway would collapse during construction, with the Scouts on the platform diving to the ground. A wee whiff of danger always added to the drama. But the gateways always worked and gave our site an impressive look.

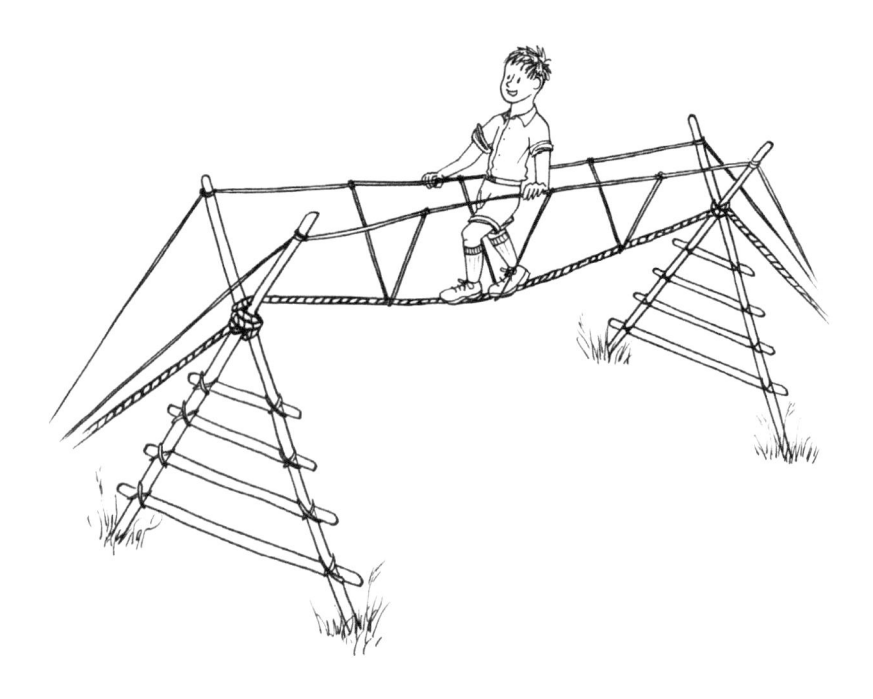

Other projects would see the 131 building various rope and wooden bridges, some of which had lifting walkways on them. We had worked hard to learn the skills needed and it was great for our morale. We could show the world that we were good at something.

One of the first purchases Jack had made was scout staves and pioneering poles. These wooden staves were four and a half feet tall. Each Scout was issued with one and they were very useful for activities such as estimating heights and distances, as the top foot of the staff was marked off in inches. Young Scouts were intrigued by this and part of their Scout knowledge was to learn what the markings meant. The staves were often taken home by keen boys – quite a useful item in Pollok.

The pioneering poles were made of bamboo and were ten feet tall. This meant that outlandish structures could be constructed indoors at Troop meetings. We would swiftly turn them into bridges, tripods and other great creations. But it was all about getting the lashings tight to prevent slippage as we had to test them ourselves and they often collapsed with us on board. Applied engineering no less.

Rafts were also built, with the knots carefully tied around the barrels. Pete McGuire loved this task, 'In our day, these barrels were metal, not the plastic, light, easy to handle containers of nowadays. We would roll these barrels from the store area at Auchengillan down to the pool and use them. They were of course sore to bump against and would take skin off the nearest Scout.'

Foot and Mouth and a Shotgun

Occasionally, the real world restricted the 131's great adventures and one of these was the outbreak of foot and mouth disease in Scotland in 1961. This caused devastation for farmers and also disruption to the Troop's normal activities. Local countryside hikes were cancelled and Auchengillan was also closed as its entrance road ran straight through a farmyard. Other places had to be found for Scout activities.

Jack started a series of hike challenges. Each Patrol had to find somewhere to visit and either hike to the destination or hike back. Needless to say, the Patrols came up with some interesting – and bizarre – projects. These involved hiking around Glasgow for 8 or 9 miles without going into any fields.

My Patrol took part in a few of these and on one occasion we decided to hike from the ferry at Bowling towards Auchengillan without crossing any farm land. But we found out that a farmer's definition of farm land was not the same as the Pollok meaning.

We only got as far as one mile from the ferry ramp along a narrow road, when we were stopped by an angry farmer carrying a shotgun – *Keep off this land!*

Panic stations all round. The Swift Patrol dived for cover behind a wall while I spoke to the farmer. This was a waste of time as he just waved his gun in the air. It was a wee bit scary. He also had two fierce looking dogs which never stopped barking. We got the message.

The Patrol retreated in good order, boarded the next Renfrew Ferry and then hiked back to Paisley town centre. But we now had a great tale to tell. One of the many daft stories which make up the Legend of the 131.

The Magic of Troop meetings

Jack Banks brought his own special charisma to Troop meetings. They were structured and purposeful, with plenty of variety, excitement and fun.

In those days, there were three levels of training in the Scout programme – Tenderfoot, Second Class and First Class. The Tenderfoot Badge involved skills such as Law & Promise, Salute, Union Flag, Cleaning a Wound, Woodcraft Signs, Knotting and Whipping (basically how to stop a rope from fraying). Each of the next levels involved more difficult activities. It would take a keen Scout six years to complete all the tests to reach the level of Queen's Scout.

'The secret of the Scout training scheme,' noted Pete McGuire, 'was that it brought the boys into contact with stuff they had never encountered before. Just to learn knots made us think that we were explorers or sailors, always something exciting.' This was echoed by Joe McEwan, 'Growing up in the scheme was miserable at times and being a 131 Scout was my escape pod. We were always learning something interesting like first aid, cooking, camping, pioneering and such like. All of this you would never find in the scheme. We felt that we were special wee guys – and I suppose we were.'

Most of the new skills would be taught by experienced Leaders and PLs. Sometimes there would be a specialist subject which needed an external tutor, such as advanced First Aid and this would be taught at the St Andrew's First Aid station at the Bundy. Scouts went there for about 7 or 8 nights (additional to Troop meetings) to learn the syllabus. They would tie bandages and practice on each other, all of this being watched and corrected by the instructor.

However, the majority of Scout skills were taught at Troop meetings. Jim Mackay commented on this, 'Most nights we came home from the Troop and had learned some new skills. Every time I was taught something new, I would make sure that it was ticked off in my card. It was a wee bit like a race as we all pushed one another to get to the end of each stage of the training. It helped us immensely in later years when we were students and teachers as we realised the importance of a structured training programme.'

A programme such as the one of 13th February 1963 looks easy and it was. It was carried out in an atmosphere of wild enthusiasm which Jack controlled by yelling *Troop!* whenever he wanted to talk. This brought Silence – or else points were deducted from noisy Patrols. Each Scout had their own personal log book. This listed all the skills to be mastered and all the badges which had been gained. Each test was signed off by a Leader:

Each Scouter will take (15 mins) each Patrol for instruction as follows:

GSM (Tommy) will take mapping and compass.
SM (Jack) – Observation.
ASM – Pioneering.
ASM – First Aid (Tenderfoot, 2nd Class).
ASM – First Aid (First Class and Emergencies).

Each Patrol moved around the various Scouters for instruction.

Mapping and compass: the First Class Scouts were OK but the 2nd Class Scouts were poor.

Observation: Skipper had 12 match boxes with various ingredients in them, e.g. cinnamon, sugar, etc. Each Patrol was blindfolded and the boxes were passed along, each Scout tasting or smelling the various boxes…

One of the most important tasks of the PL was to get his Patrol members through their Scout tests. This was all part of B-P's master plan to give full responsibility to the Patrol Leaders. A PL was capable of instructing most of these skills and this produced a good team spirit. The PL knew that his Patrol would get more points if more tests were passed. It was a carrot and stick situation and Leaders recognised its benefits as it made the PL take an interest in his Patrol instead of hanging about with his pals of the same age. It also meant that the young Scouts made good progress.

Taking a test was always exciting – and stressful. 'We used to get scared having to do some things but we just got on with it,' said Danny Houston. One of these tests involved stepping out of our comfort zone to simulate making an emergency phone call to the 999 services to report an accident. Nobody in the Troop, apart from Jack and Tommy, had a phone. The recipient for this test was normally the District Commissioner. All phone calls in those days were made from public call boxes. In Pollok this was difficult as most of these had been vandalised.

Home telephones were scarce, so this would probably have been the first phone call the Scout had ever made. A few years after completing this test, Noel Carson recalled how nervous he was. He had been scared that he would take too long to tell the story before his pennies ran out and the pips started. Noel passed, as did all these keen young telecoms pioneers. In fact, Scouts who had passed this test earned cash for camps by standing beside public call boxes, answering incoming calls and fetching the required person from the nearby houses. A truly transferable skill.

Then there were incident trails. These were simple activities; we would have to follow a trail such as string or woodcraft signs outside and tackle a series of projects on the way round – knotting, First Aid, pioneering, quiz, etc. These were intriguing challenges for the boys.

The tough kids of the 131 really loved these games and projects because they were different, exciting and fun.

Cold and Wild in Winter – the Saga of Indoor Weekends

Winter weekend camps were held in the Providore at Auchengillan, at Rowardennan Youth Hostel near Balloch and in our own Scout Hall. We ran these events when it was too cold for outdoor camping, as tent pegs could not be driven into the frozen ground.

Auchengillan was almost eight hundred feet up, straddling a rocky ridgeline. Cold weather was normal. Pete McGuire remembered the Providore layout at a winter weekend, 'One wing would be used for eating, the campfire and programme activities (with Leaders also sleeping there); the other wing was full of Scouts.

I mean full as we would normally get together with other Troops so there would be more Leaders on hand. This also meant that we could share the costs for the weekend.'

Winter wonderland at Auchengillan (Photo – D Scott)

It was not unusual for a hundred lads to be sleeping in the Providore. (Today it has accommodation for 30). And it was cold as there was no proper heating. The boys usually slept straight on the floor, but at some stage a large number of straw mattresses were introduced as beds. In true 131 style, these were converted into missiles.

These winter weekends have lived long in the memories of those 131 lads who took part in them, as Roberto McLellan recalled, 'It always seemed to be freezing when we went out to 'Gillan or the Loch Lomond youth hostel for these weekends. There was plenty of running about, snowball fights and getting cold and wet. But the most standout memory is of the clowns who would not shut up on the Friday night. On most occasions a couple of us bigger guys would get out of our sleeping bags and go over and sort them out. We gave them what you could call a team talk and they shut up.'

Winter activities were a great success as Michael O'Neill recalled, 'Any outing was popular as there was very little else to occupy energetic young lads in Pollok. For us, this was a winter weekend getaway in the Highlands!'

One of these indoor weekends was described by Noel Carson in the Curlew Log Book in December 1963. The wide game was well received by the boys:

At 10.30 pm the wide game began. This involved firing a rocket when the starting bell was rung; a corn flakes box was erected on top of a stave and a torch shone on it. The box was then to be guarded from other Patrols and we were to try to capture another Patrol's box. We did not succeed and lost our own box to the Falcon which was returned after an argument with Skipper.

This game ended at 11.15 pm. Tea and biscuits were served to the boys and they were sent to bed with lights out at 11.30 pm.

All winter weekends were like this. Lots of activities, lots of cold and wet weather, sometimes snow, and always lots of tired boys when it was over. Oh, and also burst pipes in the Scout Hall and plenty of running about in the cold trying to fix them.

At the end of one particular weekend at Auchengillan, the lads piled aboard the coach and headed home late on the Sunday afternoon. Sleep overtook them until the driver decided to drive around the Glasgow city centre streets to George Square to see the Xmas lights. This was a great treat for boys from Pollok where street lights were constantly vandalised and few families had Xmas lights.

Gang Warfare

Scouting works in a simple way. A group of pals get together and they go along every week. Just like a wee gang. The 131 were just the same. The weekly pilgrimage would set off from the top of the scheme and head for the meeting. By the time we reached the main road, we were about 20 in number.

But we still had to negotiate the most difficult part of our journey. We had to pass the Church of Scotland – the home of the BB who also met on the same night as us. It was a mad gallop as we ran past on the opposite side of the road while stones were thrown at us from the BB lads. Gang warfare no less. Sometimes we would catch a couple of BB guys and chase them back up the street.

This was a completely tribal response as Jim Mackay recalled, 'One of the BB guys was our neighbour. He lived in the bottom flat and we lived in the top flat. We saw each other every day and played happily until it was Scout and BB night. Then it changed into warfare. I last heard of him when he was a sergeant in the CID so I suppose his BB training came in useful there.'

This rivalry continued throughout the 131's existence as Gerard Doherty remembered, 'We were divided into two groups at one time: the *Tuesdays* and the *Fridays*. I think I was the former. I seem to remember that we met in the Scout Hall on Brockburn Road, although the *Fridays* possibly met in St Robert's church hall. However I must have gone to the church hall one Friday. When we left we encountered a very small BB member. Then, Jim Mullaney jokingly said, *We have a fight*. The wee lad turned round and shouted to 20 larger BB boys – *They want to fight!* – We ran away as fast as we could. Quite sensibly.'

One of the treats during these treks to and from the Troop meeting at St Bernard's School was the chip van at the roundabout. We would have money for our bus fare; I think it was a ha'penny each way but we would walk back home as we had spent the money at the chip van. We would put all the bus fares into a kitty and pass it round the gang. Sometimes if it was raining we would jump on the bus to go home and try to dodge our fare. As soon as the conductress came along we would jump off the bus and keep walking home and try the same trick on the next bus.

Another daft episode would take place when the winter weather turned to fog. This was formed from the sulphur particles from the vast number of coal fires and industrial furnaces in the city. The air became a freezing, yellow cloud, with visibility down to ten yards at the most. The Diehards made their way down to the Troop meeting by memory, normally with their neckies tied across their faces to catch the fog which made a yellow stain on the cloth. But it had a great benefit, remembered Jim Mackay, 'It meant that we could get past the BB church unseen. In fact, I don't think they would be on that night – they weren't as hard as us.'

Brotherly Love

One peaceful Saturday afternoon in 1963, about thirty Scouts were camped in Sleepy Hollow at Auchengillan. Jack had called the PLs into his tent for a briefing.

He had just started to speak when a commotion arose somewhere on site. Heads peeped out of the tent to identify the problem. Two brothers were yelling at each other. Suddenly the younger boy came racing through Jack's tent followed by his big brother who was wielding an axe!

A couple of PLs charged after them and wrestled the older brother to the ground. We were all totally flummoxed. No reason was ever produced for this colourful interlude and they both continued to entertain us for years to come – and ended up as Queen's Scouts.

This was not the first tasty incident involving the brothers. One evening we were holding a Patrol meeting in their home. One of them had rigged up an entry buzzer to his flat and when the button was pressed it was often accompanied by a small electric shock!

But the star moment of the meeting came when we were in their bedroom. From under the bed, one of the brothers brought out his latest scientific experiment. He had climbed over the fence into the local quarry and liberated a few sticks of gelignite! He told us he was going to make them into a bomb but had not yet managed to find the other parts. I chased the others out of the house and told the neighbouring flats about the problem.

The boy was astonished. He said he knew what he was doing. One of the neighbours ran to the nearest phone box and about twenty minutes later a policeman arrived.

Ah, Scouting for Boys – there is no mention of bomb-making in this marvellous book.'

A Special Night

Late 1964 and another gang of pals were approaching the end of their Scouting careers. They had become master campers and their shirts were covered by vast numbers of proficiency badges, from

Artist, Astronomer and Athlete to Swimmer, Tracker, Weather Man and Woodcraftsman.

A Scouting Display and Presentation of Badges was held in the Church Hall on 23rd December. The school was closed for the Xmas holidays and this alternative venue had been hired from the parish. Loads of parents attended and the boys ran around serving tea and answering questions, as well as showing off their Scouting skills – and being presented with even more badges.

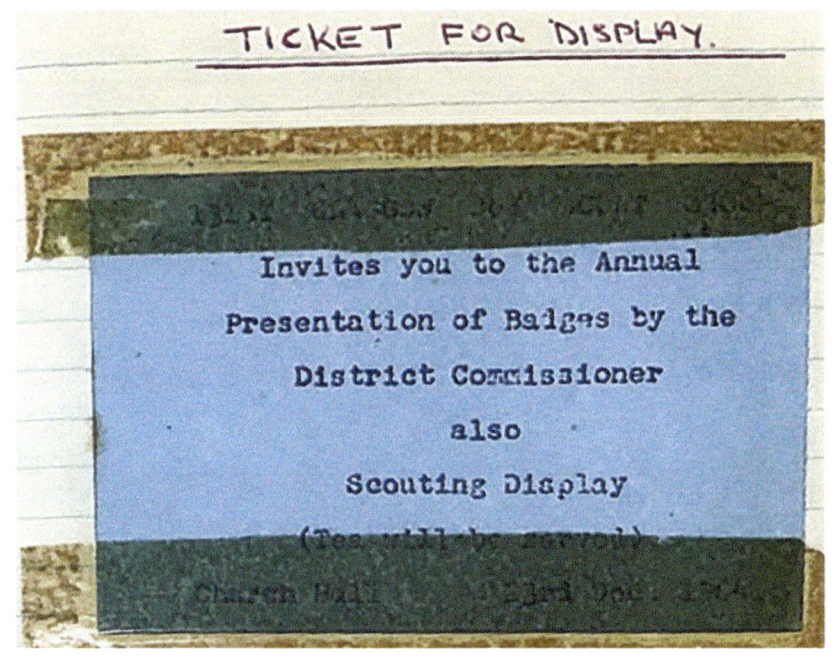

Ticket for Scouting Display 1964
(Printed on our John Bull Printing Set by the PLs)

The highlight of the evening was the presentation of the Queen's Scout Badges. Another eleven had gained the top award in Scouting – a terrific achievement. The District Commissioner, Douglas Laing, presented these after a short speech in which he pointed out the 131's great record in recent years, 'There is no doubt that your Troop is now at the forefront of Glasgow Scouting. The 131's record of Scouting excellence and public service are well known. And you have started from a harder background than many other Scout Groups. Well done.'

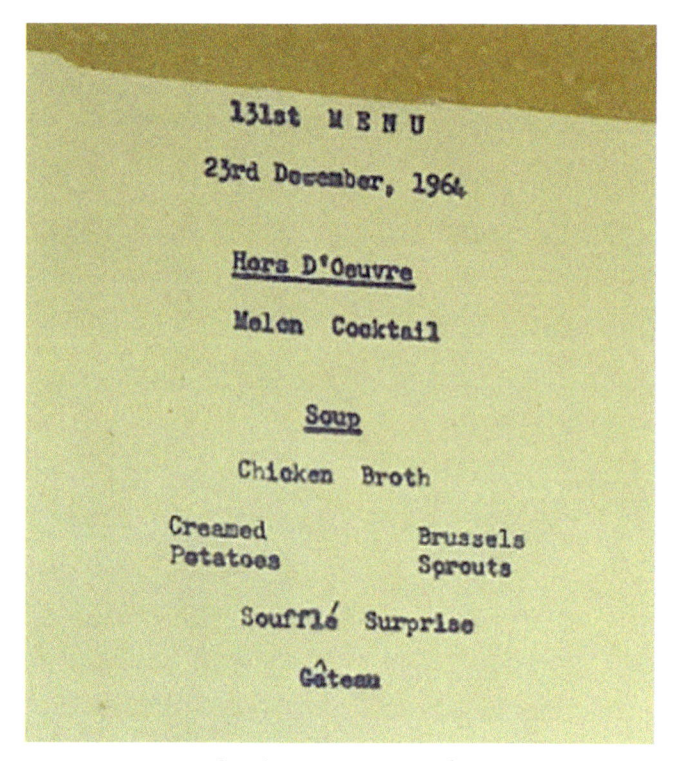

```
            131st  M E N U

          23rd December, 1964


              Hors D'Oeuvre

             Melon Cocktail


                  Soup

             Chicken Broth

        Creamed          Brussels
        Potatoes         Sprouts

              Soufflé Surprise

                 Gâteau
```

Menu for the Scouting Display 1964

The evening's activities were well described in the Curlew log Book:

The Troop met at 7 o'clock and prepared the Hall for the arrival of the parents and Cubs at 8 o'clock. There were 5 stalls – trophies, photographs, cooking, pennants and camping. Curlew helped to prepare the stalls while the Raven constructed an aerial runway and the Kingfisher and Falcon made a monkey-bridge.

The DC arrived to give some of the boys their Queen's Scout interview. The display commenced at 8 o'clock and we were put in charge of the pennant stall.

The photographer from the Observer took a photograph of the Queen's Scouts which appeared in the paper the following week. After having looked round the stalls the parents sat down and had tea and biscuits. After this our Patrol gave an ambulance display for which we received a generous round of applause.

Next came the presentation of badges which started with a speech from Father Mallan the Diocesan Chaplain. The last badges to be presented were the Queen's Scout badges which the DC presented after a short speech.

The eleven Queen's Scouts were: PL Carson, Second Mackay, O'Neill (Curlew); PL McKinnon, Second McLellan, MacCormack (Raven); PLs Watts, McLeod (Swift); PL Mallan (Falcon), PLs Mullaney, McGee (Kingfisher).

The evening ended with Father Jamieson presenting Skipper with a mug on behalf of the Troop.

On that note the very successful evening ended.

This was a great night – for Jack and Tommy and Jimmy MacNeillie, as well as for all those who received their badges. The 131 had reached the top of the Scouting tree in style. The proof was there on the arms of these Scouts. The Queen's Scouts were equally proud. It was great to get their Queen's Scout badge in front of all the parents, the Troop and the Cubs. They all sewed their badge on as soon as they got back home that night. And most of them kept their badge for the remainder of their lives, a great reminder of those happy days.

Roberto looked back many years afterwards, 'A great memory, even sixty years later, what a terrific night. I wonder where they all are now. The best thing was to get it along with all our pals. We were a good bunch and we had all helped one another. I can't ever remember any of us falling out or having fights.'

Yes, he still has his badge.

This great team spirit was one of the strengths of the 131 and it was emphasised by Graeme O'Neill, 'I learned to talk to my Scout pals if there was something bothering me. This was so useful to me in later life as I knew that chatting about problems would help me to solve them. I learned to share problems as a Scout. All things considered, it was a good time in the 131.'

For the watching parents, it was a special evening. They saw their sons show off their Scouting skills in front of an audience – even a tricky pioneering project was successfully completed. They had believed that it was good for their sons to be in the 131 and now they had achieved a national standard. Another obstacle had been overcome for these determined Mums and Dads. Their sons were heading in the right direction – upwards.

And for the younger Scouts it showed them the path to follow. This really was a big occasion and made an impact on all of them. They didn't stop talking about getting more badges for weeks on end and loved it whenever they had a new one to show off.

It also meant that more cash had to be raised to pay for the nonstop avalanche of new badges. A great problem to have.

NEVER A DULL MOMENT

Buon Appetito!

As well as introducing youngsters to outdoor activities and the countryside, the 131 discovered new food at camp weekends. Exotic items would be produced in a haphazard fashion and Pete McGuire recalled one of these incidents, 'One weekend we were in a competition and I remember Roberto bringing stuffed peppers to camp. To us in the 1960s, peppers were wee tiny black things, so how could they be stuffed?'

The interesting peppers arrived in a cardboard box and were produced for Sunday dinner. 'I didn't know how to cook them, so Roberto suggested that we heated them up in a dixie and he covered them in Italian tomato sauce from a wee tin. So, we did this and awaited the inspection,' said Pete. 'Bill Stobo, our local District Commissioner, came along and checked our cooking. He had never seen stuffed peppers either and asked us a simple question – How did you make these peppers? We were snookered and had no convincing answer, so I am afraid that we had a low score for our cooking. But the peppers cooked nicely and we ate the lot.'

Roberto roared with laughter at the memory of the peppers, 'Pete had asked me to bring some exciting Italian food to the camp. So I asked my Mum and she made the peppers. I packed them carefully and headed off to camp unaware of the consequences.'

The 131 camp menu improved overnight when four of the older Scouts, Brian McIntyre, Brendan McLeod, Tommy McGee and John Watts became apprentice chefs. They had access to a wide variety of food at their workplace. Prior to this there were lots of sausages cooked for breakfast, lunch and dinner – in big, heavy ex-Army frying pans and cooking pots. The chefs changed this tradition.

They used plastic containers, tureens and serving trays to carry the food, just taking a loan of them for the weekend and they would be brought back to the kitchen on Monday morning. Nobody ever complained and their boss always made sure that they had a decent supply of tasty food for the camp.

Anything different was exotic back then as we all supped on plain fare at home. 'Nobody in the 131 had ever heard of tomato puree in those days,' said Roberto. 'I don't think there were many people in Scotland who had, apart from Italians like me. So there was great interest when I brought out some puree to Auchengillan one weekend and added it to the mince. The other Scouts were amazed – *I hope this disnae ruin the mince* was muttered by some of them. No problem, though, they loved the taste.'

Many of the older Scouts, like Eddie Mallan, would come out to Auchengillan after they had finished their Saturday morning job. His was in the Co-op butcher's shop and the boss would often send out some offcuts for free. These would be made into soup or stew that night.

This expertise always earned the 131 top marks and we won the Scottish Scouts Camp Cooking competition. Four of the lads went down to Gilwell Park for the UK Finals, finishing third. Not bad for housing scheme ruffians.

It was not just the young chefs who could pass on good cooking tips as I discovered one day. It was a Troop camp at Auchengillan and Tommy was the Duty Scouter. I was in charge of the dinner meal and was busy around the fire when I saw him slicing a banana. This immediately caught my eye as bananas were few and far between. He was standing beside the big dixie, cooking the custard for the whole Troop. We had to mix up the separate ingredients and then carefully heat the milky mixture to boiling – without it burning or spilling out of the dixie.

Tommy explained that he was adding the banana to the custard as it would take away any burnt taste. A simple and effective solution. Another lesson learned from a wise man.

Jack also added to the sum of cooking knowledge. The Leaders were running a PL training day and the lads had to cook the old favourites – a damper (a flour and water pancake) and a twist (the same mixture wrapped around a stick). The eager lads would come up to Jack so that he could taste their offerings. One of the PLs noted that Jack would turn away from the Scout and would only bite a tiny morsel and chew it. So, he asked him why he was not eating more of it and he replied that he had been a Scoutmaster too long to eat what Scouts had cooked!

Another of Jack's rules about camp cooking was that the meal had to look good on the plate instead of just being lumped there from the pot. 'The appearance of the meal gets you as many points as the taste,' he would say.

Scouting put an emphasis on healthy living and this was appreciated by Graeme O'Neill, 'It taught us to look after our health. We cooked and ate lots of good food at camp and this paid its benefits in later years for me. Even though we used a primus stove or wood fires, we were good cooks and as far as I was concerned, the food always tasted good. The tea had a fantastic taste although this may have been because it was in a tin mug.'

We liked to cook baked potatoes. Back then, we would just pat some mud around the potato and lob it in to the fire. After about 20 minutes we would pull it out, break it open and eat it. Very tasty. We would also cook fish on a skewer – a big metal tent peg – over the open fire. The fishmonger was surprised when we bought a whole fish before going to camp but we did know how to cook them. All right, they would taste a bit smokey.

Even cooking a banana over the open fire was exciting. This would be speared by a long metal tent peg or covered in mud and thrown on the fire. Of course, it would be way too hot to eat but we would manage it anyway. Our cooking was never dull.

Once the Scout Hall was in operation, this cooking expertise was regularly used at fund-raising events run by the parents committee. We would also provide the food for some wedding receptions which were held in the Hall. We would wear cooking whites and we really looked the part. Our fame spread and we even got silver weddings and other bookings from other churches.

In fact, the parish priest even sent a message to Tommy that the Scouts were not to cater for weddings as this was a steady source of income for the parish. His instruction was ignored. The cooking skills – and confidence – gained with the 131 were used by most lads in later years, 'When we went to parties, we found out that the only folk who could cook were us, the old 131 gang and we used these skills in married life also,' remembered Pete McGuire. This was reiterated by Joe McEwan,' My Scout knowledge was so useful for me when I got married at nineteen and already knew how to budget for items and how to cook and buy food.'

Al fresco dining at Auchengillan 1965

First Aid – Serious Business

'First Aid was an important matter, and I was determined that the boys would have a good grounding in this as I had seen how well it worked when I was in the jungle in Malaya,' said Jack. So he would include a First Aid training incident at least twice a month.

The next step was to compete against other Troops for the County Ambulance Shield. 'I had won this a few times as a Scout in my old Troop in the Gorbals,' recalled Jack. 'The 131 managed a couple of second places over the years and were always in the top four. A couple of the other Glasgow Troops took First Aid very seriously and normally beat us, but one of their Leaders would be a doctor – a wee bit above our status I'm afraid.'

At one time there was also a District First Aid Shield. So, the 131 entered and won the competition in 1961. After this, none of the other Troops would enter and it was never held again.

There was also a St Andrew's Ambulance training centre at the Bundy. The Ambulance Badge course of 8 weeks was held there and a gang of us would turn up for instruction. Jim Mackay was one of these lads, 'I remember Mr Kinvig (I think that was his name) who put us through our First Aid badges. He came up to the old school and we went to his hall at the Bundy as well. A couple of us went to his house for the exam. I think he lived just off Braidcraft Road. His wife gave us Irn Bru and biscuits and we all passed.'

As far as Graeme O'Neill was concerned, first aid training brought great benefits, 'At the time I was fascinated by being able to deal with injuries and treat them. It was great stuff. Nobody else in school could do anything like this apart from other Scouts. It helped to make us special. We felt like super heroes.'

With all of this First Aid knowledge, any accidents were easily dealt with. A Patrol Leader could handle the normal ones such as cut heads, skinned knees, sprained ankles and wrists. There was no accident log book but there were also no complaints from parents whose son came home from a Scout activity with a bandage.

Probably the funniest incident was when the bold Henry Watts suffered a severely bruised backside when testing an aerial runway at a Troop meeting. He had really thumped himself when the rope sagged and he was lying on the ground groaning. But there is no treatment for sore bum muscles. In the end we had to splash water over his backside and he could only limp slowly up the road at the end of the meeting. He was back to normal the following week.

Scouting tasks were always different and some lads, like Frank Roselli, had more of an adventure than normal, 'We were always doing active things like building bridges and suchlike in the Hall. One evening, I went up a ladder to tie off a rope around one of the beams. I was only about 7 or 8 feet up. Someone was supposed to be holding the bottom of the ladder, I cannot remember his name, it was one of the other Scouts about the same age as me, but for some reason he walked away. The bottom of the ladder slipped out and down I came. I landed on my back with my right arm slightly behind me. I thought I was okay, then moved my arm around to the front of me, my hand was basically hanging and detached from my wrist. There was no pain at first, and I think it was Pete McGuire who immobilized it and put it in a sling while someone called an ambulance.'

At the hospital the doctor said Frank would need a general anaesthetic in order to set the break. But having eaten just before it happened, Frank would have to wait, 'Then the pain started. It was like a red hot poker burning into the palm of my hand. It became unbearable, and the doctor eventually told two nurses to hold me down. He took my wrist in one hand, and my hand in the other, pulled and twisted as I screamed my head off. It only lasted a few seconds, and as soon as he was done, the pain was almost gone. A couple hours later and after my parents arrived, they put me under and set the arm properly. It was a bad break, and I was in a cast for three months. They must have done a great job as I've never had a problem with it since.'

Just another night of Scouting. Frank never let his plaster and weak arm hinder him. 'The broken arm slowed me down but didn't limit my scouting involvement. I was back at the Troop the following Thursday and then off to camp that weekend.'

Fun and Games on the Bonnie Banks#

The bonnie banks of Loch Lomond were the scene of several 131 escapades as Roberto McLellan recalled, 'We used to go to a youth hostel at Loch Lomond for indoor weekends. It looked like a big castle. I think there would be about a hundred Scouts there. The 131 would always have about twenty or so. My best memory was of the time we went on to an island in Loch Lomond. We went across on a boat and had to spend the night there, hiding from everybody else. I crawled into some ferns and lay there wrapped up in my wee groundsheet, cold and hungry but cheery. The Leaders went around during the night to catch people and most of the other Scouts were caught. But I think there were only two of the 131 who got caught and they were young Scouts. We were obviously tough guys.'

'Another year I remember that we had to carry a bucket of water across the island following a rope trail. It was not really water – it was actually liquid uranium for us to make our nuclear bomb. This led us up and down various parts of the island and we went through bogs and burns and bushes. The bucket was suspended from a big wooden tripod made of Scout staves and swung about all the time. We were the winning Patrol. Great memories.'

The 131 regularly rambled along the shores of the loch and one year a group of the older lads went hiking along the east side of the water. We were completing our Queen's Scout badge with a thirty miles hike. We got the last bus to Drymen on the Friday night and then climbed over a wall in the village square and set up two hike tents. We were tired and managed to get to sleep quickly although the ground was a wee bit bumpy. Then, when we got up in the morning, we found out why – we had pitched camp on top of the hotel's rubbish dump!

Undaunted, we caught the bus to Balmaha where we followed the path along the edge of the loch. This track subsequently became part of the West Highland Way about ten years later. But in those days, it was a rocky scramble. Roberto McLellan remembered the route, 'As Scouts, we weren't bothered by this, nor by the heavy rain. This was normal weather to us. We had done wet hikes many times before and this was the final hike for our Queen's Scout badge. We were wet, singing Scout songs and having a great time.'

Michael O'Neill was one of the hikers, 'Finishing my Queen's Scout badge was very important. It was the gold standard for us and we were all determined to complete it. When I was doing the final hike up the side of Loch Lomond from Balmaha, I can remember sitting on a rock and looking out over the water while we ate the pieces of chicken we had just fried up on our stove. Simple food and a great memory.'

The tents and other kit were shared out amongst the hikers. We trudged along steadily although most of the path was a big bog. 'Truth to tell, we were probably just a wee bit fed up with the weather when we came upon a boat. This banished our blues!' chuckled Michael.

It was a wooden rowing boat. Sunk in the water close to the shore. The lads dragged it on to the beach. There was a fist-sized hole in the bottom, but otherwise it was in excellent condition. A search of the foreshore produced two good oars. As he was an apprentice joiner, Noel Carson fixed the hole. This meant that we could now travel by boat instead of trudging along the very muddy path.

The boat was launched back into the loch, rucksacks were hauled aboard and we all clambered into it, none of us having ever been in one of these boats before.

The repair was good and we started rowing up the loch. This was organised in teams of two, with a drill for every time the oarsmen had to change. This was essential to keep the boat from overturning. About an hour later we pulled alongside the pier at Inversnaid, tied up and climbed on to the shore, carrying our kit. Inversnaid was a real place where Rob Roy had roamed about many years ago and the 131 were now there!

The best bit of our stay there was being able to have an all-over wash by sitting in the burn up to the neck in cold water. This also kept away the midges. But we had to race back to the tents and tie up the tent doors when we were finished.

The next morning we had an early breakfast and we pulled away, heading across the loch to Tarbet on the west shore. The rucksacks were piled up in the bow with John Watts, the smallest guy, sitting on top. The rowing changes worked well – at least until we were in the middle of the loch. Disaster! The boat tipped heavily on one side but did not overturn. However, John slipped from his perch and clutched the prow of the boat before he fell into the water.

One of the lads leaned over and grabbed him. John held on to the boat and made his way to the stern where he was dragged aboard. The subdued hikers quietly rowed the rest of the trip and reached Tarbet where we waded ashore and left a note to thank the owner, explaining what we had done. It was important to let him know that we had not stolen his boat.

On the way out of Balmaha, one of us had spotted a grass snake and had trapped it in an empty cocoa tin, intending to study it later. While we were sitting outside the small café at Tarbet, we decided to take a look at the snake. Somebody wrapped a handkerchief round his hand and reached into the can. Out came the snake, wriggling vigorously. Its colour had now changed – there was a zig-zag pattern all down its back. It was not a grass snake. It was an Adder – the only poisonous snake in Scotland. Everyone jumped back and watched it as it wriggled into the nearby undergrowth. We all make mistakes. None of us had never seen a snake before and it was as scared as we were.

A few weeks later, a stranger came up to the Troop meeting. It was the boat owner and he had come along to meet these interesting young lads who had passed the hike and completed their Queen's Scout badge.

Rucksack Revelations!

Before going to camp, each Scout had to pack his own kit. This was an important early step on the path to self-reliance. When he reached the meeting point, his rucksack was examined by his Patrol Leader. Unnecessary clothing was removed and left behind.

This provided a funny memory for Tony McGuire, 'One of the newer Scouts turned up at the Hall with a really smart-looking rucksack. It looked very neat, not like ours which bulged everywhere. So, his PL opened it to solve the mystery. It contained a pillow, underpants and a pair of swimming trunks and nothing else. His Mum had packed it. This was daft as his PL had already told him what to bring but his Mum decided she knew best.'

'Now we come to the daftest bit – there was a note on top of the clothing which said – make sure he changes his underpants!'

Going out to roam around outdoors was the central part of camping and hiking. There were few sources of suitable outdoor wear, normally the Army surplus store, and boys had to use whatever was available to them.

But the lack of formal outdoor clothing did not deter the 131. Boys would turn up for outdoor activities, wearing a glorious hotchpotch of garments – reefer jackets, duffel coats, donkey jackets, denim jackets, windbreakers, some even had fur-collar jerkins and another strode forward in his Afghan coat. Bold, adventurous and confident. They carried their personal kit in various containers, such as duffel bags, kitbags, canvas travel bags and even a string net shopping bag. Often these bags and jackets would be emblazoned with various badges such as CND, Lion Rampants and in the case of one lad, Occupational Therapist. After all, this was the time of hippies and Pollok boys could dream.

But camping was an unforgiving environment regardless of whatever personal items the Scouts may have brought with them. The most important item at any Scout camp was a good tent. This would keep out the wind and snow and rain. Or at least that is what it is supposed to do. Gerard Doherty recalled one weekend when this did not occur, 'On another visit to Auchengillan, we went on our own, four of us older scouts and the two McCombes brothers. We arrived on the Red Bus from Buchanan Street Station with a Nijer Tent which we erected. This had been dragged all the way from Pollok on the bus and then on the Subway. Hard work but we got it to Gillan OK. So far, so good. Then the weather took control.'

'We were awakened in the middle of the night to see the open sky and stars above us and no sign of the tent which had detached from its ground sheet. There was a hurricane blowing! We scrambled into nearby tents of other groups. The camp was evacuated next day with instructions to leave the tents in position.'

But their troubles were not over. 'Once the tent was returned to the Hall, we were told off (by a certain D. Mackay) for the state of the tent! He would not believe our story and only relented when he had phoned the Warden for confirmation.'

Campfires and Bonfires

*'Around the old campfire, our rough and ready
choir will join in the chorus too…'*
(Campfire Song)

All old Scouts have fond memories of campfires. The 131 were no different. We were a musical Troop. Jimmy McNeillie was a great song leader and Pete McGuire played the guitar and the banjo. Alex Johnstone would bring his small accordion along and give us some great tunes.

Whether at camps or in the Scout Hall, the Troop would sit around the camp fire and sing all sorts of Scout songs along with Irish – and even English and American ones. Older Scouts would introduce the lads to the Red Clydeside song books. They also learned the great anthem of the *D-Day Dodgers* by Hamish Henderson. These were the years close to the war and had great resonance as members of everyone's family had been involved.

But our own Troop Song (*We are Boy Scouts of the 131 of the City of Glasgow*) also caused some problems as Alan McCombes noted, 'A lot of us were from Irish families and the sentiments of the Troop Song did not sit comfortably on us – particularly Loyal and true to the red, white and blue. So, we came up with our own parody for these words – Loyal and true to the Green, White and Gold – and we would lose points for our Patrol if the Leaders heard this version. No rancour and no drama, but that was our true background in those days.'

After a gap of more than fifty years, Graeme O'Neill smiled when he spoke about old campfire songs, 'They were terrific songs. How else could we have learned such great songs? Everybody at school only sang pop songs but we had loads of tremendous songs. My favourite was *Ging Gang Gooli*. It was a song from the Zulus in South Africa and we were singing it in Pollok.'

When the Troop met inside the Hall, a small heater which looked like a coal fire would be plugged in and gave off a red glow, but no heat. Some nights we would carry our benches across Brockburn Road and set them up on the big grass patch beside the Brock Burn and light a real campfire and make cocoa. Passers-by would often join us.

Once a year we would hold a Troop bonfire night with a controlled fireworks display. Another Troop would be invited to this event. Everyone would have a great time singing songs and doing campfire sketches. It was a happy night and then it would be time for the fireworks display. Apart from sparklers, everything was expensive so our fireworks box would only have a few rockets, a few whirly things and a couple of loud bangers.

On one particular Bonfire Night, big Frank Steele was in charge of the fireworks and had opened the box on a spare bench, some distance away from the fire. Everybody cheered as the first few fireworks went off. It was great fun. But then a spark landed on the open box. The first anyone knew of it was when a rocket whizzed across the camp fire.

Then there were lots of loud bangs and bright sparks everywhere. We all hit the deck. At first there were roars of laughter and loud cheers from the lads. It was spectacular. Then we saw flames coming from the fireworks box. A couple of the Leaders ran to the box with a bucket of water and soaked it. There were no more fireworks that night but there were lots of wild stories about the shenanigans.

Campfire sketches were always funny. These took place when a couple of Scouts would get up and perform their rehearsed piece. Sometimes it was a four-piece song when they would split the campfire gang into different singing sections. Other times it was some sort of comedy activity such as throwing cups of water over a magic wall (a blanket) and the response being a bucket full of water in reply. Solo singing was never done. Campfires were communal activities. Patrols stuck together to entertain the rest of the gang and to be as daft as possible (and gain points for their Patrol).

One of these campfire occasions witnessed a memorable performance by three of the older lads, Michael O'Neill, Jim Mackay and Ian MacCormick. 'We were about sixteen at the time,' said Jim. 'So we decided to play our musical instruments and entertain the troops at Auchengillan. Michael played the trumpet in the school orchestra; Ian played the guitar and I could pick out a tune on the recorder. We called ourselves the Pollok Trio for the sketch – copying the rather better-known Kingston Trio.'

The campfire was held in the big Campfire Hollow and the trio entered from the side, playing *Frère Jacques* on the trumpet, the recorder and the guitar. Quite musical, they thought. Michael initially believed that the reception was applause. Well, it was certainly loud. They were trying very hard to keep in tune and not trip over any rocks as they walked, trying to look like a bunch of wandering minstrels from the Middle Ages.

However, Jim's assessment was brutal, 'The campfire crowd erupted with hilarity. It was just like a bad act at the Glasgow Empire. They gave us pelters. We just ignored it, tootled away and disappeared across the campfire into the darkness. Very atmospheric we thought. The place was in uproar but I don't think our manager received any bookings.'

It can also be claimed that our renowned musician Gerard Doherty received his early musical training at 131 campfires, 'Oh yes, campfire songs seemed to get regular airings. *Ging Gang Gooli* – (although gooleys has since taken on a new meaning), *Father Abraham, Bravo Bravissimo*. We had a parents night one meeting and had to form a circle facing out towards the adults and sing various songs. I really didn't know many so I just tried miming... Conducting an orchestra was easy after facing stage fright at a Scout campfire.'

These were Scout campfire songs of their time, not polite, sanitised Ralph Reader Gang Show ditties. Some of the songs had robust lines such as – *Bring a stick of chewing gum and stick it on the floor and I'll tell you Bible stories you've never heard before.*

We would have a campfire leader, a PL or Adult Leader, who was the MC. Guys like Danny Houston and the McGuires. They would whip us up into great excitement and lead us on songs which had great lines – *There was cheese, cheese with kilts and hairy knees in the Quartermaster's Stores!*

There was also great four-part songs which would be sung by Patrols in turn – *Oh dear mother I'm to be married to Mr Punchinello.*

And then this ditty would be sung faster each time as the singers were only allowed one breath!

None of us could ever forget the vigorous refrain of McCarthy's Party, where – *Casey and his cousin paralysed half a dozen – They hit both swift and hard.*

The 131 campfires would have loads of young lads roaring out their parts. Roberto McLellan had no problem remembering the words of the Troop song from sixty years back, 'Well, we sang it at the end of every campfire.'

One of the benefits of Scout campfires was that we became interested in folk songs and a group of us would visit various folk clubs around Glasgow and Paisley. Only Pete McGuire was good enough to perform but the rest of us joined in the chorus – and the Guinness.

The 131 Take Stirling Castle

One of the most colourful 131 stories was when thirteen members of the Troop received their Queen's Scout certificates at Stirling Castle from the Chief Scout, Sir Charles Maclean of Duart on 9th October 1965.

For Jack, every Queen's Scout badge was a significant moment. He had been the first Queen's Scout in Glasgow, 'The King died on the Monday and I completed my badge on the Tuesday. It meant that I got a different badge, one with a queen's crown. I was one of many Queen's (and King's) Scouts who lined the way for the Coronation procession in London. But I had to face the crowd and had my back to the Queen's coach as she passed by. Never mind, not bad for a guy from the Gorbals.'

The 131 group made their way to Stirling by rail and were collected at the station by their host families. Travel costs were paid by the individual Scouts, with some assistance from our meagre Group funds. All of the hosts at Stirling had sons who were Scouts. The following day, inside the Great Hall, the 131 recipients met up with another seventy Queen's Scouts from all over Scotland and the Chief Scout. The 131 felt they already knew him, having camped on his land in Argyll. It was a great memory for all the boys involved.

This was a quantum leap for the boys from the scheme. They were inside a royal castle, one which had an iconic place in Scottish history. They made the most of it and had a good peep around their surroundings. Noel Carson was impressed by the ancient woodwork and for Brian McIntyre and Eddie Mallan, the most memorable bits of the castle were the gargoyles, ugly wee faces peering down from every corner.

After the presentation of the certificates, the 131 Queen's Scouts roamed around Stirling and headed back to reality to carry out work on their own Scout Hall.

The recipients were – Noel Carson, Jim Mackay, Michael O'Neill, Len McKinnon, Roberto McLellan, Ian MacCormick, John Watts, Brendan McLeod, Eddie Mallan, Hugh Mullaney, Michael McGee, Pete McGuire and Brian McIntyre.

But one of the 131 gang was not there in person. Jim Mackay was playing in an important football match, so I attended instead to receive the treasured certificate on his behalf.

This landmark achievement was written up in the Glasgow Evening Times on 8th October 1965:

The 13 lads from the Pollok troop – the 131 – have set up a Scottish record.

No other Scottish Troop has had so many members qualify as Queen's Scouts at the same time.

Queen's Scout Reception

Stirling Castle

9th October, 1965

Cub Campsite Chuckles

Like many other 131 veterans, Jim Donnelly started his Scouting career in the Cubs, 'I remember going to the Cubs at the wooden huts at the old Gowanbank St Bernard's school. All I can remember is lots of mad wee nutters like me racing up and down the hall and the Leaders trying to keep us in order. We passed lots of badges and it was a really great time for me.'

The Cub training programme included simple household matters like making beds, tidying and cleaning. The Cub Leader would take a group of boys and show them how to do these things in the Hall. But, sometimes this would go wrong, as Eleanor Reynolds recalled, 'I told the Cubs at the start of the meeting, that if their shoes weren't shiny they were to go into the kitchen and use the polish and brushes which were stored there. I couldn't believe it when I did inspection and found that several of them who were wearing black sandshoes had accepted my offer. Their shoes and socks were now covered in black shoe polish!'

At times the Cubs were allowed to come along to Scout camps at Auchengillan. Not to sleep over but to take part in a day of activities. Len McKinnon took about 30 Cubs and 4 Leaders from Pollok to Auchengillan one Sunday.

This was a trip of more than an hour in a bus with wildly excited kids. The Cub Leaders started out by singing campfire songs to try to keep them calm but this only made them noisier. Then they played some games where the Cubs had to keep quiet but this didn't work either. Eventually they patrolled the bus trying to stop them climbing over into the next seat or throwing sandwiches everywhere. When they got to Auchengillan, the driver pulled Len aside and said that Celtic and Rangers supporters never made so much noise when they were in his bus. By that time the Leaders were all hoarse and almost out of their minds, so journey's end was a relief for them.

They were marched up the track to the 131 camp site. Several big Scouts went with them but nevertheless, a few Cubs still managed to break free and dive into the farmyard to shout at the cattle in the big pen. They were then told to keep quiet when crossing the farmyard as any noise could upset the animals. We should have saved our breath. It wasn't every day that Cubs got into a farmyard and they all had a ball. Later, one of the Scout Leaders had to race down and have a chat with the farmer to apologise for the mayhem.

Once on the site they were split into groups and handed over to Patrol Leaders. The nonsense stopped there. The PLs were just like big brothers and big brothers tended to be direct with their discipline. There were no reported incidents of Cubs being thumped but there were no more lunatic escapades either. Well, perhaps there were a couple on the aerial runway…

The Cubs had to climb up the big tree to get on the slide. This was no problem for most of them as they were tied on to a rope to prevent them from falling out of the tree. However a couple of them chickened out halfway up. What a carry-on it was to try and get them up the tree or back down to the ground. Once they got to the top of the tree (about thirty feet up), they were strapped into the seat and away they went yelling and screaming all the way down. We had a couple of big Scouts at the bottom to act as a brake.

The wild day out ended with a campfire, sitting around on logs, drinking hot chocolate and eating biscuits. A pleasant end to an exciting day. Eleanor takes up the tale, 'Then Skipper asked for one of the Cubs to give us a campfire stunt or sing a song. There was total silence before wee Stephen put his hand up. He treated everybody to a full rendition of *Found a Peanut* including all hand, leg and foot movements. It was hilarious. I believe he would regularly do this turn when he moved up to the Scouts a few months later.'

Needless to say, all the Cubs – and Leaders – slept on the return coach journey. A perfect end to a grand day out.

The Cubs Invade The Zoo

Another lively Cub outing was a trip to the Zoo at Easter 1970.

Eleanor Reynolds was one of the Leaders that day. Her Cub Pack name was Baloo, 'The Cubs were fascinated by it. They did not know my real name so they thought I was called Baloo!'

'The first stop was the Polar Bear enclosure. All went well until the Cubs started feeding them. They were firing their packed lunches like missiles at the bears who were diving into the water to get them.'

Akela (Len McKinnon) and the Leaders struggled to control this madcap behaviour. It was all happening at a huge pit with a high metal fence at the top. This was to keep the bears from getting out but it was also very good at keeping the Cubs from getting in! They bombarded the bears with sandwiches and the Leaders looked on in amazement as these huge creatures glided through the water after them and the Cubs just kept on cheering and yelling away.

Fifty years later, memories of this performance still bring a smile from Eleanor, 'I was terrified in case one of these wee rascals would manage to climb over the big metal fence of the enclosure. They would probably have chased the Polar bear away. Being a Cub leader with the 131 was an all-action experience. There was always some scallywag getting up to some daft trick.'

The next part of the tour was reasonably straightforward. There were lions, monkeys, camels and even a rhinoceros. Then the Cubs came across a group of peacocks strutting around the paths. The boys raced forward in a mad rush and the birds flapped away, leaving behind a bundle of beautiful tail feathers.

Finally, the Cubs were all rounded up to board the bus. Another crackpot moment on this trip was recalled by Eleanor, 'We had just got on the bus and I kept getting tickled on the back of my neck. I couldn't see anything until the Cubs burst out laughing and showed me about a dozen big plumage feathers which were brandished all the way back to Pollok and the Scout Hall.'

This comical conduct left a permanent impression on Cub Leader Graeme O'Neill, 'I was just a young Leader at the time and the Cubs were great fun. Always noisy and up to lunatic tricks. It was great fun trying to control them. I will never forget the sight of Cubs waving peacock feathers on the bus and later on while we were walking through the city centre. Hard work but a great time and I always remember that I was only about six years older than the biggest Cubs.'

A grand day out for the Cubs, and the Leaders.

COMPETITIVE SCOUTING

A Well Worn Look

Scouting was publicised by word of mouth. When I was eight years old, a friend at school asked me if I would like to go to a Cubs meeting with him. He never came back and I never left. I had to wait a while before I had a Cub jersey, but once this was available, I spent the next two years covering it with badges. And for the following ten years, my level of skill and knowledge was displayed on the sleeves of my Scout shirt, an old Army shirt – hairy and itchy.

The second-hand Shirt and Kilt Box was an important part of life in the 131. Lads who had left were asked to bring back their uniforms to the Troop. Shirts, kilts, sporrans, belts, socks, garter flashes, hats and Cub jerseys all served the next generation. Rucksacks and hiking boots were a specially prized donation. There were no wasted items and each was given out free of charge.

'It would be no exaggeration to say that at least one-third of the Troop used hand-me-down shirts, neckies and camping kit,' remembered Jack. 'It was always welcome when an old Scout came down to return his shirt. This stuff was always needed and some of these shirts would have all the badges still on them. Even though they had left, they were still part of the 131 family.'

Eddie Mallan was one of the young Leaders who had been put in charge of the spare kit box. He would make sure the shirts had been washed and ironed and that the badges had been removed. The 131 had a well-worn look. Baggy shirts with long sleeves, a selection of outdoor jackets and occasionally hiking boots. Footwear was always the weak spot until the late 1960s when cheaper boots came on the market.

Scouting was the only place where the boys from the scheme could mix with and compete with the posh boys and do the same activities. There was no hostility towards them. Indeed not, the 131 wanted to get up alongside them as Michael O'Neill remembered, 'We were so far below these people on the social ladder that

I wonder if they could even see us. We were as good as they were – and in many cases, we were better. Class war no less, but without any nasty behaviour.'

The 131 lads had learned the hard way how to camp comfortably. We could camp anywhere in totally wild conditions and leave the site perfectly clean, apart from an area of trampled grass. Jack Banks summed it up, 'There was a high level of outdoors skill all round. And we beat all the pre-war, established Scout Troops in the process.'

Pride in the 131 showed through when the boys talked about it to their friends. According to Tommy, this acted like a recruitment advert. As a result lots of youngsters wanted to join the Troop. We were doing things which nobody else in the scheme could do.

There was also a tremendous parental input as well. Our Scout activities attracted their attention. We were showing them something completely new which was definitely good for their sons.

Scouting was not promoted in the local schools. 'We would probably have been swamped,' laughed Pete McGuire. 'When we did it later on we would have dozens of weans turning up at the Hall the next evening. A pity that adult helpers could not be recruited as easily.'

The limited method of promoting the 131 paid dividends as it ensured that all the boys felt they were part of a special, secret gang. And they were.

Familiarity Leads to Success

Glasgow Scouting was split into local Scout Districts throughout the city. Southwestern District stretched from Govan to Nitshill and there were 20 Scout Groups in it. Each year, the 131 would compete in the District camping competition against these other Troops. Jack was determined to win this title and a lot of hard work was done over the years by many of our Scouts and Leaders and we had finished second in each of our first two attempts.

Then, in 1962, the competition was held at Peesweep Camp, above Paisley, on the very top of the Gleniffer Braes, a familiar hiking ground for the 131. There were another four Troops taking part and we all had to meet at Paisley Cross, carrying rucksacks and camping kit. Each Troop had four Patrols taking part, so there were more than one hundred Scouts milling around beside the war memorial.

At the agreed hour, they all jumped aboard two double decker buses which then roared off towards the drop-off point at the foot of the Gleniffer Braes. There was plenty of singing and cheering during the short trip before everybody struggled off the buses and formed up, laden with kit. There was only a steep, narrow road to the top of the hill. The singing gradually died down as all the Scouts staggered up the road. There was an old well at the side and every Scout had a good drink from it before continuing on their way. From the top of the hill, there were another two miles to go before getting to the camp site.

This hill provided an important clue to the result of the competition, as Robert McGuire prophesised at the time. The 131 were always confident and kept marching up the hill. But the other Troops were lying about, absolutely knackered. Robert kept telling us we were tougher, more enthusiastic than the rest of them and this meant we would win. And we did, the first of five consecutive wins.

Our First Attempt at the County Flags

Camping competition stories are woven into to the 131's narrative and Jim Mackay added this one, 'I can still remember being at Auchengillan for the County Flags weekend. I think it was 1962. Each District had a team of four Patrols and the 131 were representing our District. We were tested on camping, cooking, First Aid and various other skills. But the bit I remember best was the tug-of-war. Each District pulled against the others, just like a league and we got to the final.'

This weekend was also a vivid memory for Roberto McLellan, 'Yes, it was a real carry-on. There was no flat ground as it was Auchengillan. There was only some less bumpy ground to use for the competition.'

'Ah,' added Jim Mackay. 'We were very sneaky at the tug-of-war. All the other Districts had loads of big guys. The team had an overall age limit but our older guys would have put us over the limit.

But we sneaked in a couple of our older Scouts, George Lyden and Len Ashforth, as they were smaller. But we lost in the final. The whole Troop was there and we had our own camp strip by then – we wore black T-shirts, khaki shorts and white socks.'

Pete McGuire remembered when Jack turned up at the Troop meeting with the black T-shirts, 'You have to remember that in those days we did not have replica football jerseys or any kind of football jerseys. So to have our own 131 jerseys made us feel like world champions. We even sewed numbers on them later. We made the numbers ourselves and they were all squinty.'

The County Flags event took place at the East End at Auchengillan. The 131 were tested on their camping standards and finished second in this category, a good showing for first-time entrants. Other activities included first aid – rescuing a climber who had a broken leg and lowering him down a rock face where all of the team had to be properly secured.

A huge scavenger hunt was also part of the event and one Patrol had to roam all over Auchengillan to get hold of various items. Then there was the routine incident hike which also covered the entire camp site. Plus some pioneering tasks, one of which was the construction of a tripod which then had to be raced against the other Troops.

Regardless of their skill levels in the individual events, the 131 rushed into every challenge and worked hard at it. We were very excited about being in the County Flags. I suppose it was like being in the Cup Final and we, the 131 from Pollok, were competing at the top level of Glasgow Scouting.

At the end of this weekend, the 131 were placed fourth in the County Flags out of 12 Troops who had taken part in the final of the competition. The earlier rounds had involved almost 200 Troops.

Jack was very pleased with our overall performance, 'For our first attempt at the County Flags it was a decent result. The detailed scores gave us the starting points for the skills which had to be improved. But the competition was not an end in itself as it showed the high standard of Scouting skills within the Troop. We had shown that we could do everything the big Troops could do and we could improve for next year.'

The 131 form up at St Bernard's School in 1964
for the County Flags inspection

An Important Lesson

The 131 were determined to build upon the good result of the 1962 County Flags. They reached third the following year and by 1964, our two Patrols who had qualified were confident of success. We had done more camping than any of the other competing Troops and our outdoor skills were second to none.

The 1964 final was eagerly awaited. The camping section was held at Tullochan, Loch Lomond, the farm of the great Airborne Forces war hero Alistair Pearson (himself a former First Glasgow Scout). At the end of the competition we had finished second, despite one Patrol winning the hike section and the other Patrol taking third in the camping section.

The competition had been decided on the final inspection and the 131 finished one point behind the winners. The PL of the camping Patrol, Len McKinnon, was puzzled by this as the deciding penalty had been a discarded piece of sausage wrapper found on our camp site. Sausages were not on the menu that weekend, so he hadn't a clue where this item came from. But he could remember that the judges did not spend much time inspecting his site but still managed to find this piece of paper.

The two Patrols listened to the results being read out and were pleased to have finished second but disappointed that they had not won. Surely the winners must have been super campers – even though the 131 had seldom seen this Troop at Auchengillan. We were bussed back to Elmbank Street, the Glasgow Scout Headquarters, for collection by our Scout Leaders. When Jack was told the result, he was dismayed.

However, the story is more complicated than this. It had been a three-part competition – a hike, a camp site and an inspection visit to the Troop to examine its individual progress standards and overall programme. Jack had worked very hard on this part and was confident that the 131 would score well despite not having its own Scout Hall and having to meet in a local school instead.

This visit took place before the competition weekend. Every 131 Scout was present in full uniform. The record cards were up to date and every boy had been to at least two camps that session. Summer Camp was planned for Torquay and there was a winter weekend arranged for Auchengillan. Two of the lads were Queen's Scouts and another ten were expected to complete their badge in the summer. Overall, a very good Troop programme.

But Jack's optimism was misplaced. We were marked down because of matters out of our control; kilts of different patterns, wearing Tam o' Shanter hats instead of the big bush hats, not camping in far-off places – two of the other Troops had camped at the Scout Chalet at Kandersteg in Switzerland and another was going to Germany.

Jack felt it was a simple case of discrimination by the examining team, all of whom came from well-off Troops – and wore big bush hats. Apparently these Troops ran better programmes than the 131 because they went to expensive camp sites. The 131 finished bottom of this section.

Jack, Tommy and Jimmy McNeillie were speechless when these scores were revealed but tongues were kept firmly in place. The 131's fightback over the competition weekend had just fallen short. In fact, without the programme inspection scores, we had easily won.

Jim Mackay remembered the Troop inspection visit, 'We had been fully briefed by Jack and had been preparing for the visit the previous week. We were all excited and determined to perform well in front of the inspectors. In those days such people were regarded with full respect. I feel that this was one-sided when you look at the mark they gave us.'

This annoyance was reinforced by Len McKinnon, 'All of my Patrol had the Camper badge and you had to have done 12 nights camping to get it, but only two of the winning Troop had it. And just how were we expected to be able to afford matching kilts, big stupid hats and overseas camps? But that was life in those days and we just had to take it.'

Even the Scoutmaster of the winning Troop was embarrassed by the result, as Jack explained, 'He came across to me outside Elmbank Street and shook my hand, saying that it must have been very tight for his Troop to have beaten the 131 who were champion campers.'

The County Flags 1964 highlights middle-class attitudes of the time. Camping at Kandersteg in Switzerland was deemed a magnificent achievement, whereas camping at Auchengillan every weekend was just run-of-the-mill.

This was an important lesson for our lads. Instead of losing to a better opponent, which is fair enough, the 131 had been handicapped from the start because of our economic and social status.

131 NEWS

OFFICIAL BULLETIN OF 131ST BOY SCOUTS
PRICE 3D   VOL. 1. No. 2.   JUNE 1964.

COUNTY FLAGS.

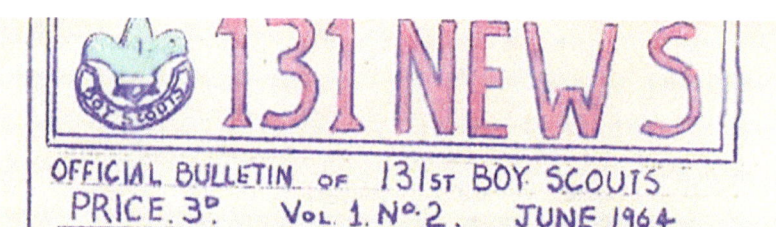

PIPPED — BY ONE POINT!

Our bid for the County Flags on 13th/14th June ended in disappointment when we finished second to the 1st 'B' who beat us by the minimum margin of one point. However we put up a great fight and are now one of the most respected troops in Glasgow. Coupled with our third position last year we have an excellent record in the County Flags.

Assistant County Commissioner Brownlie Young remarked "It was very close at the finish. A very good show by the 131".

Scout Master John Banks said "We are proud of the boys. We will be all out to win next year".

The competition was held at Rob Roy Camp site, Loch Lomond and consisted of three parts — Troop Inspection, Camping and Hiking. The first took place on Monday, 8th June, but we were not placed in the first four. The Raven Patrol camped for the week-end. They were tested on camping, First Aid, Cooking, Naturecraft and Map-making, finishing third in this section. Swift Patrol hiked from Rob Roy to Gartocharn returning by a different route and won their section of the competition.

131 News June 1964

If at First You don't Succeed...

The 131 lads put the disappointment behind them when they entered the County Flags final again in 1965. Having finished fourth, third and second, surely, this would be our year. The competition was held at Lapwing Lodge, Peesweep. It was a good, sunny weekend and expectations were high. 'If we don't win it this year we will be surprised,' said Jack on the morning of the competition. 'Any boy from the Troop could be a member of this Patrol. They'll do well regardless of the result.'

Noel Carson was the PL and was very confident as the Patrol had trained very hard for this event. They had also won the District Flags a few weeks earlier.

On the final day, the seven competing Troops formed up outside the Peesweep camp building for the results. The scores were read out in reverse order from third position. For the 131, this was agony. Second place was announced and chests tightened. The chief judge then cleared his throat and announced, 'In first place and winners of the County Flags for 1965 is the 131st Glasgow Troop.'

And there we were, the only Troop from a housing scheme to win the County Flags in 50 years. The first winners who did not have a Scout Hall and the first Catholic Troop to do so. Handshakes all round and many smiling faces. Our two great Leaders had been vindicated. Jack was the Scoutmaster who had trained us up to this high standard and Tommy had held the 131 together for almost twenty years. A good result for two lovely men.

The Leaders and Patrol Leaders trekked across Glasgow to Jack's house in Barmulloch the following Sunday. Pizza, beer and Irn Bru were consumed, many campfire songs were sung – as well as lots of Sinatra and our favourite, *Me and My Shadow* – and a great feeling of satisfaction was felt by all.

The evening ended before midnight and the visitors set out on the 10-mile hike back to Pollok. It was a lovely summer's night, dry and clear. There was no money for taxis. Just a gang of tough, happy young guys walking home with their pals. We had worked so hard to get to the top. We stood on George V Bridge over the Clyde and sang the Troop song as well as *I Belong to Glasgow*. All that remained to be done was to turn up at Auchengillan on the next Sunday afternoon to formally receive the County Flags from the County Commissioner.

The 131's long march was over. We were now on the summit and things changed after this.

County Flags Winning Patrol 1965
Brian McIntyre, Richard Crone, Pat Doherty, Robert Allan,
Iain MacCormick and Noel Carson

A Day to Remember

One of the duties attached to winning the County Flags was to represent the Glasgow Scouts at the Remembrance Day parade in November 1965. The Second World War had ended twenty years previously and there had been other conflicts since then, so this event attracted a huge crowd. It was held in George Square and hundreds took part in the parade. There were Navy, Army and RAF units, the Boys' Brigade, the Girls' Brigade, the Girl Guides, old comrades associations, Corporation bus drivers and subway workers, civil servants and many other groups and of course, the Glasgow Scouts –on this day the 131.

We provided a colour party and six Scouts for the parade. First stop that day was at Tommy's house where we excitedly collected the County Flags and had half an hour of drill on the pavement, conducted by Jack. Then, true to tradition, we climbed into a van, provided by one of the parents, and moved off to George

Square. Most of us had fathers, uncles, cousins or brothers who had served in the armed forces. In fact, many of the Troop had mothers and grandmothers who had survived the bombs which had fallen on the city. One mother's tale was typical, 'I had to hide down in the close when the German planes arrived. When I went back upstairs my wee budgie had died from the shock of the bombs.'

Jack formed up the colour party at the start point and gave them a bit more drill before the parade began, 'The lads were so keen. They were on the biggest parade in the city. None of them had ever been to it before. I made sure they were smart and they were. Tommy and I were so proud watching them march along that day – but we never told them as they would have been big-headed. Glasgow Scouting had very good representatives on the parade.'

As the Troop Leader (the Senior PL), I was in charge of the 131 squad on the parade. It was the biggest parade I had ever attended. When we were marching round I was amazed to see a mob of our Scouts who had come along specially to cheer us. We were bursting with pride that day and kept in step all the way.

There was an amazing surprise for us as we marched past the Cenotaph outside the City Chambers. We had to give a salute when we passed the group of officials who were at the saluting base. The Lord Provost was easy to see as he had a big gold chain around his neck, as did some other gent. But standing in front of them was an elderly guy who appeared to be the main man. He had lots of medals and as we drew nearer I could see that he was wearing the Victoria Cross! Good grief, a real live hero. What a yarn to tell the rest of the Troop!

Soups-a-daisy!

The River Avon wends its way through tree-lined gorges to join the River Clyde east of the town of Hamilton. Our introduction to this historic spot was in the 1960s when we went to camp on Colonel Cranston's estate for the Archbishop's Shield competition.

The Colonel was a keen supporter of Scouting and the boys from Pollok were delighted to camp on another new camp site. It seemed a bit like something from a Boys' Own story, the boys from a Glasgow housing scheme were now camping on the Colonel's estate.

The weekend started with our Patrol getting to Hamilton by train and then standing at the main crossroads to do a traffic survey. That was the first part of the competition – counting and writing. The second part was for the Patrol to hike up the Haugh Road – Scots for High Road. We had no bother straggling up the hill and then down a nearby side road to the camp site.

The site was inside a wood. It was dark and atmospheric. We quickly set up the tent and got stuck into the next round of tests. Cooking was one of our best skills and one of our top menus was going to be produced that weekend – home-made pea and ham soup, ham stew and steamed pudding with custard.

Overnight we steeped the peas and barley for the soup. The next morning the ham knuckle was put on to boil slowly and plenty of firewood gathered and laid out neatly. The masterpiece was coming along well. The peas and barley were then added to the broth and the ham knuckle removed and sliced up for the main course. The small, steamed puddings were mixed and wrapped in waterproof paper, then gently placed in boiling water. I set about mixing the custard from a dry powder with some sugar and milk added. It would then poured into boiling milk and stirred until it was thick enough. All on a wood fire.

Five minutes before the meal – with the inspection of the cooking about to take place – it was time for the soup to be poured out. My brother was my Second that weekend. He smartly removed the dixie of hot soup and made his way across to our home-made camp table. Our tin plates had been laid out. Everything was ready. Then calamity!

Jim's foot bumped against the table and he stumbled. The soup dixie swung wildly and the contents poured out – on to my back! I yelled out in pain and jumped across the fire to escape the downpour. In doing so, I managed to overturn the other dixies. Custard and steamed pudding splashed to the ground.

I still continued thrashing around, ripping off my Scout shirt. My brother looked at me and said *Sorry*! Then he started to run away as I chased him around the camp site.

COMPETITIVE SCOUTING

I was taken to the First Aid tent and the burns on my back were treated with calomine lotion. My Scout shirt was ruined and points were deducted for its dirty condition at the final inspection. We were awarded low marks for cooking and we had six very hungry Scouts.

But the smiles returned to all our faces when the results were announced and despite the setbacks, we won the competition.

Before the soup was spilled

A Welcome Surprise

The change to a much younger Troop after 1967 eroded a lot of the 131's great camping knowledge. It was now a young Troop. But we continued to enter camping competitions as this helped to raise our skills levels.

Jim Donnelly recalled the District competition in 1968, 'I remember being at a competition somewhere near Bathgate. I think the place was called The Crags. Our Patrol Leader was called Eric McKelvie and his nickname was Boris, don't know why as he was never called this at school. We did activities all weekend, like going up a hill and drawing a map of a mile radius.'

'On the Saturday night, we were sent on a late night hunt to Bathgate to obtain certain info, like the name of the main church, location of cop shop etc – stuff you now get on Google within seconds! The Sunday was a camp inspection. We had a joint of meat with veg boiling away. It looked impressive! As soon as the inspection was done, we dumped the lot and packed up for home. We came second that day!'

The Archbishop's Shield had last been won three years earlier. This was followed by two more second places, but 1969 was different, as Gerard Doherty noted, 'Skipper sent a more academic (?) bunch on that competition at Lapwing Lodge instead of our normal noisy gang. We were taught how to measure the flow of a river etc. We had to do orienteering using instructions and a compass. The maps were wrong and the compasses were broken so there were Scouts going in all directions! Well that's what we told the examiners. We managed to follow the instructions and ended up at the kitchen door opposite the Senior Scouts room. Using a bit of logic we went to the Senior Scouts door which was correct. The 131 were the only Troop to get to the finish so I think it got us a good few points.'

Their delight was summed up by Alan McCombes, 'It was a great weekend at Lapwing and we never thought that we would be the winners. We did orienteering and lots of other tests and thought that we had done OK, so when we were announced as the winners I think we were all amazed – and over the moon! We got a big shield and waved it around at the next Troop meeting.'

This victory was the standout memory for his brother Ken, 'We were actually the only Patrol available for the weekend, so we did not rate our chances highly. Some of the other Troops looked very serious and had lots of smart kit and we were definitely the underdogs. I'll never forget the utter shock for Skipper and the Leaders when we came home with the trophy. I suppose our frequent camps at Auchengillan helped us that weekend.'

A PLACE OF OUR OWN

The Hall Appears

By the summer of 1965, the 131 needed a new headquarters. The numbers of Cubs, Scouts and Rovers had risen to 120, plus Leaders; and St Bernard's School was due to become a council depot.

We needed our own headquarters where youngsters could hang about and do something useful and enjoyable. A place that was always open, unlike the school or parish hall. Somewhere which was ours. More youngsters were keen to join the Group but there was no way of accepting them.

Tommy and Jack spoke to the local councillor, initially without success, then Tommy received a letter offering the Scouts the former Community Centre. Tommy, Jack and a couple of parents turned up there a few nights later. The deal was done. The 131 Scouts were now the occupants of this property. It was a good deal for both parties – the Council had got rid of an unwanted building and the Scouts had gained a new home. The future was bright.

There was great excitement when the other Leaders and parents were informed. This was wonderful news. A real Scout Hall of our own. And one which would require lots of hard work to convert it into a proper headquarters.

The Non-stop Festival of DIY

The opening of the new Scout Hall was a low-key affair. When Tommy turned up with the keys, a whole new world opened up to us. A gang of keen Scouts and helpful parents were there, eager to get to work on the derelict building.

It was a big commitment and everyone knew it. A lot of work had to be done and constant fundraising had to take place.

Various families and local helpers were able to provide a good range of skills for all the tasks to be done on the Hall. There were bricklayers, electricians, joiners and others who gave their services free of charge. Many of the Mums and sisters got stuck in as well, mainly with the constant clean-up which was needed before any activities could be undertaken. They also made curtains for the many windows. Some of the older Scouts were introduced to basic military skills – cleaning floors, scraping paint from windows and clearing blocked toilets!

The rear wing of the Hall – the old Househillwood Library: this adjoined the main building which can be seen at the top of the picture to the right

The Community Centre was big, probably in excess of forty yards long. It was of wooden construction on a brick foundation. The roof was made of asbestos, but the dangers of this material were not known at that time. There were probably about twenty sets of windows, many of them broken. The water supply had not been turned off, leading to several burst pipes and flooded rooms. The various ceilings in the side rooms had all been destroyed and there were bare wires hanging down in most of them. A tasty challenge no less.

A joiner's assessment of the problem was provided by Noel Carson. He set the priorities as making the building wind and watertight. The internal walls were all damaged and needed repair. The complex electrical circuit had been vandalised and the six toilets were broken. There were also holes in the floor of the main hall and in the roof.

Just to add to the problems, the building was linked to the old library and this was also in a poor state. It had only been closed for a year or two, but the local hooligans had made their mark.

The 131 now had their own building. The work needed was merely a list of tasks to be done. All of these problems could be overcome.

Painting, Singing and Dancing

The Scouts and Cubs continued to meet in the school while the refurbishment work progressed on the old Community Centre complex. The parents' committee provided work squads and the Rover Scouts were a great help as several of them were apprentice tradesmen. They were even able to convince some of their work mates to come along and lend a hand. It had now become a true community activity.

Work continued nonstop for many months. The Hall was like a magnet for us and was so important to us we were always there doing some task or other. We were even working there on Xmas Day 1965.

Jim Mackay was one of the work gang that day, 'I can recall that it was freezing inside. We had no heating and Tommy, with his brother, were working to repair the electrical system. But we had a great time and when we were finished for the day we would walk back home. We were taking care of our own future. It was a great feeling.'

Although it was cold, some painting could still be done and a lot of the time was spent replacing internal walls with Gyproc. The college boys did the easy stuff like splashing paint on to walls, while the apprentice gang did the skilful stuff with tools.

Thankfully, we had Jack's expertise to call on when serious decoration work had to be done. He showed us how to mix paint and, most importantly, how to actually apply it. The lads loved the practical activity and these work sessions were always happy and exciting. 'One of my best memories of the time was when we were painting the upper walls,' said Jim. 'We fixed up a trestle and splashed the paint on the walls while singing – and dancing – to the Beach Boys. Absolute madness, but terrific fun. Much better than my day job of being at school.'

Len McKinnon picked up a useful skill – how to repair TV sets. One of the fathers showed him how to do this for one of our badges. The TV sets were full of valves and wires. These old sets were huge, almost the size and weight of a small chest of drawers. So, when old sets were donated for jumble sales, Len would have a go at repairing them. He would then take them down to Paddy's Market in the city centre and sell them in aid of the Rover funds. Other Scouts, such as Roberto McLellan, were part of this eager technical squad, 'Yes, we even managed to get one to work which we kept in our Rover Den. The reception was dodgy but we were happy with it.'

One day, there was great excitement as Roberto recalled, 'When the heaters arrived for the Hall it was great. Up till then we had been freezing every night. We would have lots of physical activities to keep us warm but it was still a cold place. When Jimmy McNeillie drove up with about ten heaters we were delighted. He had got them from his work as they were being thrown out. They were plugged into the circuit and the Hall warmed up. What a treat that was – absolutely fabulous!'

In addition to its dilapidated condition, the old Community Centre had no furnishings, tables, chairs, desks, cooking implements or games equipment. Parents and helpers became seekers for such items. Some decent stuff was identified and a group of Scouts would be sent out to collect the articles. Unwanted trestle tables were liberated from a local church hall and were carried up the road by a gang of eager Scouts. The tables were stripped down, repaired and repainted by the older lads. Various bundles of chairs arrived as a result of helpful parents asking their employers for assistance. Everything was checked and cleaned. There was no regular pattern to the Hall's contents, no matching sets or colours, but everything worked.

Probably the most ridiculous item to be donated was a full-size snooker table. This came from the youth club at St Robert's School. It was 12-feet by 6-feet, made from mahogany, with turned legs. The cloth had a slight tear, but the rest of it was in perfect order. It was also very heavy as it had a full slate top..

Snooker had just started to be shown on TV at that time and the offer was keenly accepted. A gang of older Scouts turned up at the school to carry the table back to the hall – a distance of about one mile. To complicate matters, there was also a full-size table tennis table – and only a dozen lads to carry these gifts.

It was a clear summer's evening, so the weather was dry and warm for the epic journey to the Scout Hall. Eight Scouts grabbed hold of the snooker table and the other four lifted the table tennis table. It is doubtful if Househillmuir Road has ever seen such an episode before or since.

The snooker team could only manage two minutes carrying before having to rest, while the table tennis table could be carried much further. The strange procession weaved along the road, one hundred yards at a time, with a wee rest every couple of minutes. Roberto McLellan was one of the carrying crew, 'We were absolutely knackered. We just crawled along the street and took about two hours to cover the ground to the Hall.' Passers-by were even roped in to assist and eventually the gang staggered into the hall with the precious items. 'At least, we made good use of the snooker table,' remembered Roberto, 'We played on it after most meetings and on most other nights when we were in the hall. Unsurprisingly, one of us managed to rip the cloth when trying a trick shot – that's the 131, always adventurous. So we mended it with Elastoplast and kept playing.'

The refitting of the Hall was a mammoth task as Eleanor Reynolds recalled, 'It really was in a ramshackle condition and we must have had very big hearts to take it on. Jack had lots of useful contacts who could assist and Tommy had a big family who helped with everything.'

One of the big tasks was the long line of broken windows along the rear side of the building. Each of these had six multi-panels and the broken glass still clung to them. It was definitely a messy job to sort it out. So, a special task team was set up to do this with Noel in charge.

The first step was to smash out all of the windows. collect the broken glass and clean the frames. All at the cost of a few cut fingers – and some unhappy neighbours who complained about the noise. These complainers were two men who worked as bakers and slept during the day. Apologies were delivered and they were invited to visit the Hall. One of them did so and then a few months later, he ran the Cook badge for the Troop.

Large sheets of marine plywood were purchased – another discount deal set up by a Scout parent. These were cut to size to cover the windows and painted before being fitted into the relevant window space.

Once the windows had all been repaired, the whole external wall was painted to give the building a decent appearance. 'This was done with light blue paint,' recalled Michael O'Neill. 'We had been given about thirty big tins of this paint. By this time we had learned to wear old clothes for these kinds of tasks. This was not easy as we had few items of clothing. In the end, though, we were really pleased with our handiwork.'

The electrical system needed detailed work by a qualified electrician. Fortunately a former Scout was available to do this task. He selected a couple of older lads and they climbed up into the roof space to explore the wiring in the darkness. Torches were carried up the ladders, as well as rolls of electrical wire and various other bits and bobs.

It was a wee bit scary as they could not see anything apart from those areas illuminated by the torches. The electrician knew what he was doing, but the others were just there to carry his stuff. It took more than a month to fully survey the task and sort out the complexities of the electrical system. This work was uncomfortable and cold – and occasionally comical and dangerous.

Willie, the electrician, tripped and fell straight through the ceiling. This was made of plaster board and it took us three evenings of work to repair it before we could get back to the electrical task. On another occasion, Willie arrived to switch on the power. He shone his torch into the mains cupboard only to find a rat sitting inside. As he yelled out, he dropped his metal torch. This was followed by a roaring sound and a big flash. The power supply cross-circuited, wires were burned and the rat was incinerated.

There were a lot of rats around the old Community Centre and some of these furry creatures had taken to living in our building. A rat-catching project was launched.

Traps were laid, but only one rat was ever caught by these devices. So, various other methods were used, some had great success and others were totally useless. We even took to throwing big stones at them – and they all missed. Eventually, it was decided to get a cat – a champion rat-catching cat. It had great fun at the Scout Hall and the problem was practically eliminated.

Eleanor Reynolds stills laughs at the memory, 'Whenever we went into the Hall, before the Cub or Guide meetings, we had to make lots of noise, stamp our feet and rattle brushes and things like that. I am sure we could still hear them rustling away in other rooms when we were there. Whenever we saw one, we would throw something towards it and it would retreat to another hidey hole. Never a dull moment!'

Broken pipework in the Hall proved to be a bit more of a challenge and a plumber had to be called in. He discounted his rate and his 131 assistants were Hugh Mullaney and Eddie Mallan, who worked on the problem several weekends and slept in the hall. They also laid pipes to provide a shower room at the brick built end of the building where Tommy laid a smart terrazzo wet floor. A shower in a Scout Hall in Pollok – now that was something else.

There was a constant bubble of activity and various groups of older lads would work late on the endless refurbishment tasks – or just do Scout things – and then sleep overnight in the Rover Den or the Leaders' Room.

The work took a long time to complete because only one of the parents was a fully trained tradesman. All the others were hard-working and reliable, but without the skills to move the task forward quickly. Tommy rebuilt three sets of concrete stairs as well as laying a good floor in the link to the old library wing.

This atmosphere of excitement was still fresh for Jim Mackay many years later, 'It was great fun. We were so chuffed with the Hall that we would spend a lot of time there. It was ours. No more looking for the jannie to open up the school early for us. We were a real Scout Group now. And we had something else to focus on after working so hard to become Queen's Scouts.'

A couple of nights each week, lads such as Noel Carson, Hugh Mullaney and Eddie Mallan would go straight from their work to the Hall and get on with the tasks there. They would go across to the chip van and get a fish supper for tea and then fight off their greedy pals once they were back in the Hall. It was a smashing time.

Even the PLs now had their own room and would turn up there to do some DIY work. Once the heavy work had been completed they were able to paint the walls and stick various souvenirs on them.

The last act before moving to the new place was to thank the janitor at St Bernard's for his great support over the years. He came along to a Troop meeting and received a presentation from the boys and a very loud chorus of *Bravo, Bravo, Very Well Done*.

The 131 Surrender Their Weapons

One of the big news stories in Glasgow in 1968 was when singer Frankie Vaughan met with juvenile gang leaders in Easterhouse and persuaded them to surrender their weapons. This was given maximum publicity and covered on TV.

Pollok was the same as Easterhouse. It was a postwar housing scheme and rated much higher as a deprived and vandalised locality. The publicity given to the Easterhouse event was resented by the 131. These thugs had now become TV stars and decent young guys like us were being ignored.

So we borrowed a cine camera and decided to make a film of our own at Auchengillan.

There was no script, only screenplay. It was a parody of the much-filmed scene when the Easterhouse yobs walked forward carrying their knives and other weapons and threw them into a dustbin. Our version was equally dramatic. A long line of Scouts walked towards the campfire carrying hand axes, felling axes, bush saws, Scout knives, big ladles and cooking pots. Jimmy McNeillie, played the Frankie Vaughan part and hugged each of us as we threw our weapons to the side of the fire, which was then lit and we all danced around it.

This was the 131's artistic riposte. It changed nothing but gave all of us a boost – and a good laugh.

The weapons in use –
Mackay, Mullaney, McKinnon, McLellan deal with O'Neill

An Italian Surprise

World Scout Headquarters designated 1965 as World Friendship Year. Jack agreed for the 131 to host two Italian Scouts for a 10-day visit to Glasgow.

The Hall was in much better condition and full-sized Italian flags covered up lots of holes in the walls. A group of excited 131 Scouts waited for Jack's car to arrive with the two Italian visitors. But it was followed by a coach full of 26 Italian Scouts, all of whom had to be hosted by the 131. Only one other Glasgow Troop had turned up at Scout Headquarters and they could only take four Italian Scouts. The rest were now in Pollok.

Jack explained, 'I knew we could crack it and somebody had to host them anyway. The Italian youngsters were all tired and hungry. They needed hospitality and I knew the 131 would step up to the mark.'

After the chip van was raided, runners sped around the scheme carrying the news. It was a slow process to get accommodation for all of the group. However, our great 131 Scouting family pulled together and all of the Italians were found a place to stay.

Roberto McLellan acted as translator and was the host for one of the Italians, 'When the Italians came, I naturally had one of them. It's so long ago that I can't remember his name. All that I can recall is that we cooked an awful lot of Italian food for the next week as my Mum was Italian. I helped him to cook some angel cakes and he helped me to cook spaghetti.'

Another one of the 131 hosts was Pete McGuire, 'My Italian Scout boarder was a lad called Alberto Albanese from Monza. I knew a wee bit of Italian because we had an Italian teacher at school. Alberto was a happy guy and was quite happy to eat our usual Scottish food. Porridge, mince and of course, chips. I even learned a few words of Italian from him which I used on my annual trips to Italy a few years later. I never visited him though. My own kids couldn't believe the story when I eventually told them it. But what a mad time that was – what a terrific memory!'

Every day the youngsters from Italy and Pollok would gather at the Hall for some sort of visitor activity. One day, a couple of us went on the coach with the Italians to guide them to Loch Lomond. They were very impressed and went for a cruise aboard a boat. Most of them had probably been to Lake Como as they came from Milan but they still loved the Loch.

The younger Scouts were amazed that the 131 was able to host Italian Scouts who had come thousands of miles to stay in Pollok. Joe McEwan remembered being very impressed by it all, 'I was just a young Scout and we had all these Italians staying with us. It was fantastic and we had a joint Troop meeting with them in the Hall. I think Bulldog was a bit of a shock for them but they all seemed to enjoy it anyway. We did.'

The 131 held a farewell dinner in the Hall before the Italians left Glasgow. Roberto was one of the cooks, 'I was a wee bit nervous having to cook a big meal for lots of Italians but all our cooking team was great. The two Italian priests had been hosted by St Robert's Church, so a couple of our priests came down for the meal.' Many of the Italians had bought kilts as souvenirs.

By the end of the visit, friends had been made, letters would be exchanged and another Scout badge had been earned. A couple of 131 Scouts made the return trip to Italy a few years later after fundraising by the parents' committee. Any mention of this long-ago burst of glamour in Pollok still raises big smiles – and no wonder.

The World Cup Finals 1966

Everyone was football daft in Pollok so it was only natural that the 131 wanted to be part of the crowd at the World Cup Finals in 1966. Summer Camps had regularly been held in England and three bold Scouts set off on the long journey South – Roberto McLellan, my brother Jim and me.

The first part of the tournament was held at Manchester and the trip was recalled by Jim, 'We set off from Glasgow and we got the bus to Hamilton on the first leg of the journey. We then hitch-hiked from there to Manchester – hitching was quite normal and we were picked up by kind lorry drivers. They were of course intrigued. Three kilted Scouts going to the World Cup. An early days Tartan Army, I suppose. After all, we were Jags fans, and the Tartan Army was later founded by Jags fans.'

On the other hand, Roberto was not interested in football, 'I went down to the World Cup Finals with David and Jim. There was no Summer Camp that year because of all the time we had spent working in the Hall. We needed a break from Scouting. So, us three older Scouts set out to hitch hike to Manchester from Glasgow. In those days it was very easy. A couple of lorries stopped when we had trudged up to the top of the hill in Larkhall and we were on our way. We were dropped off a couple of times and split up before we all finally got to Middlewich camp site just outside Manchester in the early hours of the following morning. This was our base for the next ten days.'

Roberto did not have tickets for the games, but he would go into town as well and have a look around before coming back to camp and preparing the dinner. 'After the first few days we managed to get better accommodation in the camp cabin and stayed there for the next week. Then it was time to get down to Gilwell Park in Chingford for the rest of the games. We went down by train and battled our way through London. The camp site was excellent and we had been there the previous year with the 131.'

The Mackays had saved up their pocket money to pay for their tickets and Jim recounted the great day at the Final, 'We were there when Bobby Moore lifted the trophy. It was a fabulous experience for a couple of boys from Glasgow, from our initial hitchhike to reach the camp in Manchester, to our walk along Wembley Way for the final. Two Scottish Scouts in kilts being pestered by spivs to sell our tickets. No chance. We both still have our tickets and the unforgettable memories which come with them.'

Oh yes, and the Mackays disagreed about England's third goal. Par for the course.

The return journey was a wee bit different as Roberto remembered, 'When the World Cup ended, David was staying at Gilwell for a Scoutmaster training course and Jim was going to stay with one of his cousins who lived nearby. So, it was just me for the return trip to Glasgow. As I was in Essex, I decided to go up the East Coast this time and then come across from Edinburgh. I just stood at the side of the road wearing my kilt and the first big car which came along stopped for me. My lucky day, I thought – it must be a wealthy bloke.' As he walked towards the big car – a Bentley as he later found out – Roberto wondered what kind of rich guy with a chauffeur, the owner was. These cars had never been seen in Pollok in those days and he had never seen a chauffeur either.

'The driver got out and put my rucksack in the boot. I jumped into the passenger seat and we moved off. I knew there was somebody in the back seat so I turned round to say hello. It was Michael Caine! He leaned across and shook my hand and said *Hello Roberto, so where are you going?* For the rest of the time he chatted with me and asked me lots of questions about Glasgow. He was impressed by the tale I told him about our great Scout Group. It's a pity I didn't ask him for a donation to the Hall Fund.'

Getting to the World Scout Jamboree

Jack had been to the World Scout Jamboree at Bad Ischl, Austria in 1952. As the first Queen's Scout in Glasgow, he was fully supported by Glasgow Scouting. He always talked about this great occasion and worked hard to get a 131 Scout selected for the Glasgow contingent.

By 1967, the 131, having won the County Flags, were now big players on the Glasgow Scouting scene and Danny Adams made the cut.

The 131 parents committee ran special fundraisers to support his trip and Danny attended the Jamboree at Farragut State Park, Idaho, USA later that year. He proudly showed his slide show to many Scouts and Cubs over the following years. Success followed for Thomas McWilliams when he was selected for the Asagiri Heights, Japan Jamboree of 1971. Two Scouts from Pollok had made it to the other side of the world.

In 1983, Jack was chosen as the leader of the Scottish contingent to the Jamboree in Alberta, Canada. A fitting accolade for this great man of Scouting, 'I got them together, about 70 Scouts, for two training weekends before we set off. They were representing our country and I made sure they would do this properly. I gave them hillwalking on Dumgoyne, canoeing, first aid and pioneering training– all the usual Scout Troop activities. It was all necessary because I had decided that we would not drive into the Jamboree site in Canada. No, we set off on a hike from thirty miles away carrying all our kit and completed it with a five miles canoe trip directly on to the camp site. I think we made a bit of an impression.'

This particular episode has been cheered by the old 131 gang every time they hear it. It was true Scouting in action, no less. Travelling the world in style, with a tough edge included.

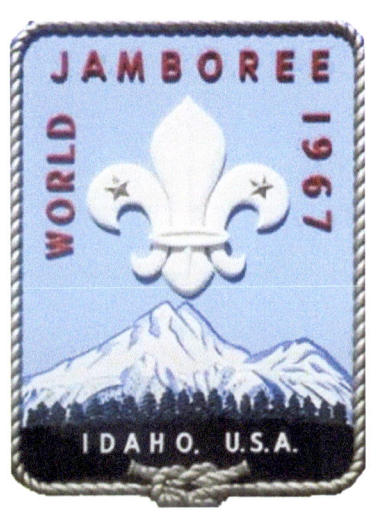

The Jamboree badges worn by 131 members –
Jack Banks, Danny Adams and Thomas McWilliams

FUN AND GAMES IN THE HALL

A Change of Leader – the Young Generation

By the end of 1966, an unexpected and major change had occurred. Jack stood down as Scoutmaster. He had been selected to become a District Commissioner in the Far North of Glasgow, near to where he lived. He was the first working-class Leader and also the first Catholic to be appointed to this level in Glasgow Scouting.

After eight years and 23 Queen's Scouts, it was time for a new team to take over. I became the new Skipper and was joined by Pete McGuire, Noel Carson and Eddie Mallan. We were all Queen's Scouts and I was the oldest at 19-years old. Tommy was still there in the background for advice and guidance.

Although there had been a change at the top of the Troop, Scouting continued nonstop as usual. Every one of these young Leaders was a very experienced Scout with dozens of camps to their name.

The change did not disrupt planning the Troop programme. The Curlew Log reported that Summer Camp 1967 would be held in Dublin, as well as the decision by the PLs Council that the Troop would join the local Oxfam council.

The 131 lads, from Pollok with all its social problems and financial hardships, were now going to help raise funds for Oxfam.

One method was to sell Oxfam raffle tickets amongst family and friends. Another was a monthly whip round on a Troop night which would see Scouts donate a ha'penny to the cause. This was enough for the individual Scout to buy a couple of sweets at the local shops but instead it was put into the pot for the poor people in a faraway country which none of them would ever visit.

Years later, I was working in Nigeria and was involved in Scouting. The local DC told me that there had also been a Scottish Scout from Oxfam who had worked with them many years before. His name was MacBrown and he had brought money which had been donated by Scouts in Scotland. I wondered if this had been linked to the 131 donations. I never met MacBrown – he had fallen down a well some years before. So, I took great care around wells after that!

Tent Pitching with a Difference!

All through the 131's existence, camping skills were taught relentlessly. Even something bizarre such as indoor tent pitching was a regular activity. This could be done in the Hall by using the interior support beams, plus some chairs and bricks to anchor the guy ropes. Most of the time it was only hike tents which were erected, but we often used to pitch the Nijer tents as well. It was important that all Scouts had handled tents before they arrived at a camp site so they would be able to pitch their tent quickly and get on with life, especially if it was raining. You didn't want a gang of wee jokers flailing about trying to erect a tent and getting soaked and miserable. Indoor tent pitching sorted out that problem.

Sometimes at camp, a tent would have to be erected in the dark. This was awkward and could only be done by good campers. When we were doing this in the Hall, a hike tent was used as this was an ideal size. The lads would be blindfolded with their neckies and would have to figure out how to do it. After a lot of practice they could be trusted to do this for real and the boys gained confidence from it.

Another skill which some older lads could perform was to erect a tent entirely on their own. One of us would carry the big tent up the track at Auchengillan and then set about erecting it single-handedly. On a good day, it could be done in about 20 minutes. I had watched my PL Robert McGuire do it a few times and learned from him. Another feather in the caps of the 131 camping experts.

Having our own Scout Hall also solved another problem. Monthly Patrol meetings could now be held there. These were an integral part of the Scout training programme, the aim being to practice the PL's organisational skills. Just having a Patrol meeting was a success for the PL and showed that he was taking his responsibility seriously.

A Full House

The hard construction work paid off and by the end of 1966, the Hall was in use every night. As well as two Cub Packs, a Scout Troop and a Rover Crew, the Hall was used by our own boxing club and a ladies dance club (foxtrot, not Zumba!). The 131 had completely transformed a wrecked building into a good headquarters. The two large meeting halls had a folding partition which could be opened, and there were also a couple of side rooms. Some nights would see more than sixty people – young and old – attend an activity in the building.

There was also a large kitchen with catering ovens which had been repaired and used at various times. One of the first occasions was when the Troop decided to have a Xmas Dinner on 29th December 1966. At the time, Xmas Day was not a public holiday in Scotland. Most people did not have a Xmas lunch.

So, the PLs organised the event. The guests were Jack and our own District Commissioner, Alistair Gibson. The cooking team was supervised by Tommy and they produced a great menu. This was a landmark moment for the 131. We had hosted a meal for about 40 people and cooked it ourselves in our own Hall.

We were so pleased with our ability to cope with cooking for large numbers that the 131's twenty-first birthday was celebrated in a similar fashion in December 1967. This was opened to the parents and the boys all assisted at the event.

The cooking activities in the Hall left a permanent impression on Eleanor Reynolds, 'I can still remember all the cooking antics which went on. Some of the lads, like Brendan McLeod, were young chefs and produced great stuff like scones and wee cakes for us.'

Having our own Scout Hall was beginning to make a noticeable impression. Many of the lads were so thrilled that they would come down a couple of nights every week to do some Scout work or just help with the general refurbishment tasks. The older Scouts, all Queen's Scouts by now, were members of the Rover Crew. They spent a lot of their time assisting with the Hall work programme but would often run their own activities. Swimming and qualifying as Lifesavers was one of these and twice a month a group of them would go to Paisley Baths. Jack himself was a Bronze Medallion lifesaver and had encouraged our best swimmers to work for this qualification.

FUN AND GAMES IN THE HALL

Another Rover activity was the new-fangled sport of ten-pin bowling at Cathcart, although this could only be done after meetings. The Rover Leader was Frank Steele and we would go along to these late-night five-pin bowling sessions. Some of us were quite good and we would meet up with lads from other Rover Crews and formed a league of sorts. When the bowling session ended, we would make our way down to the Broomielaw to buy mugs of tea and rolls and sausage at the all-night mobile cafe. This nightly finale was considered quite cool. We thought we were actually on the waterfront in New York City. Then we would walk 5 miles back home to Pollok with our pals.

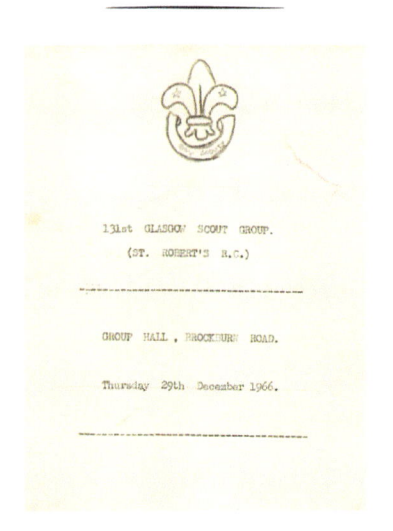

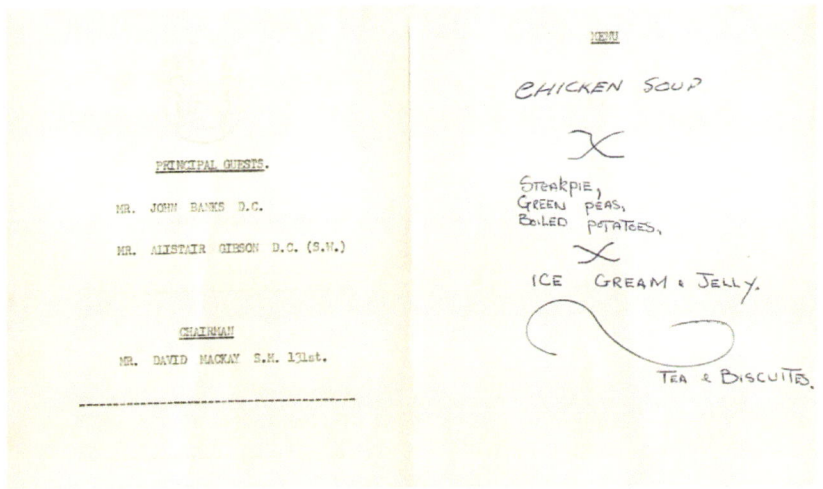

131st GLASGOW SCOUT GROUP.
(ST. ROBERT'S R.C.)

GROUP HALL, BROCKBURN ROAD.

Thursday 29th December 1966.

PRINCIPAL GUESTS.

MR. JOHN BANKS D.C.

MR. ALISTAIR GIBSON D.C. (S.W.)

CHAIRMAN

MR. DAVID MACKAY S.M. 131st.

MENU

CHICKEN SOUP

×

STEAK PIE,
GREEN PEAS,
BOILED POTATOES,

×

ICE CREAM & JELLY.

TEA & BISCUITS.

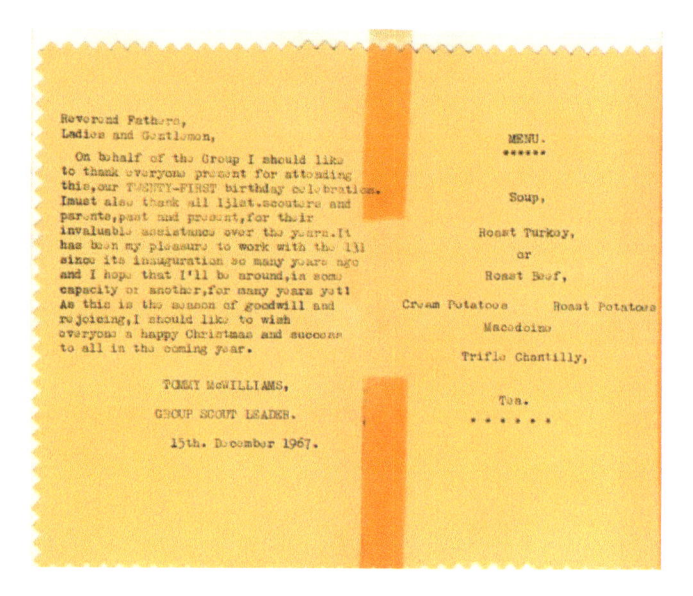

> Reverend Fathers,
> Ladies and Gentlemen,
>
> On behalf of the Group I should like to thank everyone present for attending this, our TWENTY-FIRST birthday celebration. I must also thank all 131st scouters and parents, past and present, for their invaluable assistance over the years. It has been my pleasure to work with the 131 since its inauguration so many years ago and I hope that I'll be around, in some capacity or another, for many years yet! As this is the season of goodwill and rejoicing, I should like to wish everyone a happy Christmas and success to all in the coming year.
>
> TOMMY McWILLIAMS,
> GROUP SCOUT LEADER.
> 15th. December 1967.
>
> MENU.
> ******
>
> Soup,
>
> Roast Turkey,
> or
> Roast Beef,
>
> Cream Potatoes   Roast Potatoes
> Macedoine
>
> Trifle Chantilly,
>
> Tea.
> ******

Into the Lion's Den and Tackling the Mormons

Govan Town Hall was often the scene of some of the 131's most daring – and, as some could say, foolhardy – episodes. The Rover Crew was looking for some exciting programme activities, so Tommy Maguire, the Rover Leader came up with the mad suggestion that some of us should go to an event in Govan Town Hall being held by Ian Paisley who was then in his prime of anti-Catholic abuse. So, a couple of Rovers volunteered and off they went, somewhat apprehensive but keen to hear the Big Man in person.

They thought it would be interesting to know what he was really saying as we would only get a censored version in the newspapers. They would then report back to the Rover Crew. We also asked our Scout Chaplain, Father George Bradburn, to come along but he sensibly declined the invite.

The grand meeting was full to the brim with Union Jack-waving Protestant zealots who sang their hearts out when the National Anthem was played. A couple of minor performers were on stage to warm them up – not that this was really needed. The roof almost lifted off when Dr Paisley strode on to stage – or the pulpit as it really was. Our brave threesome sat quietly in their seats, joining in meekly with all those around them. They were terrified they would be uncovered as interlopers.

All they could do was try and look as if they were part of the audience. A few of the faithful chatted to them and our heroes mumbled plausible replies. Eventually there came the inevitable collection. This was a problem as our lads did not have any cash, only bus fares, so this was handed over and they walked home.

Our three survivors made their report to the astonished Rover Crew the following week. To us, it seemed as though they had been to hell and back. But we all roared with laughter at the story. They didn't even get a badge for it.

There was another religious interlude a few months later when the 131 encountered the Mormons (the Church of the Latter Day Saints) in Pollok.

The Mormon missionaries had been swamping the local area for months. These young Americans, smartly dressed and polite, had been knocking on doors everywhere, including the Scout Hall. We discovered that they had been Scouts – Eagle Scouts – and we invited them in for a chat. A couple of Leaders listened to them and asked them to come back the following week for the Rover Crew meeting. In fact, the Mormon missionaries thought the Mackays were probably related to the high chief of the Mormons – David Omar Mackay. They were not – at least as far as they knew.

Unknown to the Mormons, the Rovers also asked Father George to come along without his priest suit and join in the meeting. The full Rover Crew turned out – about fifteen of us – and we listened as the two sides had a most interesting theological discussion. The Mormons were finally told about George's real job. It definitely wasn't a meeting of minds but it was great entertainment. After this, the Rovers would always wave to the Mormons when they saw them in the local streets. We never invited them back to the Hall, but we did get a Utah Scout badge for our collection.

Bob a Job

The change of leadership and the Dublin Summer Camp had worked well for the 131 and the Troop was in good shape by Easter 1969. There were 36 Scouts and good progress had been made in badge work. The camping season was under way and the boys had flooded out to Auchengillan for more exploits. By now, the camping kit could be cleaned in the Scout Hall and then transported to our locker at 'Gillan. This meant that the tents would have the correct poles, guy lines and pegs, as well as all the cooking dixies being in good condition. Campers could now hit the ground running instead of having to sort out all the kit at the first weekend of the season.

At Easter, there was the Annual Census. The Scout Association needed to count its membership and collect fees from every Cub, Scout, Rover and Leader. Each boy had to produce his own membership fee.

To help with the fee payment, Bob A Job had been invented. This meant that the 131 could pay the overall subscription fee for their numbers but would keep the excess collected by keen Bob A Jobbers. Some boys were excellent and would get a job fee from everybody up their close (tenement). Others, mainly the older ones were less keen, but all would have to hand over the minimum for their personal membership fee.

The Bob A Job tasks were varied. Most boys would empty bins, sweep stairs, brush shoes and even wash windows – only on ground floor houses. Others would dig gardens, go shopping and even take youngsters to the swimming pool. Rabbits were a common pet and 131 boys would clean out rabbit hutches and lure the residents back with tasty grass and leaves. A couple of the lads even cleaned out a pigeon loft. And Scouting skills were also useful to lay a fire for some locals.

The 1968 Census Figures show the makeup of the Troop:

TOTAL BOYS 1968 – 36
10 YEARS OLD – 4
11 YEARS OLD – 16
12 YEARS OLD – 3
13 YEARS OLD – 4
14 YEARS OLD – 3
15 YEARS OLD – 5
16 YEARS OLD – 1
SCOUTS WITH QUEEN'S SCOUT AWARD – 1
SCOUTS WITH CHIEF SCOUT'S AWARD – 4

A Den of Treasures

The Rover Den was the centre of attention for our Queen's Scouts who were now too old for the Troop. It was their room and they worked well to make it a special place.

Roberto McLellan has many great memories of those times, 'When I was a Rover Scout we sorted out a room in the Hall to be used as the Rover Den. As I was good at art I painted a sign for the door. It looked quite smart. We decorated the inside with various things such as neckies from other Scout Troops, pennants, post cards from camps we had been to and even an old set of antlers. But the best bit was when we raided an old pub on Paisley Road West which was being demolished. It was the Half Way Bar and the building was secured but we had a contact who let us into the old bar to collect souvenirs.'

'We took lots of different beer mats, a few old pint pots, a couple of stool chairs and the main trophy was a coat stand. Being adventurous we also unscrewed a street name from the corner of the building as it was being knocked down anyway and then we set off back to the Hall along Corkerhill Road. This was at night and we must have looked like a crowd of ruffians carrying this heavy coat stand. I remember we saw a police car and raced under the White Cart bridge at Corkerhill.' This was a tricky moment and the lads had visions of being arrested and dragged off to Govan Police Station. Something had to be done.

'So, one of us decided to try and fool the cops and climbed back up on to the road. He walked over to the cops and handed them the street sign and said that we had found it under the bridge. The cops did not know what to do and just told us to take it along to the nearest rubbish bin and then they drove off. We took it along with the rest of the stuff back to the Rover Den and slept there overnight.'

Eddie Mallan, Pete McGuire and Noel Carson loved popping into the Den. There was always somebody to meet and a few non-Scouts had joined because of this cosy wee gang hut and all the history which hung around it. A few late arrivals became Rovers – Bill Toal and Tom Shields being two of them. The Rover Crew grew in size and started its own separate programme.

For Roberto and his pals, being a Rover was an opportunity to put something back into the Group and they could help with some activities. They felt like big brothers to all the Scouts and Cubs. They were part of our own special family. They were still productive.

Accolades and Awards

A memorable occasion occured for the 131 when Tommy McWilliams was awarded the Medal of Merit in April 1968 for his twenty-two years in charge of the Group. Tommy was loved by all those who had ever been members and some of the old boys from the far distant past still stuck their heads into the Hall to chat with him. He had been so important to them. The Troop Log recorded this in proper fashion:

> *Tommy McWilliams has been awarded the Medal of Merit – congratulations Happy! (Tommy's nickname) A great honour and one which has been hard-earned.*

Tommy did not want any fuss, but we laid on a big evening with parents, Cubs and Scouts. The County Commissioner came to the Hall and pinned the medal on Tommy. The parents committee presented him with a watch. Everybody cheered, all the cakes were eaten and Tommy was embarrassed. It was a lovely night for a lovely man.

Twenty-five years later, when he was in his seventies, he was awarded the Silver Acorn in recognition of distinguished services to Scouting.

At that time he was running a Scout Group in Govan. Another really hard place. That was Tommy. He helped so many youngsters from disadvantaged areas over the years. As far as he was concerned, Scouting was about camping; boys could go off on their own and look after themselves. It was that simple.

Any adventurous activity would draw in the 131 and when in 1968, the County Commissioner issued a challenge to all Patrols in Glasgow, our PLs, such as George Coll, Joe McEwan and Eric McKelvie, stepped forward. There were various categories involved, but the 131 concentrated on the outdoor sections – camping, pioneering and hiking. All natural and affordable activities for the boys from Pollok.

The Troop was one of the few in the District which received a certificate for every Patrol. But then again, that was the 131 – one in, all in.

County Commissioner's Certificate 1968

A Tight Squeeze

Mr Murphy was the Group Chairman. He worked at the docks and was very useful when we had problems with the Hall. He was a jack-of-all-trades and could fix most things. One day he announced that he had managed to locate an old tent which would be ideal for the Troop. Two Leaders arranged to go down to Govan Docks with him and check it out.

Another tent was always useful and this looked like a good deal. It was yet another ex-Army bullet-proof tent, very large, with long tent poles – five of them in fact. They loaded it up into Mr Murphy's car, squeezed themselves inside, with the poles sticking out of the open window, and set off back to the Hall.

At the first corner in the docks there was a slight mishap. The front wheel fell off the car and rolled away across the road, bumped past a bollard and gently plunged into the River Clyde.

So, there they were on a Friday night. Marooned in Govan with a large tent and no transport. There were no mobile phones and very few people had a home phone. No other parents were available as none of them had a car, apart from my Dad who was working that night at Clydebank Docks on the other side of the river.

So, one of the Leaders, Len McKinnon, went down to the ferry and crossed the river to Yorkhill Quay. From there, he walked up to Dumbarton Road and boarded a bus going to Clydebank. When he spotted the sign for Clydebank Dock, he got off the bus and kept walking. To make life more annoying, it had now started raining. Our Leader had no jacket and was very wet when he met up with my Dad and explained the problem to him. They jumped into his car – the luxurious Hillman Imp – and headed back to Govan to complete the rescue.

However, the other two in Govan Docks had thought Len was never coming back as he had been away for more than two hours. So, one of them, Eddie Mallan, decided to board a Number 26 bus with the poles. He chatted to the nice conductress who just rolled her eyes and told him to store the poles in the space under the stairs. The bus rolled off in the direction of Pollok.

This left Mr Murphy sitting on the big tent in Govan Docks when the rescue team eventually arrived from Clydebank. With a bit of pushing and shoving, they managed to squeeze the tent into the Hillman Imp and my Dad drove it back to the Scout Hall.

There was no room for Mr Murphy and Len, so they caught the next bus back to Brockburn Road. We used the tent the following weekend. It was excellent.

Nowadays eBay would have sorted out this matter.

Fishing in the Dark

Mr Murphy was a keen fisherman and ran a fishing club for the Troop. Fishing was a very popular activity in Pollok and at Jumble sales we would often receive broken fishing rods which would be taken by the PLs and repaired where possible and then used as Troop gear.

He would take a group of Scouts up to Waulkmill Dam in Darnley. There was no age limit on joining the fishing club, but it was a special members-only fishing club – they fished in the dark. Typically, as this was the 131, there was an initiation test.

This consisted of spending a night alone fishing at the Darnley dams. Any prospective member, normally twelve or thirteen years old, would have to map-read to a specific spot at the dams, set up a wee tent and then start fishing during the hours of darkness. The reason for this, as Mr Murphy explained, was that the fish only came up to feed in the dark. Maybe they did, as he was the expert.

Whenever any boy expressed an interest in joining the Fishing Club, he was handed over to the PL who was in charge of this activity. The young Scout would ask questions about the entrance test. We would never tell them very much as it was all complete baloney. They would be told to make sure that they were happy to camp overnight on their own. Of course, they all said that they could do this.

They weren't actually on their own though, as Mr Murphy and another adult would be present. During the dark hours, they would make ghost noises and try to frighten the candidate. Sometimes the Scout would yell and shriek, sometimes they would throw stones at the noises, but they were determined to pass their Fisherman badge and this gave them a sort of Dutch courage.

One of these brave young fisher lads was Graeme O'Neill, 'It was quite windy and I was waved off by Mr Murphy and my PL at the edge of the dams. I easily got to the selected fishing spot and set up my hike tent and got on with fishing. I had no luck and gradually became aware of the ghostly sounds around me but I just ignored them and continued. Although I have to admit that I was a bit worried at times. When Mr Murphy popped up in the morning I was very relieved. And I got my badge. It was a mad and scary night but great fun looking back.'

Did they catch any fish? Of course not, the fish were all scared away by the pantomime antics. But all the boys passed their Badge.

Football Crazy

By 1968, the 131 PLs decided to set up a football team. None of them were ever selected to play in their school teams so this meant there were lots of boys looking for something to do on Saturdays when there were no Scouting activities planned.

A team was organised and the 131 were founder-members of the City Boys League. This competition involved teams from all over the Glasgow area and the 131 travelled many miles to play its games – all on public transport. They would wear their football strips under their other clothes, as dressing rooms were few and far between. The team would sport the faithful black jerseys with our home-made squiggly numbers. One of the mothers would take a turn each week to wash and iron them.

Of course, we could not compete with some of the top boys' clubs, but we held our own against others. We even had one player, John McDade, who lived in the far North of Glasgow and travelled by two buses on a Troop night.

The *Govan Press* carried match reports from our games, such as the following from a local derby:

SCOUTS WIN NEEDLE GAME

131st Scouts – 7; 58th Boys' Brigade – 1.

These local rivals met in a challenge match at South Pollok. The small BB team played the neater, more direct football and deservedly went ahead in the 12th minute. Scouts could not combine and were still behind at half-time.

A quick one-two from Smith and Coll surprised the BB. With play even and fast, Ferris slammed home a great goal minutes later. Now 1-3 down, BB began to tire and two goals from Smith ended BB's hopes.

A superb lob from Milligan and a flick by J Steele rounded off the scoring.

131st Scouts: W Steele; Coll, Davies, Ferris, Hunt, Parry, J Steele, McDade, Smith, McLellan and Milligan.

These regular football matches came in very useful in the run up to a District football tournament in 1969. We got to the final, played at Tinto Park in Govan. The game was refereed by an international official who lived across the road from one of the Leaders. The 131 tried their best but were well beaten by the Penilee Scouts (25th). This was probably due to the fact that they played one of their Young Leaders and claimed he was the correct age. 'It was a real struggle against this guy,' recalled Joe McEwan. ' All our team were wee guys and he was so big that he just ran through us every time he had the ball. We kept tripping him up. Blooming cheek as he was a year ahead of me at school and I was our oldest player!'

But the top referee chose our captain, Joe, as the Man of the Match. The 131 team received small plaques after the game. These were presented by the renowned referee but the photo, which appeared in the *Govan Press*, has long since vanished. Noel Carson made these plaques at his work and painted them with varnish a few hours before the game. Unfortunately the varnish had not dried by the end of the game and everybody had sticky hands afterwards – including the international referee!

It was a great memory for Alan McCombes, 'That football game is still in my memory, fifty odd years later. We could not get a hold of the big guy from the other team but I always recall the famous referee. Imagine that – a gang of boys from the scheme and we had a World Cup referee!'

The following season, most of the boys had improved so much that they were picked for the school team. As a result, our 131 team bit the dust, but it had been an exciting journey.

Rugby, on the other hand, was unknown to the 131. There was only football for the working class schools and their youngsters but once introduced to the oval ball game, our lads shone at it. Two of them, Bill and Pete, played rugby at Jordanhill College and were members of Scotland's champion club team.

Hell's Glen in Winter

Lochgoilhead is a wee hamlet a few miles past Arrochar. Nowadays it has timeshare cabins and a spa. In the late 1960s, it was the source of great attraction for the 131 Leaders. Most Friday evenings during winter, a couple of us would meet at the 30th Glasgow Hall in Cardonald and climb aboard an old ambulance driven by another Scout Leader, John Flockhart (Reverend).

The ambulance would head west along Great Western Road and get to the chippy in Dumbarton. Haggis suppers and fish suppers would be taken on board and eaten as the vehicle swung along the old Loch Lomond road. It would then stagger up over the Rest and Be Thankful on the old military road, before heading down Hell's Glen towards our destination. In the dark. In the snow. Singing Scout songs, as well as the hymns bashed out by the Rev Flockhart.

We were helping to build a new Scout Camp at Lochgoilhead. The Scout Association had set up a water activities centre there, the very first in the UK, but it could only be used during summer. It was on the site of a former wartime Army camp and some old wooden buildings were still in place.

The 131 and their pals were refurbishing them. Pete McGuire was one of this regular gang, 'I can remember dragging big bits of wood everywhere and sometimes digging ditches. But we would also get to climb one of the local hills. All in the winter. Great fun.' Lochgoilhead is now one of the top centres of Scottish Scouting – and has been totally rebuilt since our time, thank goodness!

These weekends were always good fun, despite the cold weather, and we knew we were helping to improve one of Scottish Scouting's camp sites.

Eventually, in May 1970, the 131 were able to use the facilities. Until then the cost for the water activities weekend was too much for Pollok purses but common sense took over and cheaper courses were organised. Some wheeling and dealing was done and Pete McGuire and I, plus six boys set off to attend a canoeing and sailing weekend at an affordable price. Bobby Moore, Tony McGuire, Alec Johnstone, Neil Gray, David Roselli and Jim McGrotty were the lucky lads. There was a full weekend of canoeing and sailing as noted in the Troop Log Book:

The weather was fine and there was a lot of activity. Sailing was brisk. The boys all enjoyed this thoroughly and it was a worthwhile venture.

The most dramatic episode was when each of the 131 gang, including the two Leaders, completed their canoeing Eskimo Roll qualification and were duly awarded their One Degree Under certificates. We had to roll over in the canoe and then get upright. It was absolutely freezing in the loch. And a lot of wet clothing was brought home afterwards.

One Degree Under Club

SPREADING OUR WINGS

Our Local Hero

Priesthill had been the site of a terrible mining disaster in the nineteenth century. A memorial had been erected at Nitshill station, but this was constantly defaced. The same fate also befell the sandstone memorial to the station clerk who had won the VC in the First World War.

Public service was a constant theme in Scouting and the 131 wanted to do a good deed in their locality. In 1968, a group of the lads went up to the station one Sunday morning and cleaned up both memorials. At first people thought that they were vandals and they had to keep explaining what they were doing. The lads were amazed that this hero had only been a few years older than them. He was aged nineteen all those long years ago. This ritual was regularly observed by the 131 – a task for the duty Patrol for their public service.

Eventually, the hero's old regiment removed the memorial and reinstalled it in a clean, healthy little town in the Highlands.

The memorial to John Meikle VC in Dingwall (Photo – D Mackay)

Mastering Mechanics

Several of the Leaders had motor scooters. Indeed Pete McGuire had already been fined for not wearing a crash helmet after driving back from the Hall one evening with another Leader as his passenger. The cops spotted them. 'I was summoned to court and turned up wearing my suit and tie. A waste of time. I was fined and three points on my licence.'

Nevertheless, scooter maintenance became an unplanned part of the programme for the older Scouts one evening when an old Vespa scooter found its way into the Hall. This machine had lived under a tarpaulin in the McGuire family's back garden for a few years. It was spotted by Joe McEwan and Tony McGuire. 'We thought this looked quite cool, so we decided to take it down to the Hall and try to get it started,' said Tony.

In those days, Peat Road was regularly patrolled by PC Shepherd who kept on top of any local nonsense. 'We pushed the scooter down a side street to avoid Old Shepherd. He would have moaned at us and he would have thought it was suspicious to have had a scooter at our age – thirteen.' The sneaky route took much longer but they reached the Hall safely. Then the fun began.

'We parked it inside the Hall and started to clean it,' said Tony. 'We knew nothing about scooters or engines, so this seemed to be a sensible thing to do. We used soapy water on the outside of the scooter and cloths on the various bits and pieces of the engine. We were soon down to the carburettor. I knew about this because my brother was always fiddling with it on his scooter. That was the limit of our technical knowledge.'

But this innocent tinkering with the engine soon took a wild turn, 'We didn't know what fuel a scooter used. We were completely clueless but we were keen to find out. So, Joe suggested that as we had some meths for using with our paraffin stoves, we could see what happened if we poured meths over the carburettor. A huge ball of blue flames no less, with wee droplets everywhere. We were not burned, but it made a mess of the wooden floor in the Hall. After stamping on the burning wood we managed to put the fire out.'

Fortunately the wooden floor of the Hall was sturdy and the effects of the scooter flash fire were only surface deep. No permanent damage was done.

The next stage for the intrepid duo was to try and start the engine, 'I had seen my brother start his scooter most days with a push start, so we decided to do this in the Hall,' recalled Tony. 'We wedged open the corridor doors and Joe got aboard with me pushing. I started running down the corridor, past the Leaders room and the kitchen and across the main Hall.' Joe took up the narrative at this point, 'I then let the clutch out and the engine fired into action. We had succeeded!'

But there was no triumphant drive on to the main road. 'The engine spluttered away for a few minutes and then died out, never to restart again. But it had been great fun. I've never forgotten about our efforts to get an old scooter working in the Hall. We were trying to get our Mechanic Badge – and we did.'

Passing the Mechanic Badge

Fun and Games at the Edinburgh Tattoo

The Parents Committee decided to organise a bus to the Edinburgh Tattoo in 1968. Hardly anybody in our part of Glasgow had ever been to Edinburgh in those days – never mind to the Tattoo. Pete McGuire and I had felt like we were explorers when we went through to Murrayfield to see Scotland play the All Blacks the previous year.

The Tattoo trip was a sell-out and there was no room left for any Leaders on the coach when it set off for the Capital of Scotland. Len McKinnon's old van came to the rescue for the Leaders who piled into this and set off following the bus. There was no motorway at the time and the land which lay beyond the Glasgow Cross was unknown to most of the 131.

One of the most thrilling performances of the evening was by the French Moroccan cavalry. We were sitting at the very front of the stands in the cheap seats and the cavalry came charging towards us, waving their huge, big swords. It looked as if they would crash straight into us but they pulled back about two yards from us and trotted away. There were loads of cheers and a few sweary words from our crowd.

Everyone was happy as we left the grandstand to head back to Pollok. The fog came down and there were constant roadworks. Although the coach driver knew how to get back, the Leaders did not. It was horrendous. Five of us were squashed into Len's van as we crawled along behind the coach.

Len was driving and I was beside him with my head stuck out of the window trying to see through the fog. The others were sleeping in the back. Suddenly we hit a really big bump in the road. There was a shout and the rear door swung open, then it shut. We sneaked along the road for about ten minutes until there was a yell from the back seat. Noel had disappeared!

The sleeping Mr Carson had fallen out of the car when the door had swung open. When he opened his eyes, he was lying in the road in the fog. He couldn't see anything and didn't have a clue where he was or how to get home. He tottered down the road for some time but in the cold and spooky atmosphere of the fog he could hear nothing – and nobody else could hear him either.

The backseat gang were startled by his disappearance as they had been sleeping away when we hit the bump. Eddie Mallan had just rolled over and tried to get back to sleep before he realised that Noel wasn't there so he grabbed Len and raised the alarm.

By this time Noel, stranded in the middle of the road, heard a lot of shouting. It was the other Leaders looking for him. Reunited with his transport, he climbed back into the wee van and off we rolled off towards the Scout Hall. The coach with the parents had long ago disappeared in the direction of Glasgow. When our van finally reached Pollok, everybody else had gone home. So, we slept in the Leaders' Room that night and dreamed about Moroccan cavalrymen in the fog.

Years later, in 1981, I was the Army officer in charge of the Tattoo. It was a long six week project but I kept thinking about my first trip to the Tattoo in my 131 days and often regaled my soldiers with the tale but they thought I had made it up.

Fight Night With A Difference

One of the most sensational nights in Scottish boxing history was witnessed by the 131 at Govan Town Hall on Thursday 6th March 1969. An amateur international match between Scotland and Morocco was taking place and was televised UK-wide by the BBC with commentator David Vine at the microphone.

The 131 had some good contacts in the boxing world. One of the local Scout Leaders, Stevie White, was a member of the Scotland team and the boys knew him from several camp weekends. Also, one of our Leaders lived next door to the chairman of the Scottish Amateur Boxing Association. Favours were granted and excitement was high as the 131 lads entered the arena.

Then we had our first treat. Free programmes for the event! This was fantastic for us and they were all signed by members of the Scotland team. Groups of boys were taken to the dressing rooms to see the boxers getting ready. The excitement was at fever pitch, despite the dressing rooms only containing chairs and tables with all the boxers' clothes strewn around.

We then took up our seats at the front of the balcony. The contest got under way to cheers and wisecracks from the crowd which probably numbered about five hundred.

Of course, our biggest cheer was produced when Scout Leader Stevie appeared for his fight. *Come oan Stevie,* was yelled nonstop by the 131 gang. All to no avail, though, as Stevie was well beaten. This decision was greeted by boos and catcalls, many coming from the maroon neckie fans, *Robbery! Wee Stevie was the winner by a mile* was one of the milder remarks.

For each fight, the referee would alternate between both nations. The judging team was made up from one judge from each country plus the referee. At the end of each bout the judges' scores were announced and it was clear that the Moroccan referee and judge had voted for the Moroccan boxer every time. By the second-last fight of the night, the crowd were not amused by this blatant cheating.

Willie Black was the Scottish boxer. He was a big lad and seemed to be thumping his opponent quite hard. The referee, a Moroccan, kept stopping the fight and warning Willie. This drew plenty of abusive comments from the crowd – and the 131, *Hey pal, gie oor bloke a chance! It's no' the Bundy here ref, this is a fair do!*

Then it happened. The ref pulled Willie aside and pointed to each of the judges in turn. This was a formal warning and any more misbehaviour would bring disqualification. At this point, Willie brought the house down!

He thumped the ref with a huge John Wayne punch, leaving him flat on his back and rendering him unconscious. Willie then bent over him, crying as he tried to revive the comatose gentleman.

The ring was invaded and cops appeared. The crowd were on their feet cheering, cursing and yelling. The 131 were hoarse with roaring and they could not stop laughing as they made their way home. That was all they could remember about the night's happenings. Even Scout Leader Stevie had been forgotten.

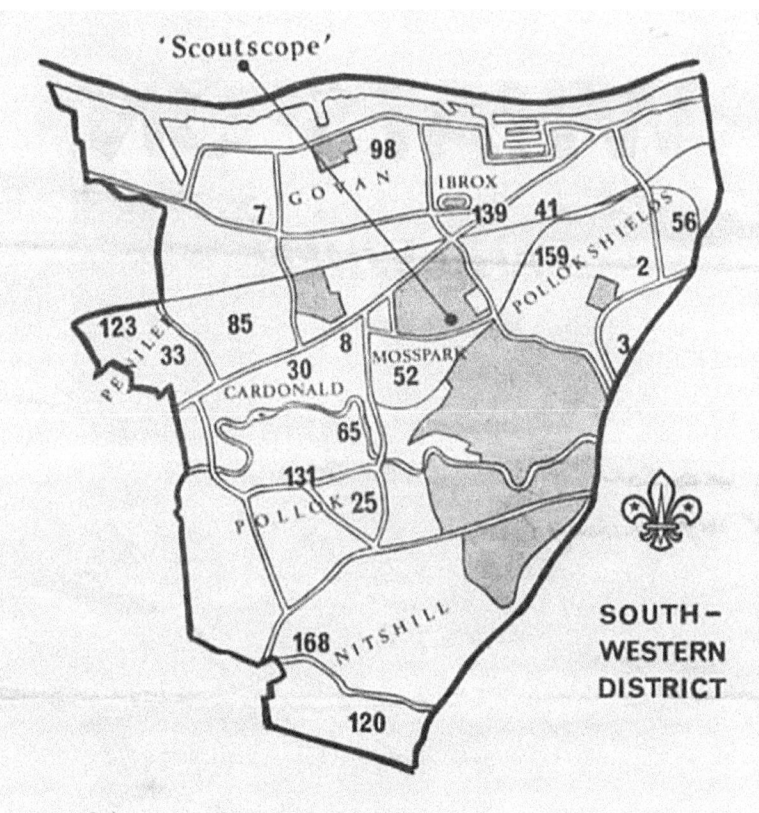

```
2nd.          73 Glencairn Drive, Glasgow S.1.
3rd.          121 Shawmoss Road, Glasgow S.1.
Govan
Scouts.       Langcroft Road, Glasgow S.W.1.
8th.          Lourdes Parish Hall, Lourdes Ave., Glasgow S.W.2.
25th.         Drumcross Road, Glasgow S.W.3.
30th.         37 Lammermoor Avenue, Glasgow S.W.2.
33rd.         St. Georges R.C. School, Hollybush Rd., Glasgow S.W.2.
41st.         5 Jane Street, Glasgow S.W.1.
52nd.         34 Mosspark Oval, Glasgow S.W.2.
56th.         175 Darnley Street, Glasgow S.1.
65th.         Scout Hall, Lochar Cresc., Glasgow S.W.3.
73rd.         (Handicapped Cub Scouts)
              Mrs. Denham, 17 Harley St., Glasgow S.W.1.
85th.         Allanton Dr., Glasgow S.W.2.
98th.         Hill Trust School, Langlands Road, Glasgow S.W.1.
120th.        South Nitshill Primary School, Willowfield Rd., Glasgow S.W.3.
123rd.        Penilee School, Penilee, Glasgow S.W.2.
131st.        Brockburn Road, Glasgow S.W.3.
139th.        Ibrox Church, Glasgow S.W.1.
159th.        240 Nithsdale Road, Glasgow S.1.
168th.        Levern School, Glasgow S.W.3.
212th.        St. Monica's R.C. School, Kempsthorn Rd., Glasgow S.W.3.
```

SCOUTING – TOMORROW'S ADVENTURES TO-DAY

Scoutscope 1969 programme

Scoutscope 69

Bellahouston Park was the venue for Scoutscope 69 and all 21 Scout Troops in the District laid on various activities for the weekend.

Each Troop chose its own demonstration activity. The 131 chose to hold a boxing tournament. Well, why not – the lads were always knocking lumps out of one another during games.

We had to get hold of a boxing ring. No Scout lash-up version would do as there would be many spectators. It had to look good, so the chairman of the Scottish Amateur Boxing Association arranged for us to collect a boxing ring from the East End of Glasgow.

There was no problem with the transport. Two fathers stepped forward. One had a small lorry and the other had a big van. Some Leaders climbed into each of these and whizzed across the city along unknown streets, before ending up at the destination. More adults were waiting there and helped to load the boxing ring onto the lorry. The other bits and pieces fitted inside the van. The collection team drove off towards Bellahouston Park in high spirits.

Halfway through the Gorbals, still five miles from Bellahouston Park, the lorry broke down. The van was way ahead, with no means of contact. The boxing ring components had to be delivered that night. Then fate intervened.

A Glasgow cop came round the corner and asked a few questions of the stranded Leaders. Within thirty minutes a small lorry from the Police Transport Division arrived. The boxing ring was lifted in and was delivered to the park about two hours later than expected. A group of Leaders and older Scouts had been waiting and they worked hard to set up the boxing ring – finishing about 3 o'clock the following morning. Some of us even slept under it that night. Everything was ready for the event.

It seemed that every Scout in the District wanted to enter the boxing tournament. Another local Scout Leader who was a GP, examined all the entrants and attended every contest. One of our team for this event was Bill Toal, 'For referees and corner men, we had some luck. Three of us were PE students at Jordanhill College, so we were ideal for these tasks.' There were probably about one hundred spectators, eating hot dogs which we had cooked. The bouts were all great fun. Some blood was spilled. A few black eyes were given out. And, amazingly, all contests ended in a draw – but this fact was not noticed by any of the boxers.

At this time, Jim Donnelly and his brothers Tom and Eugene were members of the Troop, 'One of my daftest memories is about Scoutscope at Bellahouston Park. This was a huge District camp and all the other Troops camped there for the weekend. The 131 had decided to run a boxing event and I remember training for months to compete in the boxing! Never wanted to do it! It was a comedy sketch…the other guy was a decent boxer and I wanted to get in there with heid doon 'n feet swinging.'

The 131 had its own boxing club. It never produced champions but was always attended by a dozen or more lads. The interior roof struts in the Hall were used as corner posts for the boxing class which was run by Bill and Pete. As Bill noted, 'We explained to parents that this was not to train champion boxers, but to teach their sons to stand up and fight back when thumped by some thug. A very useful ability for the local area.'

Fond memories also from Alan McCombes, 'Boxing was always a good laugh. I sort of liked doing it and got smacked a few times. But the instructors were great guys and we all got better eventually.'

His brother Ken was also in the middle of the boxing action – somewhat unwillingly, 'I really hated the boxing club but I went there as it was something our great group of guys did. The Leaders sold it to us as a way of making sure that we would not be beaten up by any neds around the scheme. In fact, I was normally given a doing by some other Scout in the boxing ring. Still, I suppose it did me some good. In any case, I managed to get my badge so it wasn't all grim.'

Out and About

Regardless of the time of year or whoever was the Leader, the 131 enjoyed regular visits to external organisations. These included a visit to the local Fire Station, as well as Darnley Fire Station to see its log book entry about Rudolf Hess, and the Daily Record offices. The purpose of these trips was to introduce the boys to different aspects of life and afterwards they were expected to describe these visits and answer questions in order to pass various badge tests.

One of these outings had been to Rangers Football Club, the great Satan of the Catholics in the city. But Skipper was a Jags fan and did not care. The visit was excellent, with plenty of cheeky comments such as – *Where's the Celtic pennant?* – and – *Youse must have stolen a' these cups.*

Transport could be a problem but it was easy to get to Ibrox Park as the Troop just had to jump aboard the Number 26 bus which passed by the stadium. For the other trips, three of the Leaders would provide their cars and these would be crammed with at least six boys in each car.

Meanwhile, the non-travelling Scouts would often be deployed on a jumble sale raid. Jumble sales were a staple element of our fundraising year. The Troop Log described this saga:

> *Evening split into 2 groups – one, under Skipper, headed for the Police Stables, and the other, with Pete, foraged and plundered for tomorrow's jumble sale.*
>
> *Despite the hazards involved none of the horse lovers managed to collect any odorous souvenirs of their visit. It was very interesting and Sgt Kirkwood provided the feat of the evening by lifting PL Ken McCombes on to the back of a horse – it now has bandy legs.*
>
> *The other party returned with all kinds of rubble and junk which was joyfully seized by members of the parents' committee.*
>
> *The late night ended with the ceremonial dishing out of Bob-a-Job cards. Let's hope we can collect more than 1969!*

The collection safari was worthwhile as recorded gleefully in the next entry of the Troop Log:

> *As usual, the 'junk' was snapped up – even 2 chairs which were on the demolition list! Despite having no teas on sale we totalled a nice profit of £45! Now for the battle with Frank Steele to spend the loot!*

A Patrol Leader Goes to Jail

Being Patrol Leaders did not mean that the lads were angels. They all loved the nonstop activity we provided but adventurous lads always crossed the line at times. It was part of the package.

Scouts can be coaxed into doing all sorts of worthwhile activities. This was frequently tested, such as on a May weekend camp at Auchengillan in 1968 when there was nonstop nonsense from some PLs.

At the end of camp, the Leaders stayed behind to sort out kit. The PLs accompanied the Scouts home on various buses. When the Leaders arrived at the Hall they were greeted with the following story.

Scout Johnstone was a real live wire. His exuberance had been too much for his 15-years old PL, who had whacked him when they got back to the Scout Hall. Wee Johnstone ran up to the police station, two hundred yards away, and reported this assault. The cops then took the PL to the cells. Normal life in Pollok.

The PL's father then turned up at the police station and began whacking his son in front of the cops. Never a dull moment. Graeme O'Neill still remembered this incident, 'There were lots of unforgettable characters in the 131 and he was one of them. Everybody seemed to be larger than life and acted accordingly. There was never any shortage of excitement or drama or mad incidents. They were a hard bunch to control as I found out later during my short spell as a Young Leader.'

Lucrative Parades

The 131 had a good relationship with the local police who were happy to help with some Scout tests, mainly because we were not the Bundy or any of the local gangs. They would also pay close attention when there was a disco or dance in the Hall.

We returned the favour in an unusual way on a regular basis. One evening, at a Rover meeting, a cop came into the Hall and asked if any of the older lads would be willing to take part in an ID parade at the police station. Jim Mackay chuckled at the next step, 'This cop mentioned that we would be paid and he was almost killed in the rush! A couple of Rovers went along and stood in a line with some other youths, including a little thug who was well known to us – he had been at our school.'

There were several tense moments as the witness came along and slowly walked past. Our lads started to worry – what if he picked out one of them? He did not and they all received payment of ten shillings, a useful sum in those days. Half of it went into the Rover Crew funds and the lads each kept the other half for risking their freedom!

Pollok Police Station

Well, as you can imagine, this became a favourite pastime for the 131. Michael O'Neill still can't believe this crazy arrangement, 'No kidding. This was Pollok and the cops would come along every six weeks or so looking for some of us older lads. There was never a shortage of volunteers. The Usual Suspects would cheerfully make their way down to the police station when required.'

Then, one day, there was a problem...

The witness for this line-up picked out one of our Rovers. A message was sent to the Hall and one of the Leaders headed off to the cop shop. Our brave lad was sitting there, perfectly relaxed, drinking tea and munching a nice chocolate biscuit. After signing a form stating that he had been on a Scout activity at the time of the incident, he was allowed to leave – with his payment. From then on, every ID parade carried a chance of false identification. This added ingredient only made it more exciting. Every time any of the Rovers left the Hall for one of these events there would be cries of – *See you in Barlinnie!*

Farewell to Rover Scouts

In 1968, the Scout Association wanted to make Scouting ready for the future. There was a significant reshuffle of the age ranges and badge syllabus – and Rover Scouts were abolished. The 131 decided to mark this change by having a special camp at Auchengillan to say cheerio to the Rover Crew.

The usual superb campsite was erected and we decided to challenge ourselves with back-to-basics camping.

Water had to be collected from the farthest water point, at the East End, about a mile away. We had to cook every meal that weekend from basic ingredients over an open fire and decided to bake bread from scratch. A large biscuit tin was set up as the oven, with the wood fire beneath it.

Making the bread was strenuous and painstaking. A couple of plastic basins were used as mixing bowls and the hard part was kneading the dough. We all had sore wrists. The bowls were laid aside in the store tent and covered with tea towels and had to be checked regularly during the night. The baking of the bread began early the next day and took forever! The biscuit tin oven couldn't get warm enough and the bread was soggy, warm and tasted grim. But we still ate it.

The only treat that spartan weekend was when Bill Toal arrived on the Saturday afternoon with cake from his sister's wedding earlier that day. The 131 gang were about to sample wedding cake for the first time. Few of the lads had been to a wedding other than a couple of Scout weddings and our involvement in these had been limited to forming a guard of honour.

One of the Cubs at Jack's wedding had been Jim Mackay, 'A gang of about ten of us went to the far side of Glasgow on two different buses on a Saturday morning in full uniform. I had to present Jack and his wife with a huge cardboard lucky horseshoe. This was already a wee bit battered from the lengthy journey. We had made it the Cubs during the week and covered it with silver paper and I took it home with me for safe keeping. It was the only wedding I had ever been to until my own.'

The Rover Farewell camp had worked well, despite the long treks for water and wood. So, we decided to liven up matters. The weekend camp staff had been a wee bit too fussy, so the Kings of Camping decided to play a trick on them. The inspection team was due to visit our site at 9 a.m. on the Sunday. The site was hidden behind a ridge and could not be seen from a distance.

An hour before they were due to arrive we removed our tent and sneaked it into the woods. But we still left the groundsheet, sleeping bags and rucksacks in position. As the camp staff came into sight one of us raced across to them – *Come quickly, our tent has been stolen!* They viewed the scene and set about searching Auchengillan for the missing tent. We let this run for a while before telling them the truth. Lots of laughter all round. A good piece of Scout nonsense.

The Rover Den became the Venture Scout Den, but the old Rovers would still turn up when available and assist. The national reorganisation of Scouting in 1968 was not to everybody's taste and certainly not for the 131. We had built up a good Rover Crew of 15 lads and they were now all too old to continue as Venture Scouts. According to the Gilwell master plan, these guys would automatically become leaders. They did not. Roberto McLellan explained the problem, 'I only wish that the bean heads at HQ had taken some time to talk to guys of our age and background. Why were we still in Scouting? Because it was good fun to hang about with a group of mates. Sure, we could assist with Scout and Cub activities, but we also had our own jobs, studies and girlfriends as well. We weren't available for a regular weekly meeting night. All our talent and knowledge was wasted by this change as only two of us became leaders.'

Flood Relief Duties

The Pollok scheme was a flood plain and this geographical reality would be shown on a regular basis during heavy rain. The Scout Hall sat at the junction of the two local rivers, the Brock Burn and the Levern Water.

When it rained heavily, these waterways would overflow and flood into the local streets. In January 1969, there was an almighty deluge. Streets and gardens were under water, which even came up around the 4-foot high brick foundations of the Scout Hall. The whole area around the Bundy was affected.

A lot of the local people who lived on ground floors were submerged to knee height. This was where the 131 sprang into action. The Fire Brigade were based about two hundred yards away and their top man came across to ask the Leaders for assistance. We agreed to set up an emergency centre.

The Hall stood well above the flood levels and had a generator which could power electrical appliances. It also had a mains gas supply, lots of space, a supply of camp beds and sleeping bags and, most importantly, a well fitted catering kitchen.

Tommy played a big part in this operation even though he had retired from the 131 the previous year. The refugees swarmed in. Scout Mums came along and helped with various tasks and the Venture Scouts patrolled the local area to check on households. Even though people had far fewer goods than nowadays, vandals could still break in and cause damage. The 131 delivered an excellent service to the community. Nowadays we would have been visited by a celebrity, but we had to make do with the local MP.

In fact, this gent was so pleased that he hired the Hall for his election headquarters the following year – and paid for it. There was also a donation from Glasgow Corporation for our flood relief work of £25 (worth more than £300 nowadays). Any income was gratefully received and wisely used.

But the locals were so impressed by our assistance during the Pollok floods that they continued to vandalise the building for the next eighteen months.

Hooked on Hiking

Regardless of weather, the full range of Scouting events rolled on unabated. Hikes were planned by the Patrols. These were serious exploits. The boys would carry supplies for a full 3-course lunch and light a fire to heat it up. George Coll described one such hike in the Curlew Patrol Log Book:

> *We travelled from the Hurlet to the Ferenese Hills – it took us about 3 hours and it was enjoyable. Our menu was – Tomato Soup, Irish Stew and hot pies, Creamed Rice and pineapples or fruit salad, then tea and biscuits.*

They were so pleased with their conquest of the Fereneze Hills that George produced his own map in the log book to show the ground covered.

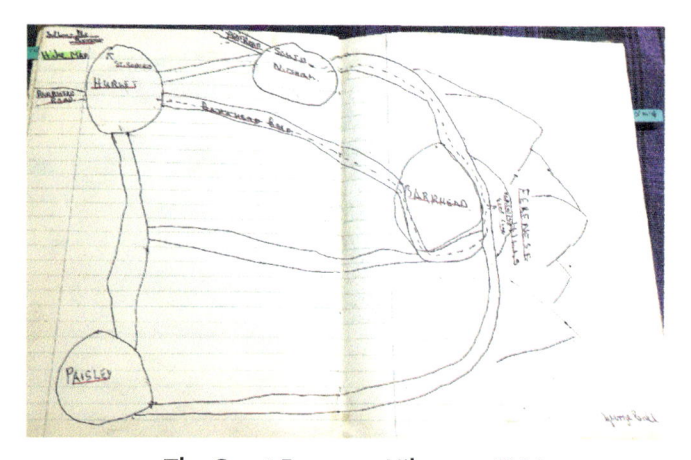

The Great Fereneze Hike map 1966

Graeme O'Neill took his Patrol on one hike, from Kirkintilloch to Auchengillan, 'I remember that Skipper and Pete were surprised at my choice. They were right as it took us most of the day to reach Kirkintilloch from Pollok. We had to catch two buses before we could even start the hike. But we all did the hike, passed some badge tests and got lots of points for our Patrol.'

Clever PLs also knew that a Patrol hike also passed as a Patrol meeting. The boys would be chattering away on their hike for at least three or four hours. So, it was a great Patrol activity. And they also managed to pass lots of Scout tests during the hike. This development was just another stage in the boys taking responsibility for themselves and organising activities. Very little planning was needed. All they needed to do was to announce that they were having a hike and tell the boys where to meet.

Of course, these were never gentle strolls in the countryside. They were full-blown exploits with various, mainly self-generated, dramas to deal with.

Patrols would head south from Pollok into the countryside and Gerard Doherty was on one of these hikes, 'One Sunday we were dropped at Moscow (Ayrshire) and had to complete a 10-miles hike to Dunlop. On arrival at the finish, we found a sweet shop and spent our pocket money there and waited to be picked up. The lift didn't arrive. A Red Bus came along and we managed to scrape together the basic fare. We sat upstairs at the back hoping the driver would forget about us and we would get into Glasgow. Eventually the driver shouted up that we had gone past our fare and we had to get off. Fortunately Jim Donnelly realised we were on Parkhouse Road, South Nitshill. We got home none the worse, apart from fatigue.'

And twenty points for the Patrol!

Turning Junk Into Cash

Once the Hall was in operation it became the site for many events. The parents' committee held jumble sales, dances and raffles to raise money, as most people's entertainment was in the local area.

Eleanor Reynolds was one of the Cub Leaders who would assist at the jumble sales, 'My Mum and I used to make some cakes for the Scout events. We had to chase away my brothers who would want to eat them before they got them down to the Hall.'

Leaflets were printed (on the Troop's old John Bull home printing set) and distributed by the Scouts. A4-size posters were also put up in suitable places and the parish allowed the Group to publicise its fundraising activities on the church notice board.

The Troop provided the collecting teams who would wander up and down the local streets looking for contributions for jumble sales. Some of the stuff we were given was ridiculous. But we would always take it as some poor soul would probably buy it. It was all cash coming in for the Group funds. We even received half a golf club. You would have needed to have been rather small to use it, but it still sold anyway.

Tony McGuire could still remember some of the details fifty years later, 'Most people had very few old items as those were the days when household items were made for life. Most of what we collected was really junk. However, there would always be plenty of stuff to sell and most of it would be bought by the customers, even broken chairs and old pots and such like. There were a few old TVs but no discarded electronic goods then.'

To publicise the jumble sales, a huge hand-painted sign was made from an old groundsheet trimmed to size. It had to fit across the outside of the hall so that it could be seen by everyone who came round the roundabout. And it had to be big – probably 30 feet long and 6 feet deep. The Rover Crew did the work and then we had to climb up ladders to fix it to the building.

Another promotional task was to decorate the outside of the Hall. This was easy, as my Dad worked at Yorkhill Docks and offered to bring some bunting which was being thrown out. It arrived inside his small car and completely filled the back of the vehicle.

To everyone's amusement it was marine bunting, the stuff which would be flown aboard a ship on special occasions. The flags were all easily the size of a door. We fell about laughing and fixed them to the outside of the Hall. You couldn't miss it now!

The jumble sales always drew a large crowd. Bargains were eagerly hunted down by no-nonsense Mums, while Dads bought tickets for the tombola stall and waited in the keen expectation that they would win the top prize – a half bottle of whisky.

The committee ran raffles, tombolas, jumble sales, bus runs and even a fashion show at one time. Good grief – a fashion show in Pollok! Scouts were banned from this event and were only allowed to serve the teas at half time.

A couple of the PLs decided to repair some broken wooden toys which had been donated for one jumble sale. They only needed painting and some minor adjustments and were bought by customers. After this, any donated broken toys would be repaired and handed in to the local primary schools for use in the nursery classes. Spontaneous good deeds by the lads. There was no input from the Leaders for these acts. They were all done by decent young guys.

Wild Times and Scout Meetings

Being a Scout was always fun. It was exciting and challenging and with the 131 it was occasionally dangerous. The housing scheme had only been built twenty years before. There were still many decent families living there, but gang warfare had taken root. The Bundy were the local gang. Most of its members were known to the 131 as they had probably been to the same school or had even been short-term members. In general, they left us and the Scout Hall alone.

Except for a couple of incidents…

The Rovers were holding a cooking evening in the Hall. A couple of the chefs had brought along ingredients and these had been carried in a large glass jar. When the evening ended the lads made their way home, some going towards Corkerhill while the remainder walked up towards Priesthill. There were probably about six of them striding along the road chatting away. Suddenly, Bill Toal and Pete McGuire spotted that they were being followed by a gang of youths. 'We knew it was the Bundy and so we all started to run. We were fast, but Henry Watts couldn't keep up,' said Pete.

The Bundy caught up with Henry, battered him in the face breaking his glasses and forced him to the ground. One of them grabbed the glass bowl he had been carrying and smashed it down on his head and started kicking him. By this time, Bill, Pete, Roberto and the others had turned round and raced back towards the scene. The Bundy scattered and ran off in every direction. The lads checked Henry and called for an ambulance which took him to hospital. He had stitches in his face, broken glasses, broken ribs and many bruises.

The following day, Pete and Bill interviewed a few locals and identified the six culprits. It had been the Young Bundy gang. Some 131 avengers paid each one of them a visit – they all went down whimpering. The point was taken and there were never any further attacks on the Scouts by the Young Bundy.

Regardless, we ended up being chased by the Big Bundy on another occasion. Once again, it was after a Rover meeting as Pete explained, 'We had stayed behind to tidy up and Bill and I were walking up Peat Road just before midnight when we heard the cry – *Come oan, let's chase them*. We looked back and saw about six Bundy clowns running towards us.'

'Although we were wearing kilts, they would never have caught us. So, we started running up the road well ahead of them and they couldn't keep up. Their numbers dropped to four, then two, then only one who was still running. At this point Bill stopped and turned round to face him as he arrived. The Bundy guy was panting and stopped in front of Bill who said to him – *Ok, pal, have you got something to say to me?* – I was completely surprised.'

While the clown thought about his answer, Bill smacked him in the face and he hit the ground. Bill grabbed him by the collar and warned him – *Any more attacks on the Scouts and you've had it.* There were no more attacks and he and his pals kept well away from us as we continued to walk home safely for many months.

Keeping an eye out for trouble was second nature for the 131. But then, it was not only the Scouts who had this problem, it was the same for all other organisations who presented a target for these hoodlums. It was a simple fact of life in Pollok.

By 1970, there was a definite sense of the Wild West in the scheme because of the vandalism, graffiti, and broken glass in the streets. Many of the street lights were without bulbs. Times had changed. It was no longer filled with people who were determined to improve their lives. Instead it was full of people who wanted to get out of the scheme and go to live in a decent area. The remainder appeared to be comfortable with their grim existence.

Show Biz

The Glasgow Gang Show dates back to 1936 and had great status. For a number of years the 131 tried very hard to break into this event. We would try out our acts in front of Jack, Tommy or Jimmy, who would normally give a thumbs-down to our efforts, including one year when a couple of us offered acrobatics.

A few of our older lads had attended the auditions but none of us was ever selected. Several of the establishment Troops would provide a dozen boys each for the Gang Show, but the 131 and Troops like us could not even get one lad into the cast.

So, in 1968 there was great glee when three of our Scouts, Brendan McLeod, Tom McWilliams and Tony McGuire were chosen. Not only that, but some rehearsals were even held in our Scout Hall. What a change. The 131 had now broken into this exclusive Scouting club.

The event was held in the King's Theatre. An evening at the theatre was a rarity, so, when the whole Troop – and the Cubs – went into town to watch the Gang Show this was a big treat. The cost of the tickets was subsidised by some cash from the Group funds.

The Leaders had to stop the Cubs from roaming all over the town, it was such an exciting event for them. The 131 gang already knew all the words of the Gang Show songs, thanks to regular campfire sessions in the Scout Hall. Joe McEwan recorded his impression in the Curlew Log on 4 April 1968:

> *We were up in the balcony which was packed with Scouts and Cubs. It was very hot and stuffy and as we were so far away from the mic we hardly heard any of the show. The part I managed to see and hear was well done.*

Pollok boys all had a bit of the Billy Connolly (another former Scout) in their behaviour. There was constant daft heckling from our row in the theatre. Nothing rude, but regular interruptions. The Leaders would try to calm them down but this had as much success as similar efforts at winter weekends.

Tony McGuire still laughs at one of the scenes in the show, 'For the finale scene, we would be dressed up in silver lame Scout uniforms. I mean, shirts, shorts and neckies all in this lurex stuff. We felt like absolute clowns! Definitely not to be worn in Pollok!'

Although the Gang Show never really figured in the 131's list of things to do, it was another target for us to aim at and we got there in the end. We just kept trying and the ones who got in were not any more talented than the guys who had failed in the past. I think we just wore down the resistance.

LEAVING THE STAGE

Securing the Hall

The Bundy was a rough area and the spread of vandalism took hold by the late-1960s. The signs of social deprivation were evident. Many families had moved out of the scheme to quieter neighbourhoods.

The 131 had occasional clashes with the local hoodlums but most of these only involved a few words. Nevertheless, we still had to secure the Hall. This work had already been started by making it burglar-proof by covering all the rear windows with marine plywood. Similar precautions were taken with all of the five sets of doors to the building. All of this had to be done before we spent any money – or time – on the inside of the building.

Despite these precautions, graffiti was regularly painted on the hidden, rear side of the building. And rubbish clearing had to be done at this area as well. This was an annoying job.

One night, there was a break-in at the Hall. This created an ominous feeling. The front door had been forced open. Some stuff was thrown about but there was no serious damage. A new door was fitted. This had two metal bars with big padlocks, as well as a metal plate. A couple of the older Scouts asked a few questions and the culprits were identified and visited. In fact, two of them joined the Scouts and stayed for a few years. There were no more break-ins.

However, we never let our guard drop and would always check the building every time one of us passed by. We certainly had to *Be Prepared* for such an incident and took all sensible precautions. There was also a routine check by the Police patrols after we had reported the break-in.

In reality, it was only a matter of time before something serious happened. Every time we locked up the premises there was an elaborate procedure to complete. But once the Hall was deserted anything could happen, regardless of any Police checks. In previous years neither the library or the old community centre had suffered damage.

The times had certainly changed in Pollok and the Scout Hall was now in the front line.

The Highwaymen

Walking home after Scout meetings had now become more dangerous. This led to one of the 131's most notorious escapades.

It was after midnight when I headed off home along a deserted main road, surrounded by playing fields and the river. I spotted two guys on the opposite pavement. One of them crossed to my side and walked towards me, as his companion kept pace on the other side – *Oh, Oh*, I thought, *this looks like a set up*. I figured that I could outrun them and pressed on. The first guy stopped a few yards in front of me. With a flourish, he pulled an axe out of his jacket.

He waved his axe at me and delivered the priceless words – *If you think this wullnae work then this will* and produced a pistol from his other pocket and pointed it at me. I had never seen a gun before and I thought it might only be a starting pistol. But it could still do me some damage, so I waited for the next instruction.

Gie us yer money pal. So, I fumbled into my pockets and handed over all my cash. The grand sum of two shillings and ninepence-halfpenny (enough to buy a pint of Guinness).

As the two robbers raced away, I spotted a taxi and flagged it down. The driver called in with the news of my drama and then took me home. The saga continued the next day when I was invited to go to Govan Police station (the real one – not the *Taggart* one) for an ID parade. A group of eight youths stood against the wall facing me as I walked along the line. I spotted Robber Number One, stopped in front of him and pointed him out. He was not a happy bunny and swore at me.

A few weeks later I was stopped by two youths as I walked away from the chip van. These guys were from the Govan Team, another set of hoodlums. They warned me not to testify against the culprit when he appeared in court.

I told them where to stick their threat and added that I had remembered their faces, so my friends (namely the other Scout Leaders) would visit them if anything happened to me. Nothing did.

I was summoned to appear as a witness at the High Court. The offence was armed robbery – the thug had also robbed another four people that night. I was shepherded into the witness room and sat beside a lady.

She told me that her son was being framed by the cops and was up for armed robbery. But she would tell the jury what a good son he really was, despite several previous convictions for similar offences (all of which were also frame ups). I changed seats rapidly.

The culprit pleaded not guilty. I was astonished. The culprit and all the witnesses had to remain in the court until the matter was settled. Eventually, after a wait of about three hours, the decision was announced. A plea bargain had been accepted and he would be going to Barlinnie for a stay of eighteen months. Relief all round, apart from his doting mother. The duty cop told me that she was just a normal mother and the court was full of them at every session.

Being in the 131 meant that we were likely to be the victims of crime, never the perpetrators. A moral victory of sorts. As Jack said on many occasions, 'I think being in the 131 had kept a lot of lads out of trouble.'

Yes it did but there were still young guys who were not members and they were still as wild as ever.

Our Big Wobble

The Year 1968 started with a bang for everybody when the Great Storm blew through the West of Scotland. Its destructive force was widespread but no damage was done to the Hall, proof that our hard work had made the building wind and water tight. The local area was not so lucky but the boys still came along to the next Troop meeting as noted in the Troop Log:

> *Miraculously the Hall has come through the Big Gale unscathed. All around the scene is one of utter and complete devastation. Many boys absent – still repairing their houses and removing debris… We ran a rather curtailed session.*

The adventures rolled along unhindered. We held indoor weekends in the Hall and the weekly programme followed a steady pattern – learning skills and fundraising.

Although there were now no older lads to maintain discipline, the PLs worked hard and organised a constant stream of hikes and camps on a weekly basis, culminating in a second place in the District Flags.

Climbing knots – Robert Brown, Eric McKelvie, Tony McGuire and Gerard Doherty being supervised by Pete McGuire

The 131 old boys kept in touch and former members of the Troop continued to visit us in the Hall – Jack Banks, no less, Tommy McGee and Brian McIntyre, both Queen's Scouts.

The Brock Burn provided the setting for outdoor pioneering projects as recorded in the Troop Log on 8th April 1968:

We built an aerial runway over the burn – not really a great success, but a chance for the PLs to tackle something hard and ambitious. Lots of laughs and a few splashes.

New ventures were introduced, such as a Troop night based on Morse code, while nature study produced lots of keen outdoor action in Househillwood Park. We also built a jetty and working crane across the pond at Maxwell Park. Then we started to get ready for Summer Camp at Beddgelert as noted in the Troop Log on 1st July 1968:

> *Start of a week's hard graft. All camping gear checked, cleaned, repaired and packed in readiness for Summer Camp.*

Following a successful two weeks in Wales at Beddgelert, we had a major change. Tommy retired after 22 years in the hot seat and Jimmy McNeillie was now the Group Scout Leader.

Although we still had a strong parents' committee, there was a severe lack of Scout Leaders. The college students could only be occasional helpers and the apprentices had to work all the hours that God sent.

Nevertheless, ten of our lads attended a District PL training weekend in Barrhead and the benefits were apparent at the next Troop meeting:

> *Active and non-stop Troop meeting. Eight projects – leaves, knots, whipping, observation, pioneering, first aid, mapping and splicing with a few games thrown in. Troop worked flat out – perhaps the PLs course has helped!*

Although this enthusiasm and good attendance continued throughout the first half of 1969, the full impact of the abolition of Rover Scouts began to be permanently felt in the second half.

Our September weekend camp at Auchengillan only attracted ten Scouts and the Troop night attendance dropped to an average of 15 Scouts by the end of October. Interest visits were still held, including a visit to the Glasgow Police Museum. Ken McCombes still remembers the lasting impression this trip made on him, 'Some of the exhibits were gruesome and quite scary. Probably a good lesson in life.'

During this period, one way to cope with the lack of Leaders was to hold joint meetings with other Troops in the District. Some of these were held with the 30th Glasgow from Cardonald, and our numbers crept up steadily.

By January 1970, our hard graft had paid off and our Troop numbers had risen to 24. Then we hit St Robert's Primary School for the very first time to tell the boys about Scouting. This worked a treat and 17 recruits turned up the following Troop night and most of them stayed. The Troop Log recorded this breakthrough evening on 6th February 1970:

> *... as a result of Skipper's mission to St Robert's during the week – 17 new boys at the ready, with another batch expected next week. The programme was rather unambitious... Main idea was to break in the rookies and let them see the Scout system at work.*

This was an important step for the Troop. It was the first time we had gone directly into a local school for recruitment. We were surprised by how helpful the Head Teacher had been. The school had the same aim as us, the development of these boys. Up till then we had operated separately. But, more importantly, it helped us to get over the big wobble and fill the Troop again. This in turn seemed to attract other Leaders on a permanent basis once more.

The numbers began to grow and by Easter 1970 we were back to a normal programme of activities. A joint camp with 33rd Troop was held at Auchengillan during Easter week, as noted enthusiastically in the Troop Log by Pete McGuire:

> *131 contingent – PL Mullaney, PL Moore, D Roselli, P Keenan, J McGrotty and N Murray.*
>
> *FRIDAY NIGHT: Scouters P McGuire and Joe Farrell got boys bedded down at about 10.30.*
>
> *SAT MORNING: After the coldest night in living memory, Scouters Farrell and McGuire arose from suspended animation. After a struggle with nature everyone breakfasted on an open fire. Inspected our Patrol at about 11 o'clock (not too good). STAs (spare time activities) took time up to lunch.*

The young boys were taken on a 6-mile hike to the Whangie and returned for tea at 7 o'clock. (131 Patrol was well organised but 33rd was a shambles.)

Campfire ended at 10 o'clock and all bedded down.

SUNDAY Another cold night. After Mass the Scouters had to make breakfast for the boys. At about 11 o'clock it started to rain. Rain lasted until about 3 o'clock when we packed up and got back to Pollok after 5 o'clock.

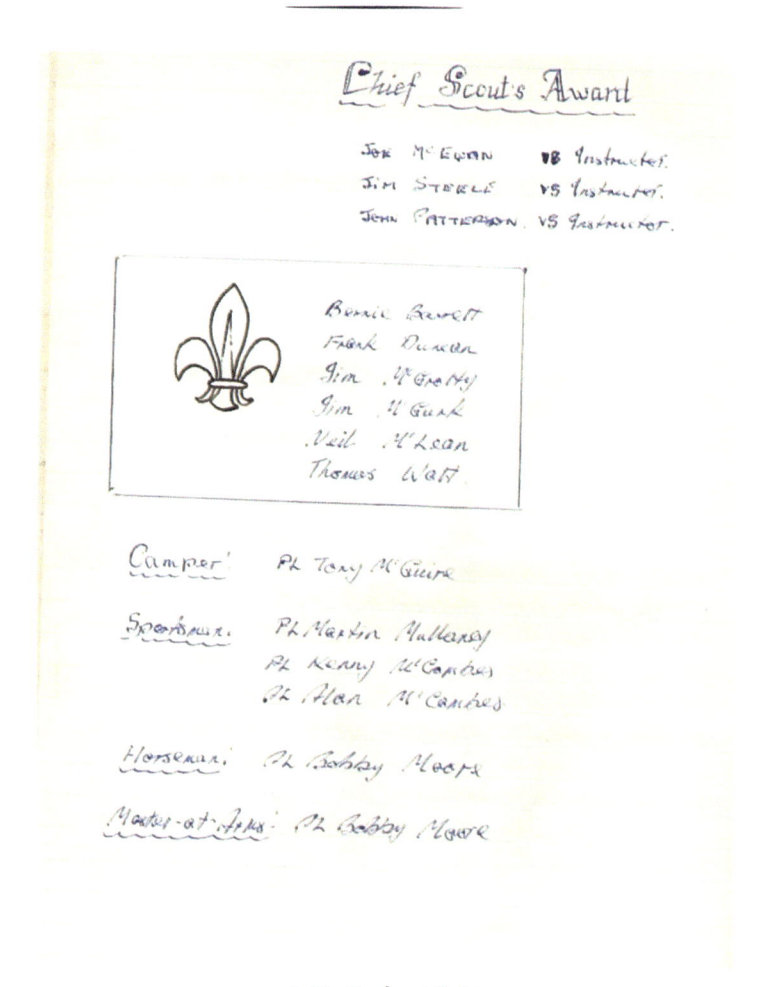

A Big Badge Night

In the 131, Scouting revolved around badges. Skills were taught and tested and badges were awarded. We believed that each one deserved its own wee place in history. Vain attempts were made to get photos of them but cameras in the 1960s, and earlier, were not readily available.

One memorable badge night was noted in the Troop Log on 20th February 1970 when our first Chief Scout Standards were awarded, as well as 12 additional badges to other boys.

Normal Service is Resumed

Joint Troop meetings continued on a monthly basis and at the start of 1970, a significant change was introduced. The 131 had always used traditional Patrol names, but being very Scottish in our outlook, the PLs Council decided that the Patrol names should be changed to show that we were Scottish Scouts. The Patrol Leaders chose the new names – Appin, Atholl, Carrick, Glengarry, Lorn and Lovat – all well-known places in Scotland. The Troop Log noted this change on 23rd January 1970:

> *New tradition of Patrol names – no more the chirping of Swift, Curlew or Eagle, instead the Caledonian cries of Appin, Lorn, Carrick etc.*

The PLs were sent to a city kiltmaker who provided suitable patches of tartan for each Patrol to wear on their Scout shirts, as well as some larger pieces to drape around their Patrol corners or even make into pennants. The Scouts then had to research their Patrol name as part of a badge. This was another bit of shop-floor education for the boys and it was quite interesting for the Leaders as well.

But we couldn't match the Patrol names with boys who were real clan members. That was just a wee bit too much for us as the majority of the boys came from Irish backgrounds. Although to be fair, a lot of them also came from Scottish families, and some of them had Gaelic-speaking parents from Lewis, Uist, Barra and Islay.

Each Patrol then had to visit its own named area. Carrick was easy as it was in Ayrshire and quite near to us. Whether the other Patrols managed to make their trips to far away parts of Scotland is unknown and remain shrouded in the mists of time.

Paul Celino is invested – also in picture Joe McEwan, Skipper, Graeme O'Neill, Jim Burton, Tony McGuire and others

On The Road

Pete had managed to save up his money from navvying during the college holidays and bought a wee Mini. None of us really knew anything about car engines but we would all try to assist with the vehicle. It could fit four Leaders and all their kit into it but it was really tight. Also it could hardly get above thirty miles an hour and that was only downhill.

Every time we got to the first hill outside Milngavie on our way to Auchengillan, the passengers would have to get out and walk behind as it struggled to get up the hill. There were lots of occasions when we would have to push it to the top. But it was a car and Pete was the only guy we knew who had one. The roof rack was crammed with our rucksacks and sometimes we had to push against the Mini to stop it from rolling backwards down the hill or we would empty the kit and carry the rucksacks ourselves up the hill.

This car story is similar to one about Len McKinnon. His uncle was a motor mechanic and he got hold of an olden days wee van for him. We all worked on it and he was able to use it when he turned seventeen and got his provisional licence. We could squeeze five or six Scouts inside and it was very handy for our trips to Auchengillan. Needless to say, though, none of us had a full driving licence and Len used to live in fear of being stopped by the cops and losing his licence.

Operation Olympus

There were only two regular Leaders by the end of 1969, Pete McGuire and me. Both Noel and Eddie had now emigrated to Canada – another two good men had escaped from the scheme. We had waved them farewell from Central Station as we sang the Troop song with them.

A positive start to 1970 was made when Operation Olympus took place in February at Auchengillan. This was a joint event involving three Troops.

We based the event on the ancient Olympics and the weekend patrols were given names of ancient Greek letters – Alfa, Epsilon, Omega, etc. It involved normal Scouting activities as well as the Olympic games such as throwing the discus (tin plate), tug-o-war and the marathon (Bulldog played on a pitch one hundred yards long).

The target for Olympus was for each boy to pass at least four tests.

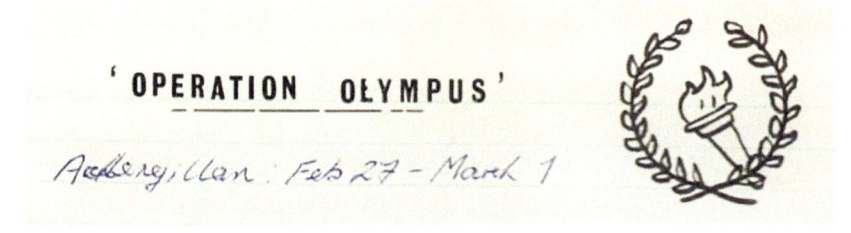

Operation Olympus

This turned out to be a massive success and it was also over-subscribed by boys – 68 to be exact! With 4 Leaders and 6 Venture Scouts the staff were worked hard all the time. Boys were evenly divided from 25th, 33rd and 131 into ten Patrols.

The usual rioting occurred on Friday night and resulted in a number of villains spending time outside the Providore. With the Warden, David Warren, on leave for his wedding, we had the run of the camp and used it to the full. Without a doubt the highlight of Saturday's campfire was the appearance of famous recording artists of the time (Leaders in disguise). Sleep was easier and even on Sunday morning at 8 a.m. no-one stirred – bliss.

The operation rushed to a close and our new DC (Mr Neil McEachran) closed up by presenting Scout Standard badges – Mark Brady receiving his – and badges to the Alpha (winning) Patrol of PL Mullaney.

At last the shattered Leaders were able to get home to a well-deserved rest!

Nothing But A Heartbreak

An upgrade to the Hall was earmarked for 1971 when a former Leader arranged for Army engineers to do work on the premises. However, on 3 August that year, the grateful locals burned it to the ground. After five years of hard slog we were left with a burnt-out shell.

There was no particular reason. That's just what stupid people do. Most of our equipment, including tents, photos and records went up in smoke.

Another casualty of the fire was our epic weapons surrender film. It had been shown regularly at the Hall, all seven minutes of its grainy colour. Nowadays it would have won a BAFTA. Alas, it perished along with the Hall. The yobs had struck back.

When the Hall was burned down, most of the Leaders were away on their summer holidays. It was only by chance that one of the parents passed it on the bus and jumped off to view the sad sight. Pete McGuire was the Scout Leader by then and noted, 'I was away in Italy and did not know until I got back in mid-August. A bit of a kick in the teeth and it really finished us off.'

At the Dean of Guild Court on 15 October 1971, approval was granted to Glasgow Corporation for the demolition of the Scout Hall. The dream was coming to an end.

The 131 Fades Away

But the 131 did not roll over and die. At least not without a fight from Pete McGuire and Jimmy McNeillie, who was now the

GSL. Within a few weeks of the fire they had managed to get access to a local school. This was a case of back to the future for the 131. 'We didn't really have much kit,' said Pete. 'But the jannie was helpful to us and found a basement store where we could keep it. In fact, it was inside the boiler room but at least it was some help.'

The 131 now struggled, as their old gang of Queen's Scouts had all moved elsewhere. They had outgrown the scheme. Fresh Leaders were needed and none were available. Then Jimmy McNeillie moved away to Wales.

Regardless of these changes, the Scouts kept turning up each week and going off to Auchengillan on a regular basis. 'There were no cars in the Troop apart from my wee Mini,' said Pete. 'I was now unable to get out at weekends as well as I ran school football on the Saturday mornings and played rugby in the afternoon.'

But the lads never wavered and many badges were gained, hikes were done and weekend camps were held.

The final Summer Camp for the 131 was held in Jersey in 1972. By this time, Frank Roselli was a veteran, 'Now the trip to Jersey was quite an adventure. A few seasick scouts on the crossing. I don't have that problem. The campground was pretty flat and unspectacular, but it was by the beach which was superb. My most vivid memory is the visit to the German underground hospital. Built by slave labour under the Nazis, it was amazing but sad to see. I was really interested that the concrete gun emplacements were still intact along the beaches.'

Tony McGuire was back for his sixth Summer Camp, 'Jersey was exciting, I do recall a couple of stories, both about our social activities! One of these is about me coming home at three o'clock in the morning from a disco in St Helier when I was less than 15 years old. The other one was about an incident in a pub next to the campsite. We were walking past one evening when group of Scousers got a bit rowdy and one of them started to hit his girlfriend. In typical 'boys from Pollok' style we warned him if he laid a finger on her he would get some Glasgow justice. As far as I can recall there was no more nonsense from him.'

Within a few weeks they were back to Auchengillan for the last camp of the season.

Ten Scouts attended, Mark Brady, Mark Campion, David Roselli, Frank Roselli, Andy Daley, Stephen Miller, Richard Lilley, Frank Duncan, Anthony Roselli and Gerry Carter.

A photograph was taken by Frank Roselli. It shows a group of confident, scruffy lads, carrying various sorts of bags and rucksacks, and wearing a wide variety of clothing. No conformity, a group of relaxed, friendly youngsters, pleased with their weekend's camp. Typical 131. No airs and graces, no fancy kit, but confident about their own worth.

It was the last camp of the 131.

The long march started by Tommy McWilliams in 1946 had ended. The 131 had lasted for 27 years. Those lads fortunate enough to have shared some of the journey were left with great memories. But more importantly, they knew that they could take on the world armed with the confidence they had gained as Boy Scouts of the 131 of the City of Glasgow.

The Last Camp (Photo – F Roselli)

The End of The Road

By 1973 Scouting was being priced out for Troops in areas like Pollok. Camping had taken a back seat in favour of sailing, archery, canoeing and ski-ing. Large joint camps were held in other parts of Scotland and the UK. All out of reach for the boys from Pollok.

'We had a few quid in the bank, probably enough to buy a ground sheet and a stove,' remembered Pete McGuire. 'But definitely not near enough to pay for these fancy programme activities. We were stuffed.'

'The camping gear we had was now old and in need of replacement and no young Leaders were coming through – thanks to the splendid decision of the Scout Association to disband the Rover Scouts section which had provided plenty of young guys of the right age. The young lads leaving the Troop were only fifteen-years old and were unable to take on serious leadership roles. The Scout Association had made a right mess for us to sort out.' Of course the 131 could not handle these pressures.

'Maybe we were victims of our own success,' said Pete. 'Most youngsters were getting out of the area to go to university or college, to better housing, etc. Really, eventually it was just me and a small number of boys (the same lads I was teaching in school). My memory is that I contacted the District and explained the situation and that new Leaders were needed. None were forthcoming so I carried on for a while.'

The parents committee had disbanded as all their sons had now left the Troop and none of the current parents came forward.

With great regret, Pete pulled the plug at the start of 1973, 'I think the Cubs carried on for a while but I'm not sure. Len McKinnon, the Cub Leader, had married and gone to the USA and Graeme O'Neill was still at school. The other Cub Leader had chucked it and that Pack closed and Mrs McLeod was too old to continue with her Pack in South Nitshill so it folded as well. Our entire support structure had evaporated and could not be replaced. This all sounds like making excuses but I had had it by this time. I had spent fifteen years with the 131 and had nothing left to give. Plus I was a young married guy trying to pay the mortgage and having to work late a couple of nights every week.'

Even Tommy could not assist as he was fully involved in a similar situation in Govan with a Scout Group which faced all the same problems as the 131. The reality of working-class Scout Groups was now becoming evident. Good intentions need physical support – adults, funds, premises. Without these the enterprise could not continue, regardless of its obvious benefits to the local community.

'I'm afraid that I have always had a slight twinge of guilt about it,' said Pete. 'But really, the 131, for which I had great affection, just died from lack of interest from all concerned – including the powers that be in the District at that time.'

The 131 was now back to where it had started out in 1946. It had no headquarters, no equipment, no funds and no Leaders. But this time there was no way back.

Jack shook his head slowly when he spoke about the 131's downfall, 'It was a great pity as we had done so much good for all of these boys and given them adventures and confidence. But you can't run a Scout Group without parental support, Leaders and money. Fine words don't cut it. And the new-fangles expensive activities added to the problem. The cost to attend one of these was far more than the cost for a weekend camp at Auchengillan.'

Vandals were taking over the scheme and many streets were dismal areas. The 131 had worked well and most of its old boys had moved on.

The great adventure was over. The boys from the scheme had reached the end of this exciting journey. But what a marvellous adventure it had been!

Our Final Flourish

The 131 Cub Pack continued fitfully for the next ten years. As there was no Scout Troop, boys would leave the Cubs and some of them would go down to the Govan Scouts (98th) as Tommy was now running this Group.

Attempts were made in 1981 to try to re-establish the 131 Troop again with the help of some of the 98th Leaders, Tommy Maguire, one of the 131's Queen's Scouts, was now Scout Leader of this Group.

John McCusker was one of this team who made the journey to Pollok, 'Our involvement was quite short-term and although hard work at the time, was all to restore local Scouting with local leadership.'

Alas, even with such superb assistance, the 131 was not feasible and soon reverted to a Cub Pack and then closed a few years later.

Fifty Plus Years Later

Some former 131 Scouts were tracked down and asked to give an assessment of the benefits of their Scouting years. Their replies are heartwarming.

Michael O'Neill – Director of Education…

'My Scouting skills and attitudes were in use in later life in many unusual circumstances. I have very fond memories of the 131 people and the skills and attitudes they gave me. I don't think Jim Mackay and I would have had the courage to do our three-week tour to the south of France in 1969 were it not for our Scout experiences. I remember that we only had our two-man tent, some cooking equipment and a few pounds to make it happen. We even agreed to meet David on the beach in Barcelona when he had finished off the Troop's Summer Camp in Cornwall and hitched his way across. None of us had been to Spain before but we met up on the beach!'

'I did organise a barge trip when I was a teacher, for a group of third year boys, split into two patrols, each on a barge with two teachers per barge. We sailed (if that's the right word) along the Avon Canal doing our own cooking on board and mooring each night at a quaint little village. The boys operated the lock gates and did various other onboard tasks. It was a great trip, and in true 131 fashion, the punishment for misbehaviour was emptying the chemical toilet!'

'When I was a Head Teacher, I fully supported all the outdoor activities that were available for my pupils and this continued when I was Director of Education; I secured funding to put 1,000 youngsters through every year. All because of the great times I had experienced as a 131 Scout. And the kids in my school were from the tough end of society, just like the 131 boys, and could not have afforded the fees.'

'Many years later when I was a board member of the Outward Bound Trust, I would visit Buckingham Palace for board meetings with Prince Philip. I often wondered if he knew anything about my background. I always knew that I had one over him as I had been a Boy Scout of the 131. Perhaps I should have told him.'

Ken McCombes – Social Worker...

'We had an amazing group of lads and we all went on to achieve great things. There was so much talent in the boys, including Gerard Doherty's great musical ability. My experience as a Scout helped me to take on the big bad world and feel confident. In my later career as a social worker I was able to relate to my similar experiences as a Scout in Pollok.'

'We would have a go at anything and not worry about being unable to do it properly first time round. Second time round we would really do it well. The Scout lifestyle gave us a feeling of adventure and we applied this to everything.

Henry Watts – Marine Engineer...

'I visited Japan, New York, Montreal, Boston and South Africa on my travels. My old Scouting background helped me to settle in to uncomfortable living quarters aboard ship. Eventually, when I came ashore I re-joined Scouting, becoming the DC for East Kilbride.'

Alan McCombes – Conservation Manager/Journalist...

'For us it was brilliant to be going off to the Highlands to camp. Nobody in the scheme did that. We were all in the dark streets of Priesthill but the 131 took us away from there. We got out of Glasgow and started to see the rest of Scotland. We saw real mountains and Loch Lomond – great excitement, great drama! It planted a seed and I carried this love of camping for the rest of my life and still go camping a couple of times each year with my daughters.'

Joe McEwan – Aero Engine Technician...

'I was in the 131 and it was a great time of my young life. I have said to my wife on many occasions, that I should write a book. But not specifics, just about my growing up in Priesthill, with 9 siblings and all the stuff kids get up to. The 131st St. Robert's Scout Troop holds many great memories for me. It had been my safe place when I was younger and I loved being in the Hall sorting out Scout kit. As I have said before, it was one of the best periods of my life, and those experiences and skills set me up for life.'

Frank Roselli – Police Chief…

'My brother David and I were in the 131, around 1967 till 1973. We went to lots of camps and other exciting places. It was great going up to the Hall for the fun and games. The Leaders were great guys and we all enjoyed the journey. In the last year or so my kid brother Anthony was also a member. My scouting in Scotland only lasted till 1973 when the family emigrated to Canada, but I enjoyed every minute of it. I'm certain it helped build character too, it kept my brothers and I out if trouble, and I went on to be Deputy Chief of the third largest municipal police service in Canada.'

'When I came back to Glasgow recently, I met up with my old Scout pals. The bond we formed in the 131 has lasted throughout all of these years. We all looked back and had a good laugh at our mad escapades in those bygone times.'

Graeme O'Neill – Area Sales Manager…

'Our Scout games of the time were robust and hopefully educational. Some forced the lads to think and pay attention while other games were active and physical. One great game was loved Port and Starboard. You had to listen to the call and get there as fast as possible. Half the Troop could be out on one call as they all ran in the wrong direction. But I loved all the games we played. They were different and where else could we play such great games? My time in the 131 was excellent for me as I learned how to take on the world with confidence in my own ability.'

Tony McGuire – Optometrist…

'I was ill for about two years and was in hospital a lot but the 131 would visit me and Skipper even gave me his mandolin. He was useless at playing it anyway but I taught myself to play it. It was a great day when I was fit enough to come back to the Troop and get on with all the crazy times we had. Even though I had to be careful what I did, I was back in the 131, amongst my pals. We all had such a positive approach to life as a result of this great spell in our young days.'

David Mackay – Army Officer/University Tutor…

'Army service proved to be no problem for old 131 lads as I personally discovered. After 15 years in the 131, my military career seemed to be just an extension of those Scouting days. First of all, I attended the officer entrance board. This was straightforward as it was just a series of test incidents which we would do as Scouts and I also had great confidence in standing in front of others and saying my piece after years of practice with the 131. Then I was sent to officer training school. I did not have a clue about the Army, unlike all of the other cadets, but I found it simple because of its outdoor component. So much so that I was the top cadet at the end of six months training.'

The 131 was just a bunch of lads who could have become tearaways but ended up as excellent young citizens. We were brash and confident and tackled every challenge wholeheartedly. Even our encounters with the local gang were positive. They would be a menacing presence for most others who walked the local streets, but we did not fear them. And most of us had been on the wrong end of a punch in the face without any adverse consequences. We were lads of our time and place who brought pride to our local community.

A Long Look Back Along The Camping Trail

In 2019, many years after our Scouting years had ended, I organised a wee reunion for those old 131 guys I had been able to unearth. At that time, I could only find Jim, Bill, Pete and Jack. Not many, but more than enough to recall our madcap exploits of sixty years past. It was a bright day; everyone had a great time and we all told tales from yesteryear. Plenty of laughter and a few moments of sadness as we recalled friends who had passed away.

The Mackays, Jack, Bill and Pete in 2019 (Photo – D Mackay)

Although we were all fiercely proud of being *Boy Scouts of the 131 of the City of Glasgow* as our Troop song stated, we had lost contact in later years. So, this was a memorable day. The ladies smiled as the old guys relived their youth. And we sang the Troop song as well as our classic campfire ending song –

*These are the times we will dream about
and we'll call them the good old days.*

But the most poignant moment had already occurred at Helensburgh Railway Station. Pete was waiting there to collect Jack. They had not seen one another for more than fifty years. Pete watched as the passengers came off the train. Which one was Jack? Now, remember, Jack was six feet two the last time Pete had seen him.

He could not see anybody who fitted that description. So, when an elderly gent stopped in front of him, he took a chance and asked if he was Jack. The old guy looked up at him and then said, 'You're a McGuire!' A perfect reunion. Scouting memories last a long time. From a bygone age in fact.

FINAL THOUGHTS

Being a PL in the 131

Without doubt, the best job in Scouting is being a Patrol Leader. Jack would always have a PL training camp at least once a year and the lads loved these. These were backed up by training nights in the school.

These sessions were very enjoyable and they were also essential. The 131 came from the scheme and being given any responsibility was unusual. Jack commented, 'We came from the working-class and in those times, all decisions were made by our betters.'

Michael O'Neill added his own observation, 'Thankfully, Scouting in Pollok was in the vanguard of demolishing these archaic practices. There was no focus on young people's needs in those days and there were few courses to introduce them to such matters as leadership and planning.'

Glasgow Scouting, though, was aware of this requirement and regularly held PL training courses and as a result was leading the city in youth work. But the 131 courses were much more fun. Jack would pick a Sunday for this training and we would hike up to Neilston or somewhere else and have lots of projects to do. These all involved some planning and we all had a chance to be in charge and learn something as a result.

Jack was blunt, 'Being a PL wasn't easy. It needed to be done properly and if the PL was not up to the job after training he would sometimes be removed. But this was always the last resort. We worked with the lads to help them to improve but some of the boys were very hard work. I would never really sack the PL for being hopeless. No, I would make sure that one of the ASMs paid close attention to him and kept him on the right track.'

If a PL had been removed, there was the problem of what to do with him. This would be solved by making him an Instructor, although one or two of them sorted themselves out and gave good service and got back to being PL of another Patrol.

This process was the 131's in-house HR method and it paid off as Roberto McLellan recalled, 'Often these sacked PLs would come back to the Troop a few weeks later, so we had actually resolved a problem without throwing a lad out of the Troop. But in any case, we seldom had to sack a PL as they were all dead keen in my time.'

The simple truth was that we wanted every older Scout to be a PL and learn from it. Some were excellent, some were competent and some were calamitous. But we would always help them to carry out their responsibility.

There were always some Scouts who would be missing at the start of the Troop meeting which meant fewer points for the Patrol. So, the PLs were sent to look for them. Often this search was a waste of time, but on some occasions the culprit would be rounded up to enjoy the remainder of the meeting.

Fifty years later, Joe McEwan still recalled this daunting task, 'Sometimes we would have PLs attending absentees at their homes and dragging them up to the Scout Hall. It was tough love in those days. It was nae fun for any of us – the PL or the absentee, but we did it. I think that's why we were such a tough bunch. If he said that he was not coming back we would try to get him to donate his Scout shirt and neckie as these were in short supply. Most of the Troop wore second-hand kit and I was one of them.'

Like Joe, I dreaded having to go round chasing up absent Scouts. Sometimes I just went up the road and wasted time before coming back and telling Jack that the missing boy was not at home. I suspect this also happened when I was the Scout Leader.

Jack talked about his days as a PL in early post-war Glasgow, 'It was no fun. I had to go up closes in the Gorbals when it was at its wildest. But it was part of growing up and having to do jobs which were not pleasant, just like real life.'

The 131 Leaders would visit parents at home to introduce themselves and give a report on their son's progress. Jack started this policy, 'Before I arrived, everybody knew Tommy and he would bump into parents most days and chat about their son's progress in the Scouts. I didn't live locally and none of the parents knew me so it was important that I got to know them. Tommy and I would visit a couple of parents on a Sunday afternoon and let them know what their son was up to in the 131. The parents were delighted and we often got offers of assistance from them. We were a sort of travelling sales team.'

Some of the PLs still have their old Scout shirts. Joe McEwan is one of them.

Joe McEwan shows his 131 shirt in 2023

'It was great being a PL. We were a tight knit team and looked after each other all the time and even at school. If one of the Patrol was being bullied I would step in and sort it out. We were all members of a very special gang.'

FINAL THOUGHTS

Scouting Comes First!

Being in the 131 was often an alternative classroom for the lads. School education was formal and strict. It was 'sit down, be quiet and learn these facts.' With the added ingredient of the belt being applied liberally.

But Scouting managed to produce some great learning sessions which are still remembered after a gap of more than fifty years. Roberto McLellan was still excited when he recounted his tale, 'We had gone to Auchengillan, me, Len McKinnon, Eddie Mallan and Len Ashforth. We only had a rather small tent, probably a two-man version, and I rolled out of it during the night.'

The cold air woke Roberto and he stared around, 'The sky was sensational. It was a Milky Way sky. I had never seen one so clear and I woke up the other guys to look at it. We were almost hypnotised by the clarity. This was because we were well out of the city and away from the street lights. It is something I always remember when I see a clear night sky.'

On Jim Mackay's first camp, Auchengillan was once again a classroom. 'We had wandered all the way around Auchengillan and were down at the East End. The camp seemed to be miles long to me, but many years later, when I went to a Cub and Parent camp with my son, I realised it was much smaller! Anyway, I was peering into the distance to see the city of Glasgow. After all, it was big enough, there were about a million people in it in those days and we were high enough up on this hillside to be able to see it.'

Patrol Leader Brian McGuire was pointing out various points of interest, including Glasgow. This puzzled Jim who said, 'Well, where is it? I can't see it.' The answer was short and educational, 'See that gap between those two hills there? Well, you can see a big yellow cloud there. That sits above Glasgow.' That was in the days before smokeless coal came to the city. The 131 were in the vanguard of observing climate change activity.

Some Scout badges involved skills which were not taught in school but were useful in later life as Jim Donnelly pointed out, 'My brother and I did the Astronomer Badge in 1969. The course was held in the Cardonald Scout Hall and we went there for 8 weeks. I remember it was very interesting and I still use the skills as a landscape photographer when doing night photography.'

Any time there was a clash between school matters and Scouting, 131 lads chose the Scouting option. Even when exams came round, any clashes with Scout activities were easily resolved in favour of Scouts.

Pete McGuire remembered a bit of nonsense from one year, 'I think I was doing my O Levels and there was a Scout camp at the weekend. My Dad said that I could only go if I studied hard during the week, so I started to do this but soon drifted along the street to speak to one of my Scout pals. We hatched a plan and I asked my Mum if he could come up and study along with me, as this would help us both to learn faster. In actual fact all we did was to plan various activities for the weekend camp and did no swotting at all. By some fluke we both managed to pass our exams. Years later as a teacher I would chuckle when it came to the exam period and I watched the keen Scouts trying to combat the call of the wild.'

Scouting fever affected everyone in the 131 and I was no different. My favourite subject at school was History and I won the prize every year for six years at secondary school. But I never once went to the prizegiving as it always clashed with Scout meetings. I never told my Mum about my academic success because she would have wanted to come along to the school to see me receiving the prize. Some years later after I had gone in to the Army to become an officer, the head teacher invited her along to the school and spoke about his memories of me, especially my absence at prizegiving days. My Mum couldn't believe it when she heard this news. The head teacher just smiled and remarked that he had also been a Scout.

In fact, some of the older Scouts would get together for joint swotting for Highers or university exams in the Scout Hall in later years. This activity would of course include a sleepover. Scouting ties were strong. Unfortunately there is no record of the success rate of these Scout swotting sessions.

Scouting definitely came first for Noel Carson and Eddie Mallan in September 1967. A Troop weekend was planned for Auchengillan but Noel and Eddie could not attend until the Saturday evening. They were working on the Queen Elizabeth 2 (QE2) which had been launched with them on board three days earlier at John Brown's shipyard in Clydebank.

Noel explained it at the time. The joiners, and other trades, needed to be on board to finish all the snagging jobs, such as fitting door handles and fitting plugs into sinks. These things were always left to the last minute on a ship build as they would have been pinched if they had been fitted before the launch. Only a couple of weeks earlier, some fly boys had nicked a huge carpet from the ship's ballroom. These guys had been dressed in overalls and everybody assumed that they were just another gang of shipyard workers.

This information was fascinating. We were amazed at this level of thieving. It was probably the first insight the college boys had ever had into the realities of the big, bad world outside. But worse than that, our Troop camp arrangements were being mucked up. As ever, we struggled through and Noel and Eddie finally came out very late on the Saturday night.

Both of them had made a decision that they would be going to the Troop camp and had only agreed to work until Saturday midday. They could have worked on until Monday morning but going to camp with the 131 was more important to them than earning a lot of money.

A Pint and a Singsong

Pubs in Glasgow were grim places in the 1950s and 1960s. They were dark drinking dens for men, as women were not allowed to enter. There was no colour, no food and no TVs or music either.

There were plenty of pubs around Pollok, but none in the scheme. In fact, these old pubs had been part of the local area far longer than the local houses. Most young lads would sneak into pubs from about the age of fifteen. They would travel into town or to Govan or to Pollokshaws to remain incognito – or so they thought. The other drinkers knew they were under-age and the bar staff probably did as well. But nobody cared.

And certain Scout pub escapades were recalled by Danny Houston, 'We were not always the nice little boys when we were camping and we visited the Carbeth Inn most weekends. You can take the boys out of Nitshill but you can't take Nitshill out of the boys.'

Roberto McLellan also remembered this Auchengillan cultural rite of passage, 'One weekend, Jimmy McNeillie came with us. Normally, we would go down to the Carbeth Inn and buy pints of Guinness. None of us was eighteen years old, so Jimmy told us that we were to say that we were engineering apprentices from his work at Queenslie, if we were challenged. But this excuse was never used as we were never asked our ages.'

It was normal for the older Scouts and Leaders to sneak into the Carbeth Inn for a pint and perhaps join in the singsong with the other patrons. Sometimes this would spill over and they would all go up the hill to one of the huts for a party.

But there was always one Leader at least who did not go down to Carbeth, the Duty Scouter. This was for supervision reasons and had been instilled in us by Tommy when he reminded a group of young Leaders that one pint of Guinness smelled the same as ten pints of Guinness. It was rigorously applied to all activities. A wee bit of common sense from a wise man.

Regardless of age, the Irish pubs were explored by the 131 lads at the Dublin Summer Camp and there was a pub on the road which led up to the camp site at Larch Hill.

Jim Mackay has a special memory of this establishment, 'It was a miserable night near the end of the camp and we went down to the local pub. The power failed and the pub was in darkness. However, candles were soon produced and we had a great night listening to traditional music and the craic from the locals. At closing time the barman locked the door and we stayed on for another hour and a half before heading back to camp in the dark and pouring rain. We had a great night.'

After Troop nights in the Hall, we routinely headed up to Nitshill to the Railway Inn. We would get a pint of Guinness, a packet of crisps and a cheese roll and sit in the snug next to the fire. Old Mary, the licensee, was about eighty years old, and she would look after us and give us cups of tea for free.

At closing the door would be locked but would then be opened for locals. Often the local cop would come in or even a couple of priests from St Robert's. Never any trouble or nonsense.

The Volunteer Arms nearby would supply barrels of beer for Group fundraising activities. A couple of the fathers and older Scouts would act as bar staff for the evening and, as draught beer was cheaper than bottled beer, it made sense to get a barrel for sale. It obviously made more profit for the event.

The Secret of the 131

Being in the 131 was the first step on the journey out of the scheme.

It was also valuable for character-forming purposes. Without this outlet, few of the lads would have tasted any of the great adventures they encountered as a member of our gang.

This was certainly the case for Michael O'Neill, 'Being in the 131 was the formative experience of my life. The skills we learned were all practical and the games were wild. I always loved playing Bulldog. We didn't worry about being thumped by the other Scouts when we were doing it, all we thought about was struggling through the mob to the far end of the hall. A bit like rugby training! Life in the Troop made us all truly competitive, not in the ugly sense but in the sense that we developed self-belief which enabled us to tackle the world on its terms – and succeed.'

Our tough environment featured a discipline game called Guard of Honour. This was called up when some Scout had broken the spirit of Scouting – a serious offence. It was in reality a punishment given out by the whole Troop. When somebody had cheated or acted in a dishonest fashion, one of the PLs would shout *Guard of Honour!* The Troop would form up in two parallel lines and link arms across. The culprit would run up and leap on to this human cradle and would be thrown up and down until they reached the far end. Most of us sampled it when we stepped out of line.

Of course there were some disagreeable incidents, after all, this was Pollok and life was rough and tough. Pete McGuire was blunt about this, 'If anyone started throwing their weight about, they were sorted out quickly, either by the Patrol Leaders or the Adult Leaders. These pests only stayed a short time in the Troop. We didn't need them and they couldn't handle our toughness.'

The common factor in all of this physical endeavour was that the lads who remained in the Troop were all good pals. Many had never met until they joined the 131, but once they became Scouts these friendships grew. Michael O'Neill pointed to this, 'We were fortunate in that we had a group of boys who were very able. We could tackle most things and do them in a good fashion. We were very comfortable with one another and everyone was helpful.'

Roberto McLellan agreed with this observation, 'I think the secret to our great times with the 131 was because we were all pals and most of us went to the same school. There were no arguments or fights. We all got on so well together. We had a great bunch of guys.'

Former Scouts would call at Tommy's house for a cup of tea and a chat with their old mentor. They kept in touch in this way and turned up at fundraisers and at other times provided a van to remove the unsold items after a jumble sale. They were a sort of unofficial old-boys club, always there. Regardless of how long these lads had been in the Troop, they were all happy to assist. The 131 had brought a great deal of pride to the community and had shown how well the local boys could do when given the chance.

Being a Scout in the 131 produced a core resilience in the boys. The support and patience provided by Jack, Tommy and Jimmy McNeillie ensured that we pursued a vigorous and demanding programme which bred personal strength.

Family Heirlooms

Throughout its existence, the 131 worked as a good team. The boys were mad keen and attended in large numbers, but the parents also played their part. There were some excellent official charitable sources, but these had been set up by well-meaning people who had no experience of life on a housing estate. And in any case, the 131 did not have a clue about how to access these funds. The parents committee did not moan. It just got on with the job and fully supported the Leaders and Scouts over the years.

Although the Leaders, Rovers and parents worked closely together at fundraising events and Hall repairs, they did not know each other on a social basis. All they knew was that they were somebody else's Mum or Dad. Michael O'Neill recalled one of the fairy tales about parents, 'We used to think that Mr Mackay was rich because he had a car. It was a Hillman Imp, probably the second-smallest car available at that time. The smallest was a Mini and Pete McGuire had one. We never thought that Pete was rich because he was one of our Scout gang but Mr Mackay was the Chairman and he always wore a tie with a tie pin. We didn't know he wore a boiler suit at his work!'

The 131 was well-run. It had built all the components for a successful Scout Group. There were loads of boys who joined and stayed for many hilarious – and hair raising – moments. There were excellent unpaid Leaders who spent lots of their own time running these the events. But, above all, there was a great group of parents who contributed to this success. Without their efforts, this great Scouting journey would have been much harder.

All of our parents came from working-class backgrounds and had never been involved in running any organisation. The Mums ran most of the fundraising events and the Dads were mainly involved in refurbishing and decorating the Hall.

Many parents assisted at short notice when the 131 were carrying out flood assistance duties and they were particularly impressive when the Italian Scouts arrived unannounced. They fully supported all of the Group's activities which became part of their own social calendar.

In 1970, we found a way to thank them. We asked for donations from the Scouts and then purchased Scout Thanks Badges. There was no formal event to present these enamel badges, the PLs just handed them over at the end of a parents committee meeting one night.

The parents were overwhelmed. It was the first time they had been thanked formally for their efforts. These badges became family heirlooms for proud sons and daughters in later years. 'My Mum and Dad wore theirs every day,' remembered Eleanor Reynolds. 'It was almost like a lucky charm. I still have my Mum's but Dad took his with him.'

Fundraising was crucial for the 131 and Jack summed it up succinctly, 'The most important thing in Scouting is money; without it you are always struggling and with it the world's your oyster. That's why the 131's achievements were so significant – they had so much more to overcome.'

Our parents provided the platform for their Scout sons to live out their dreams. We were so proud of them. This was Pollok and life wasn't easy but they always did their bit.

For These Are The Times We Shall Dream About

Our 131 Scout journey uncovered our hidden talents and helped to produce a flood of new occupations for us.

We produced…

>Police Chief,
>Senior Fireman,
>Two Joiners,
>An Aero Engine Technician,
>The Conductor of the Royal Scottish National Orchestra,
>Motor Mechanic,
>Toolmaker,
>Two Plumbers,
>One Director of Education (OBE),
>An Academic Doctor,
>An Optical Instrument Maker,
>Four Head Teachers,
>Two Senior Civil Servants,
>Two Chefs,
>Farmer,
>An Oil Tanker Chief Engineer,
>One Senior Nurse,
>An Area Sales Manager,
>Three Army Sergeant-Majors,
>An Army Bandsman,
>An Optometrist,
>One Lawyer,
>A Broadsheet Journalist,
>A Shop Steward,
>A Master Carpenter,

A Conservation Manager,
A Parachute Regiment Officer,
A University Tutor,
A Fast-Jet RAF Pilot,
Social Worker.

All of us refer to the crucial role that being a Scout in the 131 had played in our development. But that is what Scouting is supposed to do. It has been tried and tested for more than one hundred years.

The 131 existed for a brief twenty-seven years and served its purpose. As Jack said quite simply, 'I think we were good for lots of the boys. It gave some of them a real home environment where they were part of a great gang of pals. Otherwise they could have gone the wrong way and ended up in prison – I had been saved by the Scouts when I lived in the Gorbals.'

Scouting was a unique arena of opportunity for us. It gave us a stage where we, working-class boys, could mingle on equal terms with middle-class boys. This could not have taken place elsewhere, not through schools, sport or leisure activities, as we inhabited parallel cultures. We realised that we were as good as they were. It was a fundamental building block for later life.

We were not expected to improve our social position but we worked hard and supported each other. We never filled in a form to do anything, we just had a great trust in one another and we all pulled in the same direction.

We thank all those adults who gave up their social time to run these marvellous activities. Their good work had a profound effect on all of us. They gave us challenges and we responded. They helped to raise our self-esteem and certainly raised our self-belief. Sadly, we never had the chance to thank them properly.

So, to Tommy and Jack and Jimmy Mac, thank you for giving us so many wonderful memories – and a great basis for our future lives.

For these were the times we still dream about
and we call them the good old days.

Epilogue

When Glasgow Scouting had a major problem in 1992, they turned to two old 131 Skippers for help.

Camping nights at Auchengillan had dwindled to worrying levels. There had been a drop of 80 per cent from the totals of ten years earlier. Camping had now become an occasional event. Action was needed and a special project was set up to make camping, once again, the prime Scout activity.

Jack Banks and I agreed to run two concurrent projects – one for the Leaders and one for the Scouts. We wrote to every Scout Troop in Glasgow and visited more than 50 of them. We needed to put our message across about the fundamental importance of camping.

We designed a badge for every Scout who took part in the project, a shield for every Patrol and a pennant for each participating Troop. Erskine Hospital made some trophies as many of the old soldiers had been young Scouts.

Leader training weekends were held at Auchengillan, 'It was great to see so many young, inexperienced Scout Leaders,' noted Jack. 'Especially the female Leaders who were becoming Scout Leaders but had no experience of camping.' One of those ladies became the Chief Commissioner for the Clyde Region, Dr Marion Rankin. This was the start of her Scout career, 'I well remember that weekend. The years have certainly passed quickly!'

A full-scale PL Training Course was also held at Peesweep Camp. Almost 150 PLs from Glasgow attended, along with the Chief Commissioner for Scotland and the Chief Constable (a former Scout from the East End of London).

The overall project was a roaring success: more than 40 Leaders were trained and camping nights at Auchengillan rose to their old level. Over 600 Scouts crammed into Glasgow City Chambers to receive their badges and the pennants for their Troops.

A new Sassenach Trophy was made free of charge by Erskine Hospital. It replicated its predecessor which had been won so often by the 131.

It was awarded to the Troop with the highest number of camping nights. The winners were a working-class Troop from Easterhouse, with no Hall, little funds but lots of enthusiasm – a new bunch of boys from the scheme.

Tony McGuire Remembers Len Ashforth – A Boy Scout of the 131

A member of the 131 in the late-1950s and early-1960s until he departed for America, Len Ashforth, became a great friend of my brother Robert, another member of the troop who also emigrated, but to Australia.

Len's family had settled in New Jersey in the States, but he delayed his departure to the United States until he finished his apprenticeship as a motor mechanic. He arrived in the middle of the Vietnam War era and was required to enlist in the Army. I don't know if he volunteered or was conscripted, but after his basic training, he was sent to Korea and not to Vietnam. His family probably saw this as a blessing as the Korean War had been over for some years, and the Vietnam War was still in full swing, with the casualty figures frighteningly high.

In July 1967, the Troop was in Ireland on its annual camp when the news came from Jack Banks that Len had been killed in an attack by North Korean infiltrators. Until then, as young boys and young men, we had been spared any great awareness of death and were still at that age when immortality was not out of the question. The news of the violent death of one of our friends was a shocking reminder of the fragility of life.

Some of the lads did not know Len, and others were close friends, but our common bond through the 131 meant we all felt a strong sense of loss. It was important that we paid tribute to him, and so we changed into full Scout uniform and stood in our patrols outside the tents with the troop flag lowered to half-mast and remembered a young man who left Scotland for a better life but paid the ultimate price for doing so. Len now rests in Arlington Cemetery. If you are ever there, take time to seek out his grave and pay silent tribute to a Boy Scout of the 131 who has gone home.

The Quiet Man and the Great Organiser Go Home

When Tommy was in his sixties, he was awarded the Silver Acorn in recognition of distinguished services to Scouting.

At that time he was running a Scout Group in Govan. Another really hard place. That was Tommy. He helped so many youngsters from disadvantaged areas over the years. But he was worried about the expensive activities which were now being introduced into Scouting and cautioned that these must be kept in check. As far as he was concerned, Scouting was about camping; boys could go off on their own and look after themselves. It was simple.

Tommy's final days were spent in a local hospice. A 131 neckie was pinned above his bed along with his Silver Acorn award from the Chief Scout. Jack would sit at Tommy's bedside most Sundays. Some other old 131 lads would also turn up and campfire songs were sung, with a couple of the other patients coming along to join in. They were old Scouts too. 'It was just like being back at Auchengillan,' Jack said.

Jack and a few of us attended the funeral Mass along with Tommy's son and son-in-law, both former 131 Scouts. The Troop had long gone but it was still a Scout occasion. Many in the congregation gave the Scout Salute as Tommy, the quiet man from Sutherland, left the church to Go Home and various elderly local gents came across and introduced themselves to his family.

These guys had been 131 Scouts fifty years earlier, before either Jack or any of us had arrived and they all wanted to say farewell to their old Skipper. At the wake, there was a lusty singing of Scout songs, particularly *Riding Along On The Crest Of A Wave*. We were all saying cheerio to a lovely man. A man who gave all of us so many lovely memories from our youth. A real gentleman. A true hero. The 131 were so fortunate that he had stepped forward in 1946. At that time, he had no knowledge of Scouting. But he was a good learner and the rest is history.

Then, to the dismay of the author and contributors, Jack Banks, the last link to the 131 golden years passed away before this book was published. He was 88 years old and had regularly kept in contact with his old Scouts.

Constant in his role as the great organiser, he had been his local Scout District Chairman and an active fund raiser for the local hospice. He ran the annual Poppy Day collection as well as many Rotary Club events.

His funeral was held in the midst of a winter storm, something he would have chuckled at, and was well attended. His family was joined by mourners from all his various activities.

His obituary in *The Herald* summed up Jack superbly –

Leading figure in the Scouts who broke down barriers in Glasgow's poorest communities.

A senior Scout Commissioner, who had worked with Jack for many years, described him as 'a wonderful individual.'

Three former 131 lads, now in their seventies, attended Jack's funeral. Others had wanted to be there but were unable to do so.

As Jack was carried from the church, Scouts salutes were given to their Skipper by the proud trio as they thought back to their youth and carefree days at Auchengillan. Jack's daughter, a Queen's Scout herself, returned the salute.

The 131 boys imagined their Skipper looking back, telling them to smarten up and smiling.

Their mentor, their pal, another great hero was going home.

Winners of the 131 Inter Patrol Shield

1958–1959	Falcon	PL Len Ashforth
1959–1960	Swift	PL Frank Rodden
1960–1961	Kingfisher	PL Robert McGuire
1961–1962	Curlew	PL George Lyden
1962–1963	Swift	PL David Mackay
1963–1964	Swift	PL David Mackay
1964–1965	Falcon	PL Eddie Mallan
1965–1966	Falcon	PL Brendan McLeod
1966–1967	Curlew	PL George Coll
1967–1968	Falcon	PL Tom Donnelly
1968–1969	Raven	PL Eric McKelvie
1969–1970	Glengarry	PL Bobby Moore

Troop Leaders

1958	Jimmy McNeillie
1959	Brian McGuire
1960	Danny Houston
1961	Len Ashforth
1962	Robert McGuire
1963	Jimmy Carson
1964	Henry Watts
1965	David Mackay
1966	Noel Carson
1967	Robert Allan
1968	George Coll
1969	Joe McEwan
1970	Martin Mullaney

FINAL THOUGHTS

Our Queen's Scouts

Queen's Scout Certificate

Becoming a Queen's Scout was the ultimate target for 131 Scouts. This could be regarded as the pinnacle of Scouting but for us it was the eventual outcome of our great adventure. The journey took six years and there were no shortcuts. Every step was hard work alongside great pals and it was well-earned. Many keen lads started the journey and some got there in the end:

Brian McGuire, Jimmy McNeillie, Tommy Maguire,
Danny Houston, Frank Rodden, Len Ashforth,
George Lyden, Robert McGuire, Jimmy Carson,
Henry Watts, David Mackay, Pete McGuire,
Noel Carson, Eddie Mallan, Jim Mackay,
Michael O'Neill, Len McKinnon, Roberto McLellan,
Ian MacCormick, Hugh Mullaney, Brendan McLeod,
Michael McGee, John Watts, Tommy McGee, George Coll.

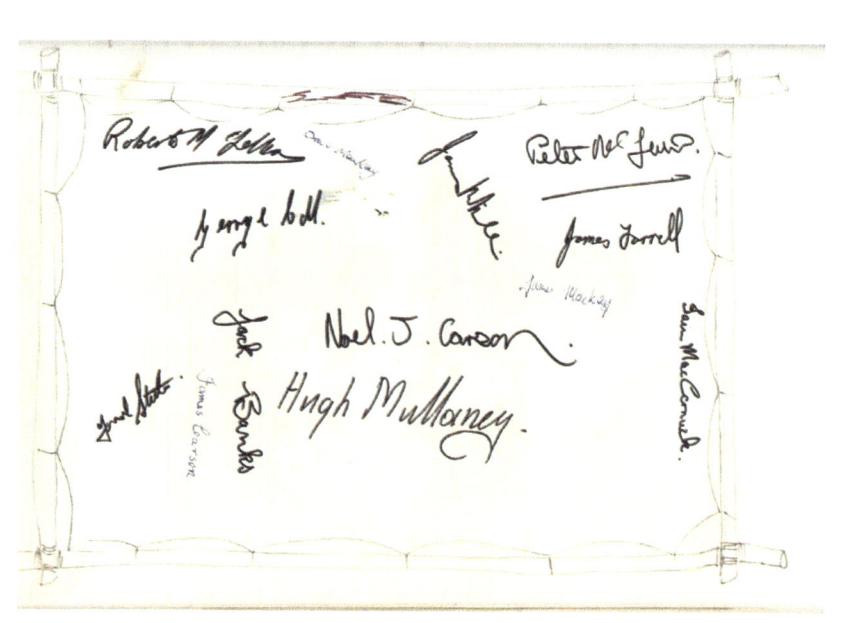

A few autographs from 1970 – add your own

BV - #0177 - 191124 - C0 - 234/156/14 [16] - CB - 9781917056168 - Matt Lamination